Everyday Life Matters

UNIVERSITY PRESS OF FLORIDA

Florida A&M University, Tallahassee
Florida Atlantic University, Boca Raton
Florida Gulf Coast University, Ft. Myers
Florida International University, Miami
Florida State University, Tallahassee
New College of Florida, Sarasota
University of Central Florida, Orlando
University of Florida, Gainesville
University of North Florida, Jacksonville
University of South Florida, Tampa
University of West Florida, Pensacola

Everyday Life Matters

✳ ✳ ✳ ✳ ✳ ✳ ✳ ✳

Maya Farmers at Chan

CYNTHIA ROBIN

UNIVERSITY PRESS OF FLORIDA

Gainesville/Tallahassee/Tampa/Boca Raton

Pensacola/Orlando/Miami/Jacksonville/Ft. Myers/Sarasota

First cloth printing, 2013
First paperback printing, 2016

A record of cataloging-in-publication data is available from the Library of Congress.
ISBN 978-0-8130-4499-6 (cloth)
ISBN 978-0-8130-6210-5 (pbk.)

The University Press of Florida is the scholarly publishing agency for the State
University System of Florida, comprising Florida A&M University, Florida Atlantic
University, Florida Gulf Coast University, Florida International University, Florida
State University, New College of Florida, University of Central Florida, University
of Florida, University of North Florida, University of South Florida, and University
of West Florida.

University Press of Florida
15 Northwest 15th Street
Gainesville, FL 32611-2079
http://www.upf.com

To my parents,
Edward and Gloria Robin.
You always told me that I could be
whatever I wanted to be.

Contents

Figures

Tables

Acknowledgments

This book represents the culmination of a journey that began when I first entered the world of academic archaeology as an undergraduate and has continued across my career. In this time I have dedicated myself to studying the everyday lives of ordinary people and demonstrating their importance in the constitution of human societies.

My thinking about everyday life has been influenced by ongoing conversations with mentors and colleagues: Wendy Ashmore, James Brown, Liz Brumfiel, Micaela diLeonardo, Tim Earle, Clark Erickson, Bill Hanks, Mark Hauser, Julia Hendon, Matthew Johnson, Art Joyce, Rosemary Joyce, John Lucy, Nan Rothschild, Jeremy Sabloff, Robert Sharer, Payson Sheets, Gil Stein, and Mary Weismantel. Wendy Ashmore taught me that peopling the past is a valuable and doable project in archaeology. Liz Brumfiel always reminded me just how critical that project is for understanding the diversity of past human life.

The first draft of part 1 of this book benefitted greatly from the critical reading and conversation in my Social Theory and Archaeology class, in which Santiago Juarez, John Millhauser, and Lisa Overholtzer were class participants. I am indebted to the careful reading that Elizabeth Brumfiel, Matthew Johnson, my father, Edward Robin, and my husband, René Rivera, gave to the whole book and that Laura Kosakowsky, David Lentz, Chelsea Blackmore, and Andrew Wyatt gave to sections of the book. The initial ideas for the book solidified during an Alice Berlin Kaplan Center for the Humanities Fellowship from Northwestern University.

I dedicate this book to my parents, Edward and Gloria Robin, who have always been an inspiration for my work, because this book represents what I have been working toward in archaeology all of these years. My parents and my husband also were important editors for this book. Since I was a child, my father has helped me in editing my work, and if there is clarity in my writing it is because of him. My husband, René Rivera, not only edits my work but also, as a software developer, now makes the difficult task of producing images simple. René and my three-year-old daughter, Lyra, inspire everything I do, and I would not be able to do everything I do without them.

This is the second book that I have published with the University Press of Florida, and I cannot imagine a better press to work with. Director Meredith Morris-Babb made the book a reality in more ways than one. I was reunited with project editor Catherine-Nevil Parker and copy editor Sally Bennett, and it was a pleasure to work with both of them again.

I began writing this book a number of times but was never able to finish it. I did not figure out why this had happened until I completed the Chan project in 2009. It was then that I realized that the farming community of Chan was the key case study that allowed me to explicate broader concerns with the analysis of everyday life through archaeological data. With this case study in hand I was able to complete the book.

The Chan project was part of my everyday life for nearly a decade. Between 2002 and 2009 I worked with an inspiring team of 123 project members who came from all over the globe, mostly from Belize and the United States, but also from England, Canada, and China. Chelsea Blackmore, Bernadette Cap, Nick Hearth, Angela Keller, Caleb Kestle, Laura Kosakowsky, David Lentz, James Meierhoff, Anna Novotny, and Andrew Wyatt directed research at Chan, and the story of Chan is very much a story that we all worked together to build. I would additionally like to thank the colleagues, students, and volunteers who worked on the Chan project in Belize and in various labs in the United States, including Michelle Abtahi, Yasmine Baktash, Doug Bolendar, Margaret Briggs, Jeff Buechler, Pamela Cardenas, Jonathan Dattilo, Kristin de Lucia, Brian Dema, Brian Dubin, Laure Dussubieu, Elise Enterkin, Krista Garcia, Mark Golitko, Chris Hetrick, Angela Hood, Iram Izam, Serena Jain, Tegan Jones, Santiago Juarez, Ethan Kalosky, Kate Kanne, Kalina Kassadjikova, Shelley Khan, Colleen Kron, Kristin Landau, Michael Latsch, Lisa LeCount, Megan McGee, William Middleton, Alex Miller, James Morris, Mary Morrison, Marcus Murph, Elizabeth Nolan, Lisa Overholtzer, Brad Phillippi, Jessie Pinchoff, Tamas Polanyi, Jeffrey Schecter, Elizabeth Schiffman, Holly Schumacher, Kate Stephensen, Anthony Tedeschi, Ana Tejeda, Carmen Ting, Bob Trombello, Sally Woods, and Dan Wyman.

My Belizean counterparts on the Chan project, colleagues and friends, made sure that my daily life in Belize was fruitful: Everaldo Chi (foreman), Marta Puc (laboratory director), Glenis Smith (project manager), Joyce Tun (Institute of Archaeology intern), and Silvia Batty (student intern). My thanks also go to the excavation supervisors: Bernabe Camal Sr., Edwin Camal, Ifrain Chan, Ismael R. Chan, Eduardo Chi, Venura Cocom, Placido Cunil Jr., Abel Goodoy, Virgilio Goodoy, Ciro Hernandez, Manuel Kent, Jose Lopez, Mariano Lopez Jr., Jose Luis Panti, Cruz Puc, and Nasario Puc. In addition, I thank the excavation, survey, lab, and project assistants: Merle Alfaro, Nestor Alfaro, Sylvia Batty, Theresa Batty, Bernabe Camal Jr., Jonny Camal, Eduardo Chan, Heriberto Chan, Ismael Chan Sr., Ismael F. Chan Jr., Elvis Chi, Jaime Chi, Omar Chi, Roberto Cunil, Ismael Ernandez, Reina Ernandez, William Hofman, Elvis Itza, Roberto Jimenez, Sergio Jimenez, Gumercindo Mai, Susan Mai, Rosita Marin, Lazaro Martinez, Rosa Martinez, Oscar Mejia, Eder Panti, Alma Patt, Salvador Penados, Elvin Puc, Ricky Puc, Ronnie Puc, Sandra Puc, Sandra Aurora Puc, Ediberto Reyes, Carlos Salgueros, Julia Sanchez, Alex Smith, David Smith, Horace Smith, Ken Smith, Feliz Uck, Elmer Valdez, and Gerald Valdez. Theresa Batty, Museum of Belize curator, has always been a friend.

As I discuss in the book, I was fortunate to have wonderful support from the landowners who today own part of what used to be the ancient community of Chan. Ismael Chan Sr. and Derric Chan, the owners of the central portion of the site and for whom the site is named, became my friends and partners in this endeavor as their lifelong interest in protecting and understanding Chan inspired the work that I did. Forty-seven additional landowners allowed the project to survey and excavate on their property, including Rosita Aguallo, Jose Alfaro, Armando Bautista, Thomas Chable, Benigno Chan, Calixto Chan, Francisco Chan, Guadalupe Chan, Ventura Chi, Adele DesRochers, Rogelio Gamez, Virgilio Goodoy, Jose Hiron, Edward Jenkins, Virginia Jenkins, Irene Jimenez, Michael Jones, Valentin Ku, Abelio Leon, Estela Leon, Ireno Magaña, Jose Mai, Amalio Matus, Fidel Matus, Domingo Mesh, Antonio Morales, Francisco Morales, Humberto Morales, Pastora Morales, Leandro Pacheco, Feliciano Panti, Glis Penados, Santiago Gonzalez Pinedos, Antonio Puc, Felipe Puc, Lorenzo Puc, Nasario Puc, Julian Requena, Manuel Reyes, Jovita Guermina Sanches, Ishil Shish, Polo Shish, Felix Uck, Monico Uck, Silvario

Uck, Julio Valencia, and Santiago Yacab. Pedro Gonzalez and Maria Jilma Sosa were the landlords of the Chan lab house and residence in San Ignacio, but they were also so much more than landlords to me.

The Chan project would not have been possible without the generous support and permitting of the Belize Institute of Archaeology. Director Dr. Jaime Awe, associate director Dr. John Morris, and associate director of park management Brian Woodeye permitted the project over the years. I would like to thank all of the staff of the Belize Institute of Archaeology who helped me with various aspects of the project work at Chan.

The excavation seasons at Chan were majorly funded by two National Science Foundation grants: a National Science Foundation Senior Archaeology Grant (BCS-0314686) and a National Science Foundation International Research Fellowship (INT-0303713). The laboratory seasons were funded by a National Endowment for the Humanities Collaborative Research Grant (RZ-50804-07). The initial survey seasons were funded by a National Geographic Society Grant (2002–3), an H. John Heinz III Fund Grant for Archaeological Field Research in Latin America (2002), and two anonymous donations. Additional funding for research at Chan was provided by three University Research Grants from Northwestern University (2002, 2005, 2009), two Alumnae Foundation Grants from Northwestern University (2002, 2006), and an AT&T Research Scholar award (2005). A subvention was provided by a University Research Grants Committee award from Northwestern University to assist in the publication of this book.

All of the figures and tables in this book are original work of the Chan project and copyrighted by the Chan project. Chelsea Blackmore holds the copyright for figures 6.7 and 6.8. David Lentz holds the copyright for tables 6.2 and 6.3. Andrew Wyatt holds the copyright for figures 6.5 and 6.6. Jack Scott is the artist who produced the beautiful reconstruction drawings in this book, figures 6.3, 6.4, and 6.12. A website for the Chan project can be accessed at www.anthropology.northwestern.edu/chan/.

Prologue

In 1986, I went on my first archaeological dig in Belize, where I have worked ever since. Belizeans live among the ancient Maya ruins and are deeply connected to these places. When people found out that I was an archaeology student, they were always eager to talk with me about the ancient Maya. Over and over I was asked the same questions: What was everyday life like in the past? What would life have been like for an ordinary person like me? The magnificent temples of ancient kings and queens overwhelm the observer in Belize today as they must also have done in the past. They remind viewers of the glorious pomp and circumstance of the ancient Maya past, but as glorious as this may have been, it does not illuminate how ancient people lived their daily lives.

Although I had taken only one undergraduate Maya archaeology class at that time, I had been interested in archaeology and the great ancient civilizations of Egypt, Greece, and Rome since third grade, and I knew that the focus of traditional archaeological scholarship was on grand monuments rather than on everyday life. I was taken aback to realize that what many Belizeans wanted to know about their prehistory was not what the field of archaeology had defined as its focus.

I decided that if I was going to work as a foreigner doing archaeology in a foreign country I wanted to do an archaeology that would be relevant for people there. This archaeology for people would make everyday life and ordinary people the focus of analysis. In this way, I felt that my intellectual pursuits in archaeology would be enhanced as my studies of ancient daily life would provide a meaningful history for people today. After receiving my undergraduate degree I joined the United States Peace Corps in Belize, in part to facilitate these goals by spending more time with Belizeans and learning what interested them about archaeology. But I also joined to enjoy my new friends and a country I came to love. I worked for two years as a volunteer in the government branch that oversees archaeological research in Belize. At that time it was called the Belize Department of Archaeology (DOA), but it has since been renamed the Institute of Archaeology (IA). Although I did not realize it then, this kind of engagement and collaboration with people beyond the traditional disciplinary boundaries of Western archaeology was something that philosophers of science and feminist theorists were writing about as being significant for enhancing scientific research both conceptually and empirically (such as Smith 1987; Wylie 2008). I certainly observed this to be true over and over again in my own research.

After completing my Peace Corps service, I started graduate school at the University of Pennsylvania to follow the pursuit of understanding everyday life in the past. Entering the archaeological field as a graduate student in the 1990s was an exciting time. There had been some significant developments in archaeological scholarship in the 1980s that were reaching fruition in the 1990s. In the Americas the fields of feminist and household archaeology were developing. These archaeologists were trying to focus more on ancient people, women and men, and the ordinary things they did in their daily lives and within their homes. I sought out Wendy Ashmore, a pioneer in the field of household archaeology, as my adviser at the University of Pennsylvania. In Europe, postprocessual archaeology was invigorating interest in people, actions, and meanings in the past. I was inspired by what I was learning in archaeology because it highlighted to me that the direction the field needed to go in was getting answers to all of those questions I was being asked in Belize. While in graduate school, I stumbled upon Michel de Certeau's (1984) famous text *The Practice of Everyday Life*. Through his writing, seeing whom he cited and who cited him, I discovered that there was a rich social theoretical literature on everyday life. As I explored the works of the everyday life thinkers, I uncovered broad support for the kind of intellectual project that I wanted to pursue.

In my case, I did not come to the study of everyday life out of a grand exploration in social theory. I came to the study of everyday life out of my experiences in the world, which led me to develop a perspective on society that embraced the importance of everyday life. Using everyday life to inform a critical understanding of society is an approach that I now realize is very much allied with the critical everyday life project of the everyday life theorists as I discuss in this book.

Across social science and humanities disciplines there has been burgeoning interest in studies of everyday life and the less-known works of a group of social theorists now called the everyday life theorists. Just over the past decade, syntheses of everyday life approaches as well as anthologies of writings by everyday life thinkers have been produced in fields as disparate as sociology, history, media and film, and French literature (some examples include Gardiner 2000; Highmore 2002a, 2002b; Lüdtke 1995; Sheringham 2006). Works by everyday life theorists have been reissued as new editions, and works not previously translated into English are now seeing their first English translation (some examples include Giard et al. 1998; Lefebvre 2004, 2008). Simply perusing this literature made it clear that everyday life was rapidly emerging as an interdisciplinary dialogue across the social sciences and humanities.

The social theoretical literature provided me with a set of conceptual tools through which to think about everyday life, but it was incomplete. It was certainly a body of literature that archaeologists could engage with to aid in conceptualizing their studies, but it was also a body of literature that needed to engage with archaeological research. The voice of the field of archaeology was largely missing from broader social theoretical and interdisciplinary dialogues on everyday life, and I found this problematic for two reasons. First, everyday life thinkers have developed general theories about everyday life that encompass long-term histories of daily life from premodern to modern times. This was done without considering archaeological research, and it has led to problematic assumptions about the nature of premodern everyday life rooted in a false dichotomy between modern and "primitive" times. Viewed from this perspective, people and everyday life in the premodern (primitive, ancient, traditional) world were part of nature, that is, people's daily lives were a passive reflection of the rhythms of nature and cycles of the day, year, and life course (see Lefebvre 2008; Smith 1987). As inspiring as such utopian visions of a past where people and nature were in concert may be, they do a disservice to the understanding of the depth of human history. Archaeologists have exposed the complex, cultural, and constructed nature of premodern societies, which only from a cursory or Eurocentric perspective might appear to approximate a primitive, natural, or unsophisticated human state.

How can researchers know what the past was like prior to studying it? For any scholar—archaeologists and others—seeking to understand the full extent of human history, the false dichotomy drawn between primitive premodern and modern times is an issue.

Second, the emerging interdisciplinary dialogue on everyday life has highlighted how ordinary spaces (houses, yards, streets, and so forth) and ordinary materials (cooking pots, clothing, tools, and so forth) are a key means through which people learn about their world. These are often referred to as "the spatial turn" of the 1990s and "the material turn" of the first decade of the twenty-first century, wherein researchers across the social sciences and humanities "discovered" the importance of the spatial and material world in understanding social life. Given that the archaeological record is a spatial and material record of human life, archaeologists have long explored the roles of objects and places in human societies. It often seems that nonarchaeological scholars are re-creating knowledge, particularly in relation to such studies. The material and spatial configuration of the archaeological record provides a powerful means for archaeologists to contribute to the broader project of developing social theory (see also Preucel and Meskell 2004: 17).

This book is intended to bring studies of everyday life and archaeology into fruitful dialogue. Through its attention to the spatial and material dimensions of human life, archaeology is particularly suited not only to engage but also to further critical discussions of everyday life. Archaeology has an important role to play in providing nonarchaeologists, both academics and laypeople, with a credible history of premodern everyday life. Exploring these themes is the subject of this book.

1 ✳ Introduction

Understanding Everyday Life

She woke up on a warm morning in AD 750. The Maya farming community of Chan was thriving, and more and more people were moving into the community. This meant clearing new land for agricultural fields. As her grandparents had taught her, and their grandparents had taught them, she went to help clear the fields nearby her home with some new neighbors after a warm meal of corn gruel prepared from freshly ground corn from her family's fields. Working with her chert adze, she carefully cleared the understory but was always conscious to leave the productive mature tropical-forest canopy trees—fruit trees, mahogany trees, *chico zapote,* and many others, standing. Agriculture and the forest could exist together. As she may or may not have been aware, this was one of the reasons why health remained consistent in her community, and why health was declining at this same time for people living in the nearby Maya city of Tikal, where much of the mature tropical forest had been depleted.

I woke up on a cold midwestern morning in AD 2012 with a wind chill factor of 30° below. I went to the kitchen and poured myself a bowl of organic cereal, a product of Canada, for breakfast. Like countless other people from all walks of life and all across the globe, I went outside and got in my car to drive to work. I usually don't drive to work in the morning, as I live only one mile from Northwestern, but when it is 30° below, I drive that one mile. As an individual act, my getting in my car in the morning and driving to work seems inconsequential. But because this act is repeated by a multitude of others and across time, its consequences are, in fact, far from trivial and have quite a dramatic effect on our world. Still, we get in our cars and drive to work.

※

Both today and in the past, the things people do in their everyday lives are not as mundane as they first appear. They are sometimes quite extraordinary, and they are always profoundly implicated in what is going on in the world and the long-term social dynamics of societies. The two vignettes presented above illustrate the critical explanatory power of exploring the everyday. In the ancient Maya case, the way people cleared the forest for agricultural land affected both the health of the forest and human health, which had significant implications for both human societies and the natural world. In the contemporary case, the act of driving to work produces transformations in climate, economy, and power. Scholars can learn much about people and society by understanding ordinary acts of everyday life.

※

This book is about everyday life and why it matters. The title of the book, *Everyday Life Matters,* is a double entendre. First, everyday life matters because what people do on a daily basis is critical in the construction of their societies. Second, everyday life is the matter of much of archaeology—archaeologists dig up the minutiae of what people did on a day-to-day basis.

In this book I develop theories and methods for a critical analysis of everyday life in the past through the engagement of recent thinking in archaeology and social theory. I then draw upon my archaeological research on the two-thousand-year history (800 BC–AD 1200) of ancient Maya farmers at Chan, Belize, to explore the importance of everyday life in understanding human societies. I developed a collaborative, international, multidisciplinary archaeological research project at Chan between 2002 and 2009 (Robin 2012a). Chan is located in the upper Belize Valley region of west-central Belize, a peripheral part of the ancient Maya world. Its two-thousand-year occupation spans the major periods of political-economic change in Maya society (the Preclassic, Classic, and Postclassic periods), making it an ideal place to explore how everyday life intersects with broader transformations in society. During this time, the great lowland Maya cities of Tikal, Copán, Calakmul, Palenque, and many others rose, flourished, and fell, while in Europe the Roman Empire rose and fell and prehistory gave way to the Middle Ages.

For two millennia, while the fortunes of nearby major Maya civic-centers waxed and waned, the farming community of Chan flourished. Although the Chan community can be characterized as unremarkable, in terms of the size of both its community and its architecture, Chan's farmers made notable innovations in sustainable practices, religious knowledge, and political strategies. Investigating the lives of Chan's farmers prompts new considerations of how power operated in ancient Maya society. Across their daily lives, Chan's farmers constructed a socially and environmentally sustainable community. Traditional notions of peasants as a passive, backward, and simple folk are not upheld in the archaeological record of their everyday lives at Chan. Developing a critical understanding of farmers' everyday lives at Chan challenges researchers to rethink and to reformulate a wide range of anthropological theories about the constitution of human societies and the nature of human agency and consider a greater role for ordinary people in the past. Thus, in a final sense, this book demonstrates that studying everyday life in the past matters for understandings of human societies. Interpretations of the past may be flawed if researchers do not take daily life into account, as I illustrate in chapter 7, by comparing and contrasting the Chan study to archaeological analyses of farmers in complex societies that do not consider day-to-day life.

Everyone, from rich to poor, has an everyday life. By using an ancient Maya farming community as the case study for studying everyday life, this book is also about ordinary people and the importance of their daily lives. I have found that studying everyday life is particularly useful for understanding the roles and relations of ordinary people in past societies. A society's textual record often focuses on the grand events of history and is often written by and for elites. Such records can leave out the histories of ordinary people, and when they do discuss ordinary people, they often do so from an indirect perspective. But everyone in the course of their day-to-day life leaves some material and spatial traces in the archaeological record. The archaeological traces of ordinary people's daily lives can provide the missing social information to understand the past. An analysis of everyday life can reveal the *hidden transcripts*: the social perspectives developed by members of society through their lived experiences, which are omitted from *public transcripts*, the overt and public representations of social life inscribed in the texts, art, and architecture of society's dominant groups (sensu stricto Scott 1990).

A focus on everyday life underscores the crucial role that archaeologists can play in reconstructing the lost voices of traditionally neglected social groups. Rather than being a part of the anonymous masses, in Michel de Certeau's (1984) writing on everyday life, the ordinary person doing ordinary things is the one who is the "common hero" of human history. Chan's farmers' daily lives might be overlooked in grand narratives of human history, but the existence of twenty centuries of sustainable lifestyles illustrates the consequential nature of understanding "common heroes" in the study of humanity.

Why Everyday Life?

Everyday life is at the core of human existence. People walk, they talk, they dwell, they meet, they play, they pray. It is through these daily practices that humans construct, perceive, and modify their world. A typical day involves spending time with families, doing work, and interacting with others in homes and across communities. These activities constitute the social fabric around which people create enduring memories and relate to others and the world around them.

While these insights at one level might seem obvious, the major intellectual traditions of anthropological theory—such as structuralism, functionalism, cultural ecology, cultural evolutionism, symbolic anthropology, existentialism, big man theory, and so on—assigned people's everyday practices a passive position in understanding human societies, because daily practices were presumed to be guided by external systems that are beyond people's grasp or presumed to be determined by individual subjectivities, particularly the will of important people in society, who are often men. This lack of attention to ordinary practices is amplified in archaeology, particularly in the archaeology of the world's ancient civilizations, with its traditional focus on excavating the exotic and monumental remains of temples and tombs.

Grand narratives of human history do not just overlook everyday life: they trivialize it and make it invisible. They do so by presenting a narrative of a society as dependent upon broader powers and dynamics, denying and mystifying the things people do and the structural causes that develop through everyday actions.

The seeming routine and ordinary nature of everyday life, such as waking up each morning to a bowl of cereal or corn gruel, is what leads it to be taken for granted not only by social theorists but also often by people living their lives (Bourdieu 1977). However, given the multiplicity of actions possible in any one context, the very routines and ordinariness of daily life that at first make it seem unremarkable are actually what make it quite remarkable.

Despite its ordinary appearance, everyday life comprises the complexity of the experiences and interactions that people have with others and their world. These day-to-day experiences are a nexus of activities and interactions that both give shape and meaning to the world and give people the ability to shape their world and make it meaningful. While humans live in a world that has been historically constructed, they also live in a world that becomes anew as they reconstruct it through their daily actions. Rather than everyday life being simply mundane, out of the richness of everyday life arises a remarkable commentary on social and mental phenomena of the human world. It is at the daily level of people's lived experiences that the micro (self, interaction, experience) and macro (institutions, power relations, societies) levels of social life intersect.

Scholars such as Pierre Bourdieu (1977) suggest that researchers can look to everyday life to identify how people are socialized into existing social relations. In this way, studying everyday life can provide a means to understand stasis and tradition—how and why things may stay the same through time. Stasis and tradition are not a condition of inaction. Staying the same requires the continued reproduction of existing relations. For other scholars, such as Michel de Certeau (1984), everyday life additionally constitutes a haven for the development of countercultural acts that can lead to change. Thus, by studying everyday life, researchers can explore both how things stay the same and how they change: people learn about and critique their world through the ordinary practices of everyday life. Reproduction and improvisation are two dimensions of everyday life that I bring together in this book, particularly in chapter 2: everyday life is simultaneously a haven for the reproduction of tradition and the production of innovation in society.

Because everyday life comprises the ordinary practices, objects, and places that make up a person's world, the dual potential of everyday life to be habitual and surprising is clearly visible in the archaeological record of people's daily material and spatial practices, as seen in two case studies from the pre-Columbian Aztecs and eighteenth-century Jamaicans. Aztec girls began to learn to weave from their mothers and older sisters within their homes at a young age (Hendon 2010: 129–35). The backstrap loom, the pre-Columbian weaving device, could be scaled down to their size. As young girls learned to hold their bodies in particular ways to develop their elaborate craft, through the repetitive day-to-day acts of weaving on the backstrap loom, across days, weeks, and years, they shaped their bodies and their selves as Aztec women and weavers.

In eighteenth-century Jamaica, street markets were part of everyday life of the enslaved who exchanged crafts and foods through these informal markets (Hauser 2008). But these markets were not just economic in nature; they were places where enslaved people met, passed on information, and developed social networks beyond the plantation, which at times enabled them to organize armed resistance such as the 1831 rebellion. As seen in these two examples, everyday life provides the possibilities for the development of both normative and counternormative actions. Seemingly ordinary day-to-day actions are central for the production and reproduction of society and also for its transformation.

A central question of archaeological research is the question of change—how and why do cultures, societies, and people's lives change? Traditional social theoretical inquiry focused on the dramatic catalysts of social change, such as culture contact, wars, revolutions, and the will of great men. Indeed, dramatic catalysts may be few and far between in either the course of human history or the course of a person's life. This is not to say that dramatic catalysts are unimportant, but it is to say that they are not the singular prime movers of change in human societies. Scholars such as Henri Lefebvre, de Certeau, and James C. Scott encourage researchers to see that social change happens throughout people's daily lives as they accept and question, consciously or unconsciously, the meaning of existing social relations. The dynamic undercurrents of daily activities—the variations and contradictions that are inherent in the plurality of simultaneously occurring day-to-day practices—are instrumental in social change. If researchers refocus their interpretive lens onto the ordinary events of human history, they can begin to make sense of how people organized and changed their world. Researchers can begin to understand not just that social change has happened, but how, why, and with what meaning change has happened. In this light, the *longue durée* (Braudel 1972) of the everyday imprints that constitute the archaeological record provide a fertile ground for understanding how everyday practices are embedded in long-term histories.

While it is obvious that daily lives are deeply embedded in local experiences and interpersonal interactions, it is also the case that everyday life is just as deeply implicated with broader social, political, and power relations. Everyday life is not some lesser opposite of political life in a simplistic dichotomy of the private versus public sphere or domestic versus political domains. Everyday life is the locus through which political and power relations are constructed and operate. Thus, any analysis of power and politics in society must also be an analysis of everyday life. In this sense, the goal of taking an everyday life perspective on human societies is not just to describe daily life but to use it as a lens through which to develop critical knowledge about the world. Such critical studies of everyday life expose both the possibilities that daily practices engender and the structural constraints and power relations in society that curtail them.

Because archaeology is a discipline that explores human social and cultural life through the study of the material and spatial remains of the past, its material and spatial focus is particularly suited to studying everyday life. Indeed, one could ask, what is archaeology if not the study of everyday life? Archaeologists study—in James Deetz's (1977) famous words—"small things forgotten," the taken-for-granteds and left-behinds of past daily life. Much of the archaeological record is a palimpsest of the minutiae of past day-to-day practices: "it is the little routines that people performed day in and day out that produced much of the pattern material remains recovered in the archaeological record" (Lightfoot 2005: 17). This ordinary nature of the archaeological record "compels us to recognize the impact of the everyday decisions made by ancient people" (Monica Smith 2010: xiv). Archaeologists do not typically find random, unique, or idiosyncratic events, because these occurrences may not endure, given the potentially ephemeral nature of their singular traces. The materials and spaces that often endure the ravages of time and nature are the remains of people's repetitive day-to-day practices. In this sense a substantial part of the archaeological record comprises the material and spatial imprints of daily life.

Although archaeology's initial focus was on macro phenomena (chronology building, identifying regional cultures, and documenting the opulence of great civilizations), the study of ordinary things has always played a role in archaeologists' understanding of these macro phenomena. The culture historians' interest in chronology building led to the investigation of the mundane aspects of the archaeological record, such as ceramics and stone tools. The classificatory, typological, and stratigraphic analyses of these materials, which form the foundation of disciplinary work in archaeology, allow for the chronological ordering of the long history and prehistory of the archaeological record. But these provide only skeleton histories that, while based on ordinary objects, are ultimately devoid of everyday life. Despite the everyday "nature" of much of the archaeological record, the models that archaeologists have used to interpret this record have often been inconsistent with the specificity of the record they study and the questions they ask. Archaeological borrowings of geological models to define cultural stratigraphy, biological taxonomic methods to create typologies, natural selection theory to model how human populations adapt to their environment, systemic and statistical models to define how societies function and operate, and structural and symbolic anthropology to infer mental templates have all required that archaeologists systematize the detail of the archaeological record into an abstract system (such as a typology) already defined in the imported model. These borrowings have productively pushed forward certain aspects of archaeology (Willey and Sabloff 1980). But subsuming the details of the archaeological record into an abstract system that itself becomes the object of study implies that the archaeological record is composed of macro categories, structures, or systems rather than the remains of everyday practices (also see Monica Smith 2010: 13). Rather than subsuming the details of the archaeological record into systemic or statistical models, archaeologists can use these details to provide evidence for human organization and change that links the micro and macro levels of human society. An archaeological approach to everyday life is essential because ordinary objects and spatial arrangements formalize the relations that people create, use, and modify and through which they learn about themselves and their social world.

About Chan

I developed the Chan project between 2002 and 2009, bringing together a team of over 120 archaeologists, botanists, geologists, geographers, chemists, computer scientists, artists, students, workers, and volunteers from Belize, the United States, England, Canada, and China to collaborate on a study of the everyday lives of Maya farmers (Robin 2012a). The Chan project received a half a million dollars in funding from two National

Science Foundation grants, a National Endowment for the Humanities grant, a National Geographic Society grant, a Heinz Foundation for Latin American Studies grant, and Northwestern University grants, among other awards. Roughly half of the project funding came from archaeology grants, and the other half came from collaborative research grants: highlighting and strengthening the role of collaboration in the archaeological project, which became particularly important for developing methods for studying everyday life, as I begin to discuss in the prologue and continue to discuss in chapter 4.

The Maya farming community of Chan is located in the upper Belize Valley region of west-central Belize, in an undulating upland area between the Mopan and Macal branches of the Belize River. Its ancient inhabitants constructed a productive landscape of agricultural terraces and homes across its rolling hills surrounding a small community center. This agricultural base supported Chan's two-thousand-year occupation (circa 800 BC–AD 1200).

The eight-year Chan project documented the remains of 274 households and 1,223 agricultural terraces in a 3.2-square-kilometer area surrounding Chan's community center. To gain an understanding of Chan's long history and the social, economic, and vocational diversity of its residents, project participants excavated a representative 10 percent sample of Chan's households (26 households) and associated agricultural terraces. We also excavated all ritual, residential, and administrative buildings at Chan's community center. These archaeological remains, along with roughly half a million artifacts of everyday life, one of the largest archaeological samples of Maya farming life, make up the comprehensive data set of life at Chan, from which I am able to document the two-thousand-year history of the community and the importance of studying farmers' everyday lives.

The majority of Chan's residents were farmers, and their agricultural terraces were the most ubiquitous and substantial constructions at Chan. Farmers constructed terraces up and down hillslopes and across channels. Chan's farmers lived in the midst of their agricultural terraces. Thus, rather than being a densely nucleated community, the Chan community consisted of clustered farmsteads around a community center. But there were also many others who lived in the community: craft workers, diviners, and community leaders. By exploring the homes, workplaces (which were often in homes), and meeting places of Chan's varied community members, we were able to identify shared understandings of home and community that rooted people in place, as well as the different and conflicting understandings of life and society that led to changing dynamics within the community.

Chan's community center is architecturally rather unremarkable: six buildings dedicated to community-level ceremony, administration, and adjudication surround a plaza at the center of the community and an associated open plaza to the west. On the east and west sides of the Central Plaza are an E-Group, a distinctive type of paired temple architectural complex common throughout the Maya area that was an important location for ritual and ancestor veneration. The east structure of the E-Group is the tallest structure at Chan, rising to a height of 5.6 meters.

The Belize River valley region where Chan is located was a peripheral and provincial part of the Maya world. Not until the end of the Late Classic (AD 670–800/830) was this area unified under the short-lived and late-flourishing Xunantunich polity capital, with its towering forty-three-meter-high main temple, El Castillo (LeCount and Yaeger 2010; Leventhal and Ashmore 2004). Xunantunich's rise to power was rapid, and so was its decline. This regional history further makes the Chan community an interesting case study by which to monitor how everyday life in a farming community is transformed through its interaction with a polity capital—but also the less explored corollary, how a polity capital may have had to accommodate to preexisting contexts of everyday life within farming communities. As I discuss in this book, Chan's residents, across the community's long history, developed resources and production and complex webs of sociopolitical and economic relations with multiple centers within and beyond the Belize River valley. These resources, production, and sociopolitical relations constrained the network of power that the rising Xunantunich polity capital hoped to dominate, such that Xunantunich achieved domination only for a short period of time.

Exploring farmers' daily lives at Chan reveals the ways in which they developed twenty centuries of socially and environmentally sustainable lifestyles. Chan's residents innovated conservation-wise agricultural technologies and forest management strategies that enabled them to establish a long-lived community. Cooperating farm families constructed Chan's terraced agricultural landscape, and the agricultural system they developed expanded through time. Farmers' terraces avoided soil erosion and maximized water infiltration, incorporating complex small-scale irrigation and water storage systems. A forest maintenance strategy maintained a diverse mature, closed-canopy tropical forest even as population expanded during the Classic period (AD 250–900) and farmers had a growing need for fuel, construction material, and agricultural land. The type of sustainable forest management practiced by farmers at Chan is distinct from the more extractive practices seen at larger Maya civic-centers, where royals culled the mature forest across the Classic period.

In social terms, the community avoided extremes of wealth and power, as all residents from humblest farmer to community leader had access to a similar range of exotic items and lived in perishable houses with similar outward appearances. Residents' health remained consistent across Chan's two-thousand-year history, in contrast to that seen at larger Maya civic-centers, where residents' health declined by the end of the Classic period. Residents were involved in community-wide ritual and political practices that focused on celebrating the community as a whole, rather than individual community leaders. Some of the ritual and political practices innovated at Chan were adopted by Maya royalty and incorporated into state practice, while others were avoided by royals. Avoidance of extremes of wealth and power, more equitable distribution of goods, consistency in health, and communal focus on ritual and politics are some of the socially effective strategies that residents established to help ensure that their community endured.

From a traditional archaeological perspective, Chan would be considered a minor center, unremarkable in terms of size and architectural elaboration, but this perspective misses the richness of everyday life at Chan. Opulent Maya civic-centers, with their towering temple pyramids that usually are the focus of Maya archaeological research, may have been impressive in their time but had rising and falling political histories. Comparing Chan's longevity and its social and environmental strategies with much more opulent centers and their inequitable distributions of wealth, hierarchical political institutions, declining health, and deforestation illustrates the ways in which some of the most important lessons about human societies, and the importance of social and economic sustainability, may be learned from everyday life at a seemingly unremarkable place such as Chan.

About This Book

This book proposes a *critical everyday life approach* to studying the ancient world that brings together social theory and archaeology to illustrate how studying everyday life can reveal a critical commentary on the nature of human societies. The project of the book is to undo the trivialization of everyday life that resulted from the development of grand narratives of human history. Toward this end, this book is organized into two parts: "Theory and Method in Everyday Life" and "Everyday Life at Chan." Part 1 proposes theories and methods that address questions of everyday life, ordinary people, places, and things, and social change. Part 2 illustrates the multiple ways in which a critical everyday life approach is central to archaeology through the exploration of a case study on the everyday lives of Maya farmers at Chan.

Part 1 brings together three lines of inquiry: (1) social theoretical perspectives on everyday life, (2) archaeological theories on households, space, gender, and historical archaeology, and (3) archaeological methods that are intensive, collaborative, and detail oriented that expose past daily lives. I propose this constellation of perspectives and methods to further an understanding of the importance of the ordinary for broader interpretations of human societies. Chapter 2 explores a selective set of scholarship within the vast social theoretical literature on everyday life that develops *critical* studies of everyday life. The theoreticians I discuss in chapter 2 are explicitly eclectic and polyglot, drawing from a wide range of theoretical perspectives such as Marxism, phenomenology, feminist theory, developmental biology, critical theory, and subaltern studies, among others, but without a dogmatic adherence to a particular theoretical perspective. Loosely speaking, these scholars could be seen as working through ideas put forward by pioneering everyday life thinkers Henri Lefebvre and Michel de Certeau and include Mikhail Bakhtin, Pierre Bourdieu, Fernand Braudel, André Breton, Sigmund Freud, Michael Gardiner, Erving Goffman, Agnes Heller, Ben Highmore, Tim Ingold, Alice Kaplan, Alf Lüdtke, Hans Medick, Daniel Miller, Kristin Ross, James Scott, Michael Sheringham, Dorothy Smith, Raymond Williams, and Susan Willis, among others. Many of the most prominent social theorists discussed in contemporary thought are missing from this list, and this is intentional. Everyday life scholarship highlights the overlooked, not only in human life but also in the scholarly literature.

Chapter 3 explores the intersecting dimensions of household, space, gender, and historical archaeology research in archaeology. Household archaeology draws attention to how past peoples organized and made meaningful their domestic spaces (e.g., Allison 1999; Hendon 2004, 2010; Hutson 2010; King 2006; Robb 2007; Robin 2003, 2004). Space, place, and landscape research expands this agenda to understand how all living spaces are meaningfully constructed and experienced by people across their daily lives (e.g., Ashmore 2002, 2004; Ashmore and Knapp 1999; David and Thomas 2008a; Johnson 2007; A. Joyce 2004, 2010; Robin and Rothschild 2002; Smith 2003; Tilley 1994, 2010). Feminist and gender archaeology have drawn explicit attention to the importance of incorporating all social groups into archaeological analyses—not just different genders, but different class, ethnic, and age groups (e.g., Brumfiel 1992; Gilchrist 1999; R. Joyce 2000, 2004; Meskell 1999, 2002; Meskell and Joyce 2003; Pyburn 2004; Robin and Brumfiel 2008). By studying the material remains of past societies that also produce historical records, historic archaeology draws particular attention to the material dimensions of past everyday life (e.g., Deetz 1977; Hall and Silliman 2006; Hauser 2008; Hicks and Beaudry 2006; Johnson 1996; Lightfoot 2005; Voss 2008a).

By situating the production of archaeological theories of everyday life and broader social theories of everyday life on equal footing in chapters 2 and 3, I hope to develop a dialogue between the two. While I am critical in the prologue of nonarchaeological scholars for re-creating studies of ordinary materials and spaces that have long been central in archaeological research, I am equally critical of myself (Robin 2002a, 2006) and other archaeologists who have prioritized the theoretical knowledge borrowed from outside of the discipline of archaeology, which has the end result of making archaeology appear to be a discipline that borrows theory rather than one that creates it.

Because data and theory are mutually implicated, critical everyday life thinkers are as concerned with methods as they are with theory. They constructively combine empirical and theoretical work. From a methodological perspective, an everyday life approach is quite suitable to archaeological inquiry, because of the material and spatial nature of the archaeological record. Chapter 4 is the first chapter to begin an in-depth exploration of the Chan research, as I designed research and collaboration and developed methods for an archaeological inquiry into everyday life. This chapter explores the importance of methodological issues such as collaboration with local communities, horizontal excavations of the contexts of everyday life, investigation of the vast expanses of open spaces that are locations for daily interactions, and engaging new scientific analyses that are revealing ever more detailed information on past daily life. It highlights the critical role collaboration plays in everyday life research, both multidisciplinary research collaboration that develops robust and independent multiple lines of evidence about past everyday life and collaboration with local communities that can challenge and transform existing research frameworks. As a unit the first section of this book illustrates how theoretical and methodological perspectives can be effectively brought into concert to critically explore people and their everyday lives in archaeological analyses.

After this theoretical and methodological ground for the study of everyday life is developed, part 2 of the book proceeds to explore the case study of Maya farmers at Chan. Chapter 5 develops the background information and history of the Chan community. Chapter 6 details the everyday lives of the Maya residents of Chan who were farmers, craft workers, diviners, and community leaders, and explores the developments and changes in the community across its two-thousand-year history. This chapter exposes how the details of ancient everyday life are far from mundane and comprise a diverse array of actions and interactions that are critical for interpretations of organization and power relations in human societies. Residents' everyday practices are a fertile ground for the development of complex systems of knowledge and the innovation of new technologies. Many of these developments and innovations have long been attributed to Maya elites and high culture, but as seen from the Chan study, they were existing practices that elites adopted from farmers. Other ways of understanding the world and organizing a community developed at Chan are in stark contrast with that seen at major Maya centers. Ultimately, everyday life at Chan reveals powerful lessons about social and environmental sustainability in the world. The Chan study, with its two-thousand-year history, illustrates how the meaning of long-term changes in society can be better understood through a detailed investigation of everyday life.

Chapter 7 illustrates how understanding everyday life at Chan facilitates a critique of the nature of human societies and challenges researchers to rethink and revise prominent anthropological concepts about the constitution of societies and nature of human agency. This chapter explores anthropological ideas such as the role of population pressure and state control in the emergence of intensive agriculture; the relationship between ideology, false consciousness, and power; the nature of political economies; the relationship between cities and rural producers; and the nature of human agency. This chapter concludes by comparing and contrasting the Chan study to archaeological analyses of farmers in complex societies that do not consider everyday life, to illustrate how interpretations of the past may be flawed if researchers do not take everyday life into account.

Although this book is divided into two sections—the first being more "theoretical" and the second being more "empirical"—the two sections are not isolated entities. Theoretical and empirical research are dependent upon one another. There is a constant interplay between theoretical issues that develop from empirical studies and empirical problems that relate to theoretical arguments. This plays out across the book as chapter 4 interjects empirical evidence into the more broadly theoretical first part of the book and chapter 7 interjects theoretical issues into the more broadly empirical second part of the book. The interrelatedness of theoretical and empirical work is a central aspect of an everyday life approach. An academic understanding of people cannot be found at the abstract level but must be located in the practice of studying people's everyday lives. The book concludes in chapter 8 by returning to the three meanings of the title of this book: (1) everyday life matters because what people do on a daily basis is critical in the construction of their societies, (2) everyday life is the matter of much of the archaeological record, and (3) studying everyday life matters for archaeologists' interpretations of human societies.

I ✳ Theory and Method
in Everyday Life

2 ✳ Social Theory
   and Everyday Life

In recent years, studies of everyday life have become a central aspect of multidisciplinary social theoretical discussions (Gardiner 2000; Highmore 2002a, 2002b; Lüdtke 1995; Sheringham 2006). The aim of critical everyday life theorizing is not just to describe daily life but also to show how understanding it provides a critical knowledge of human societies. Critical perspectives on everyday life demonstrate how people construct their social world through daily practices and expose the structural constraints and power relations that exist for and among individuals in society and how these practices affect and are affected by day-to-day interactions.

A focus on everyday life allows exploration of the intersection of people and their societies and cultures, because culture and society are not abstractions that are exterior to people: people create and experience social structures throughout their daily lives. It is this sense of everyday life that Raymond Williams (1989: 4) gets at in his influential essay "Culture Is Ordinary" where he states, "Culture is ordinary, in every society and in every mind."

Taking everyday life seriously allows scholars to move beyond Cartesian and Platonic dualities (objective/subjective, body/mind, macro/micro, structure/action, material/ideal, and so on). These dualities have been at the heart of traditional theorizing in the West and have forced theoretical developments to fracture into opposing camps that, for example, address material or ideal aspects of social life (for example, cultural ecology versus symbolic anthropology) instead of modeling social life as a place where the material and ideal intersect. For the past thirty years, scholars have paid heightened attention to the question of how to break down dualities (e.g., Bourdieu 1977; Ortner 1984), but as Williams (1973) discusses, dualities are so deeply embedded in Western society and culture that they are difficult to forsake (also see Ingold 2011; Joyce and Lopiparo 2005). But as Kaplan and Ross (1987: 3) note, "Everyday life is situated somewhere between the subjective, phenomenological sensory apparatus of the individual and reified institutions. Its starting point is neither the intentional subject dear to humanistic thinking nor the determining paradigms that bracket lived experience."

Understanding everyday life not as some impoverished domain of habitual activity but as a means and medium through which people simultaneously construct (objectify) and experience (subjectify) their world dissolves Cartesian and Platonic dualities.

This chapter explores critical social theories on everyday life by focusing on and bridging five strands of everyday life thinking across the twentieth and into the twenty-first centuries: (1) Henri Lefebvre's pioneering work in the mid-twentieth century on the centrality of everyday life, (2) 1970s to mid-1980s work by practice theorists and feminists, particularly Pierre Bourdieu and Dorothy Smith, who develop a rationale for how everyday living can socialize people into existing social relations, (3) postcolonial and feminist theory at the end of the twentieth century, particularly the work of Michel de Certeau, James Scott, and Susan Willis, who explain how everyday life can provide a space for creative or counternormative actions that can question the status quo and lead to change, (4) work across twentieth-century everyday life scholarship from German, Hungarian, and Russian schools as well as the previously discussed French and Anglo-American traditions that focuses on the emancipatory potential of everyday life (particularly highlighting the work of Alf Lüdtke and Hans Medick and the *Alltagsgeschichte* [history of everyday life] school, Agnes Heller and the Budapest school, and the Bakhtin Circle), and (5) as a segue to chapter 3, this chapter concludes by looking at recent work of the first decade of the twenty-first century by archaeologically trained anthropologists Tim Ingold and Daniel Miller, who are furthering perspectives on the spatial and material dimensions of everyday life.

The everyday life thinkers I highlight in this chapter are not meant to exhaust the gamut of social theoretical perspectives on everyday life, and in this sense this chapter is not a literature review (for reviews see Gardiner 2000; Highmore 2002a, 2002b; Sheringham 2006).[1] The scholarship I present represents strands of everyday life thinking, which can fruitfully combine to develop a critical theory of everyday life. Together with archaeological theory (chapter 3), the ideas in this chapter can further develop an understanding of the material and spatial dimensions of everyday life.

I begin this chapter with the work of Henri Lefebvre, but not because he was the first thinker on everyday life—his work arose within a panoply of early- to mid-twentieth-century thinking on everyday life from the work of Surrealists, Dadaists, Freudian psychopathology, microsociologies, and Annales School historians (e.g., Aragon 1926; Braudel 1972; Breton 1924, 1928; Freud 1914; Goffman 1959). Lefebvre's work on everyday life takes thinking in a new direction focusing on the critical power of everyday life. For Lefebvre, everyday life is not an impoverished domain of life from which humans must escape to reach higher levels of critical thinking. Everyday life is the means and medium through which people live higher and ordinary lives.

Perhaps the most prominent perspective on everyday life at the time Lefebvre began writing was promoted through the work of the Surrealists (e.g., Aragon 1926; Breton 1924, 1928). In the mid-1920s, Lefebvre met with other writers and artists at the "Bureau of Surrealist Research" (15 Rue de Grenelle, Paris), and he had a lifelong, albeit at times lukewarm, engagement with surrealism (Gardiner 2000: 72–73). The Surrealists brought attention to everyday life through their work but maintained a dichotomy between the everyday and the non-everyday, the real and the surreal: from the everyday springs forth the marvelous. Although Lefebvre drew upon surrealism in his work, he also critiqued its adherence to an ideal/real dichotomy and its notion that a truer reality than everyday life exists—one that could be grasped only through higher mental capacities. Lefebvre noted that "superior, differentiated and highly specialized activities have never been separated from everyday practice, they have only appeared to be so" ([1958] 2008: 86). The experiences of human subjectivity are always situated in everyday life.

In a similar vein, Freud's (1914) *Psychopathology of Everyday Life* delineated the important relationship between psychoanalysis and everyday life, work that was influential in the later writing of de Certeau. Freud explored how consciously suppressed events could reemerge to produce troubled everyday lives. The Annales School historians explored how the *longue durée* of history could affect everyday life (Braudel 1972). Erving Goffman's (1959) microsociology of self and everyday life provided a decisive critique of macrosociological analyses of social structure. All of these perspectives prompt a serious discussion of everyday life but still maintain a dichotomy between everyday life and other higher, conscious, mental, historical, and macro structures of human existence, which Lefebvre's notion of everyday life sought to dissolve.

There is perhaps no need to justify beginning a discussion of everyday life thinking with the work of Lefebvre, as he was the first thinker to specifically problematize everyday life as a topic of study in and of itself. This attempt to problematize everyday life may indeed be what led Lefebvre to question taken-for-granted notions of everyday life as other to higher, surreal, ideal, and macro domains of life.

Henri Lefebvre and the Centrality of Everyday Life

The French Marxist philosopher and sociologist Henri Lefebvre is best known for his work on space and urbanism, as read by social geographers, particularly David Harvey and Edward Soja. His work critically engages perspectives from independent Marxism to existentialism, phenomenology, surrealism, and structuralism. But for Lefebvre, everyday life itself was one of the most mysterious and substantial aspects of human existence (Gardiner 2000). Lefebvre remains one of the most prolific writers on this topic, to which he returned over and over again across his career, most prominently in his three-volume *Critique of Everyday Life,* with original volume publication dates of 1947, 1961, and 1981, as well as *Everyday Life in the Modern World* (1968) and the posthumously published *Rhythmanalysis: Space, Time and Everyday Life* (2004). Lefebvre's first volume of *Critique of Everyday Life* (1947) was reprinted in 1958 with a new introduction, which is equivalent in length to the original volume. The 1958 reprint is key to understanding Lefebvre's conception of everyday life.

In the 1958 foreword, Lefebvre states that "we need to think about what is happening around us, within us, each and every day" ([1958] 2008: 14). But Lefebvre knows that this is not as easy a task as one might imagine. Citing Hegel's oft-quoted maxim "The familiar is not necessarily the known" ([1958] 2008: 15, 132), Lefebvre draws attention simultaneously to the complex nature of everyday life and to its prominent absence in mainstream social theory. For Lefebvre, the task ahead is not simply one of documenting everyday life but one of achieving a critical knowledge about the world through understanding everyday life.

To convince scholars not to take everyday life for granted, Lefebvre reminded them that everyday life is where people enter into relations with the world around them and others in the world, where both subject and object are constituted and materially realized in human practice. Everyday life can be seen as the foundation upon which all other aspects of human society are constructed. In Lefebvre's words, a "landscape without flowers or a magnificent woods may be depressing for the passer-by; but flowers and trees should not make us forget the earth beneath, which has a secret life and a richness of its own" ([1958] 2008: 87). An analogy that Lefebvre used to make this point is that of walking in the French countryside—where a person can "discover the immense human wealth that the humblest facts of everyday life contain" ([1958] 2008: 132). In this example, Lefebvre explores the materiality of the agrarian history of France, which is at first hidden in the countryside but becomes visible for a walker who pays attention to the material details of that countryside. This materiality of thought and action in everyday life was pivotal in Lefebvre's thinking and lends his ideas to archaeological analyses that develop understandings of past lifeways through exploring the material record of human thought and action.

For Lefebvre the centrality of everyday life is in its constitution of the totality of human social life. Everyday life is not some impoverished form of mundane, domestic, or personal activity; it is "profoundly related to *all* activities, and encompasses them with all their differences and their conflicts; it is their meeting place, their bond, their common ground" ([1958] 2008: 97). Higher institutions such as political authority or higher ideas such as ideology, religion, and worldview are not outside of or separate from everyday life. The externality of these institutions and ideas, for Lefebvre, involves nothing more than "a measure of illusion" ([1958] 2008: 94). Everyday life includes political life, which is formed within it, takes place within it, and requires knowledge of it. Political life only appears detached from everyday life, as politicians or historians focus on privileged political events such as elections and regime change. As Lefebvre put it more pointedly—failure to examine everyday life is akin to a philosophical or historical naiveté; it is falling into a trap laid out by the great men of this world. Scholars know that great scenes of history are staged, but when they ignore everyday life in their studies they are like the awestruck onlookers who are "all but ready to start believing in the divine nature of kings" ([1958] 2008: 136). For Lefebvre, any theory of "superhuman moments is inhuman," as it is "in day-to-day life that the truth in a body and a soul must be grasped" ([1958] 2008: 127).

Lefebvre took a similar stance on the relationship between higher ideas and everyday life as ideas are produced, maintained, and transformed within everyday life ([1958] 2008: 94–98). Thus, rather than being seen as mundane, routine, and devoid of meaning, everyday life should hold a privileged role in understandings of human societies, because "it is in everyday life and everyday life alone that . . . general and abstract terms are concretely realized" ([1958] 2008: 95). Ultimately, meaning is found within life, not beyond it. Meaning is not separate from being ([1958] 2008: 144).

Just as everyday life is not some impoverished domain of action, it is also not some static and unchanging entity. Across the actions and interactions that constitute everyday life there is both a potential for the maintenance of traditional structures and a potential for revolutionary change ([1958] 2008: 45–49). Thus, Lefebvre situates everyday life as a perspective from which researchers can develop a social understanding of both transformative action and the maintenance of social norms.

A stated goal of Lefebvre's position on everyday life is "To confront philosophers with life" ([1958] 2008: 85). And life certainly confronted Lefebvre's thought. Scholars of Lefebvre's writing note that his early work, which anticipated popular uprisings in France, is optimistic about the emancipatory capacities of everyday life, while his later work more cautiously states everyday life's revolutionary role as it can be limited by social constraints (Gardiner 2000; Highmore 2002a; Trebitsch 2008). Because Lefebvre's everyday life approach entails concomitant attention to theoretical and empirical research (which he saw as necessarily entwined), I think he would have viewed such commentaries on his work as evidence of the working out of his approach.

While Lefebvre's work draws together strands of many of the leading theoretical positions of his time, he eschewed a blind faith in any specific theoretical perspective. Playfully he summed up his position by stating, "Dogmatism is a great evil which comes in countless forms. If we are to exterminate it we must hunt it down in every nook and cranny and drag it from its hiding place by the tail like a rat" ([1958] 2008: 56).

Volume 1 of Lefebvre's *Critique of Everyday Life* takes on the very essence of Western philosophy. In his attempt to confront philosophy with life, he posits that philosophy as constructed since the Enlightenment has trivialized everyday life in contrast to higher intellectual traditions such as philosophy, science, and art. He is critical of a philosophy that is seated in the mind and avoids human existence and the plight of ordinary people. He sees such a philosophy as deeply rooted in the Cartesian and Platonic dualism of mind and body, ideal and real, so dominant in France at the time he was writing and still a conundrum for social theorists today. A notion of everyday life transcends this dichotomy by unifying the mind and body in the daily lives of ordinary people.

Lefebvre's attention to everyday life is attention not just to developing theory but to the concomitant development of methods and empirical research. Researchers must develop a deep commitment to furthering empirical studies of everyday life in their work—a position he first addresses at the end of his first volume of the *Critique of Everyday Life* ([1958] 2008) and takes up more fully in his second volume ([1961] 2008). He critiques theoretical analyses, which he sees as supporting an extreme intellectual position, such as structuralism, and here he cites Claude Lévi-Strauss's statement that research could involve "'just a quarter of an hour alone' with a man from a distinct or extinct culture" ([1958] 2008: 7 and fn.13). For Lefebvre, a quarter of an hour of intellectual conversation is not enough for understanding another culture. Ultimately, Lefebvre and other everyday life theorists, while not antitheoretical, stand in a contentious relationship with traditional modes of theorizing because they embrace the search for an abstract truth—as something that can be divorced from the materiality of life and its experiences. Thus, methods and empirical research become as central as theory, in order to, in Lefebvre's words, "supplant the ramblings of philosophers" ([1958] 2008: 196). These methods include detailed attention to everyday life and its materialization of thought and action and the use of precise cases and examples ([1958] 2008: 196–200). Thus, an everyday life perspective is one that must combine empirical and theoretical research ([1961] 2008: 5). Ultimately, the goal of an everyday life approach is to develop a new kind of humanism, "a humanism which believes in the human because it knows it" ([1958] 2008: 252).

Having established the centrality of everyday life in understanding human societies and critiqued leading epistemologies of his time that had not thought through the crucial role of everyday life, Lefebvre's work serves as a foundation for future thinking on everyday life. Highlighting the material reality of thought and action in everyday life makes his ideas particularly amenable to archaeological practice.

Everyday Socialization: Practice Theory and Feminist Approaches to Everyday Life in the 1970s to mid-1980s

Philosopher, anthropologist, and sociologist, Pierre Bourdieu is perhaps the most influential scholar highlighted in this chapter. His theory of practice, first articulated in the *Outline of a Theory of Practice* (1977), brought the concept of practice (what people do on a day-to-day basis) to the center of social science research. At the heart of Bourdieu's writing, published in twenty-five books, is the idea that human experience is rooted in people's daily practices, not some outside structure that is imposed upon them.

Presaged by Lefebvre's interest in everyday life is Bourdieu's argument in *Outline of a Theory of Practice* that everyday social routines have been largely overlooked in social theoretical writing, which still in the 1970s was informed by dualistic Cartesian and Platonic logics. The two dominant theoretical paradigms in France at the time, Lévi-Strauss's structuralism and the still-prominent Sartrean existentialism, both interpreted daily practices as an impoverished form of human life, but in quite different ways. In structuralism, people's practices are nothing more than reflex automatism; they reflect objective structures of which actors are unaware (Bourdieu 1977: 22–30). In existentialism, practices are created through the subjective genius of actors (Bourdieu 1977: 73–76). Thus, like Lefebvre, Bourdieu saw understanding practices, rather than taking them for granted, as a means to move beyond polarizing debates in the field between objective and subjective positions.

To address these issues Bourdieu asked a seemingly simple question: if what people do on a day-to-day basis is not the product of rules or consciously rational decisions, then how is it that everyday activities often are regular or coordinated? He found the answer in practical knowledge that is acquired through embodied practices (Bourdieu 1977: 3–9). Bourdieu's ideas about practical knowledge are most fully elaborated in *Practical Reason: On the Theory of Action* (1998). Like Lefebvre, in *Practical Reason,* Bourdieu argues that abstract, theoretical knowledge can never fully capture everyday life and further enacts symbolic violence on it through misrepresentations.

Bourdieu was interested in the question of how regularized daily practices are generated. He sought to find the logic of practices, a generating logic of practices, which could explain the existence of daily routines. He located this generating logic in the *habitus*—acquired patterns of thought, behavior, and taste that externalize themselves in concrete material and spatial ways in society and are thus internalized by people living in that society (Bourdieu 1977: 72–95). Through the process of socialization in homes, schools, and so on, children and adults acquire socially learned dispositions through everyday living, experiencing, and interacting with the ordinary materials and spaces that make up their world. Through the socialization of habitus, the home takes on a new dimension in social life: no longer an impoverished domain of private life, in comparison to the active world of public, political decision making, the home becomes a critical arena for the production and reproduction of social life. The attention to the home, and in particular to the material and spatial dimensions of daily life through which people learn about their world, has made the theory of practice particularly amenable to archaeological thought.

Feminists writing from the middle of the twentieth century onward were also deeply concerned with how regularized daily practices were generated. Women's roles in the private realm of the household as caretakers of their children were taken for granted as the natural state of women's existence in the middle of the century. From Simone de Beauvoir's *The Second Sex* (1953) to Betty Friedan's *The Feminist Mystique* (1963), among others, questioning the naturalness of women's lives as mothers and wives led feminists to expose the problematic nature of traditional assumptions about the public/private, domestic/political dichotomies of modern society and led to discussions of how it came to be that certain patterns of daily life are presumed to be natural.

British feminist sociologist Dorothy Smith, a prolific writer who has analyzed the work of symbolic interactionists, phenomenologists, Marxists, and ethnomethodologists (Smith 1987: 8), most directly takes on the question of how certain daily routines come to be seen as natural in *The Everyday World as Problematic: A Feminist Sociology* (1987). This book is a compilation of a decade of writing and provides a cogent discussion of the relationship between feminist thinking and everyday life from theoretical and methodological perspectives. In formulating a feminist problematic of everyday life, Smith's work draws on the writing of Lefebvre and Bourdieu.

As a feminist, Smith has emphasized two facets in her intellectual work. First, she presents a feminist critique of the central tenets of established sociology, which she sees as implicit in replicating the dominant structures of contemporary society (particularly gender and class structures). And second, in following through with this critique, she attributes the occlusion of sociological research to sociology's attempts to look at society as if outside of it, "ignoring the particular local places in the everyday in which we live our lives" (Smith 1987: 2). Thus, her feminist critique leads her to uncover the importance of understanding everyday life, an importance she has gleaned not only from her academic work but also from her work in the women's movement (1987: 89).

She identifies the separation of the public and private spheres in contemporary capitalist societies as processes that have created a historical association between women, the domestic sphere, and "everyday life" (1987: 5, 18). In the binary oppositions male/female and public life/everyday life, women and everyday life fill the "lesser" sphere of activities in Western capitalist societies while men, production, and politics constitute the dominant sphere. Thus, for Smith, being a feminist implies paying attention to everyday and domestic life.

Smith identifies the everyday world not as some lesser sphere but as "the matrix of our experiences," which "is organized by relations tying it into larger processes in the world as well as by locally organized practices" (1987: 10). People understand their world through their experiences in it and with others in the world, experiences and interactions that are located materially in activities of everyday life. Daily activities are not only brought together in local experiences but are also implicated in extended social and political relations (1987: 133). Thus, everyday life is not merely some degraded domestic domain inhabited by women that capitalism has marginalized and separated from the realms of work and politics.

The study of everyday life not only enables exploration of any aspect of society from a historical and embodied position of lived experiences but also exposes the power relations and political processes of society. Power and everyday life are not isolated or isolatable domains. Power is always created, constituted, and practiced through the interactions of everyday life; thus, any analysis of how power works must also be an analysis of everyday life.

Smith (1987: 91–92) allies her project with the work of Bourdieu, in that her particular concern is to show how practices reproduce preexisting social and power relations. She draws upon Bourdieu's concept of *doxa:* the learned, deeply felt, unconscious beliefs and values that people hold as self-evident. Doxic situations favor the worldviews of dominant groups because people internalize the external structures of the social world as self-evident. A doxic state is what has led to modern assumptions about women's roles in relation to their children and the private sphere as natural. Through doxa, existing power relations in society are constructed in, work in, and impose upon everyday life.

Drawing upon the work of earlier feminist writers, Smith (1987: 61–65) feels that additive feminist work (that is, projects that simply suggest adding women as subjects of study to traditional topics such as political institutions or social stratification) and critical feminist work (that is, projects that simply critique and expose male bias in research) are important steps but not ends in themselves in feminist analyses. This is because these approaches still accept the agenda of disciplines as something that is given. For Smith, creating an alternative agenda begins with analyses of the everyday lives of women (and other marginal groups in society). This provides the necessary step to move beyond society's and sociology's hidden assumptions because methodologically, if researchers select their research questions from those that are constituted in everyday life rather than those that are imposed on it by their disciplines, they open the possibility that a new set of questions that have not yet been posed might be possible (1987: 91). Here Smith's project, like those of other everyday life thinkers, is not simply situated at a theoretical level but is deeply aware of the need for new methodologies and new research strategies from which to think through new questions.

In her 1987 work, Smith's specific goal is to create a sociology *for* women, one that takes a women's perspective seriously, and as such her work is a hallmark of feminist standpoint theory. Feminist standpoint theory has been critiqued, because its suggestion of a unitary female perspective could be seen to imply that women form an essential or even biologically determined category. But Smith responds that any essential female character that she sees today is the result of historical processes (such as the separation of the public and private sphere) rather than being the mark of biology (Gardiner 2000: 192). Smith has always been interested in analyses that foreground not just women but any marginal group in society (1987: 107). In this light, and perhaps in light of critiques of her work, her most recent work talks about creating a sociology for people rather than a sociology for women (Gardiner 2000: 203).

In the 1970s and 1980s, scholars were questioning how established social norms came into being. This question arose from feminist critiques and critiques of both objectivist positions (structuralism) and subjectivist positions (existentialism). Feminists were interested in understanding how women's roles in the private realm of the household as caretakers of their children became taken for granted in society as the natural state of women's existence. Critics of structuralism questioned how there could be regularity in what people do if their actions were not the product of an objective set of rules of which they were unaware. Likewise, the creation of practices through the subjective genius of actors seemed an unlikely mechanism to produce regularity. Within these wide-ranging critiques, everyday life reemerged as a central but overlooked aspect of human life. Within this literature, everyday life becomes the arena where people learn about their world through their surroundings and are socialized into the social life of their societies. The home, rather than being an unimportant domain, becomes a central, but not the only, location of everyday socialization.

Everyday Creativity: Postcolonial and Feminist Approaches to Everyday Life at the End of the Twentieth Century

Next to Lefebvre, the French social theorist, historian, and theologian Michel de Certeau has perhaps made the most significant contributions to the study of everyday life. *The Practice of Everyday Life* (1984), along with the posthumous collaborative second volume, *The Practice of Everyday Life II: Living and Cooking* (de Certeau et al. 1998), develops many of Lefebvre's insights and shows how practice is central to understandings of everyday life. De Certeau was an interdisciplinary scholar of rare dimensions—drawing on anthropology, history, classics, sociology, philosophy, linguistics, and psychoanalysis with equal depth. Bringing myriad theoretical perspectives into productive concert, he engages modern and postmodern thought in a way that few scholars are able to duplicate.

De Certeau read Lefebvre closely and was influenced by his work. But there are significant differences between the two. For Lefebvre, everyday life constituted the totality of human existence. Although Lefebvre was critical of abstract theorizing and abstract truths that envision society devoid of an understanding of everyday life, he still saw theorizing everyday life as a way to represent the totality of the social world. But for de Certeau there was no such unitary totality of social relations, only a plurality of relations as lived by people. Drawing on his training in history and ethnography, de Certeau paid close attention to the details of daily practices as actually lived, the practices that are often only hinted at or noted as loci for future study in Lefebvre's work (Gardiner 2000). In this sense, de Certeau's work finally gets down to mundane acts of everyday life.

Another important thinker for de Certeau was Bourdieu, with his ideas about practice. Both Bourdieu and de Certeau saw practice as central for understandings of human societies. But as de Certeau (1984: 50–60) explained, there are significant differences in their perspectives on everyday practices. While Bourdieu (1977) was interested in the logic of how practices are generated, de Certeau (1984: xv) was interested in what practices produce or do rather than how they are generated, because for de Certeau practices may not only follow existing cultural logics but also disrupt logic. Bourdieu and de Certeau's differing stances on practices can be summed up in the respective titles of their most influential works: Bourdieu's (1977) *Outline of a Theory of Practice* attempts to elucidate a theory that shows how people's practices are produced and reproduced, whereas de Certeau's (1984) *The Practice of Everyday Life* attempts to show how people's everyday practices produce and are themselves the theories through which people understand their world.

De Certeau dedicated *The Practice of Everyday Life* to "the ordinary man." This ordinary person is both ubiquitous and unremarked and is the "common hero" of human history, "walking in countless thousands on the streets." For de Certeau, then, it is ordinary people and ordinary practices that make up the core of social existence. They are the absences of human history that only haunt the stage of traditional thinking and must be taken seriously if researchers attempt to understand human societies.

Like Lefebvre, de Certeau was not one to miss an opportunity to mock what he saw as the abstract and universalizing tendencies of traditional philosophies that neglect ordinary activities. Quoting Wittgenstein, he noted that "when we do philosophy . . . we are like savages, primitive people, who hear the expressions of civilized men, put a false interpretation on them, and then draw the queerest conclusions from it" (1984: 13). Instead of working from up high in philosophy and creating models from the top down, de Certeau (1984: 28) encouraged researchers to practice an ordinary art through the exploration of common situations. In this way scholars can avoid the dilemma posed by Kant, who stated, "That may be right in theory, but it won't work in practice" (cited by de Certeau 1984: 74). For de Certeau (1984: xi), the importance of everyday life comes to light in the study of the details of practices. In the most ordinary of everyday practices there are profound implications for understanding the order and organization of human societies.

Even the most mundane and seemingly repetitive of daily practices are potentially active arenas of social life. While everyday life operates within socioeconomic (1984: ix) and power relationships (1984: 34) that put constraints on what is possible, everyday life is not simply passive and never wholly constrained by power structures or preestablished rules. With a nod to Lefebvre in a footnote, de Certeau identifies the hidden political dimensions of even the most seemingly mundane tasks, which can evade total reduction to a power structure through their potential for creativity. Everyday life invents as it poaches on society (1984: xii, 165–77). It can recombine the rules and products that already exist in society in a way that is influenced by but never wholly determined by these.

Throughout *The Practice of Everyday Life,* de Certeau utilizes a series of interrelated sets of oppositions (which, after reading de Certeau, we can see are not oppositions at all) to frame his discussion of everyday life. Production/consumption, voyeurs/walkers, and place/space are three of these.

Given the wealth of previous research on production in society, de Certeau calls upon researchers to be equally serious about studying use and consumption in everyday life (1984: xii–xiv), a position he certainly holds in common with Bourdieu. In traditional theorizing, production is seen as the active creation of something, someplace, or some world, whereas consumption is seen as the passive use of that which is produced, guided by the agendas of production and producers, who are often great men, elites, or conquerors. But serious investigation of use and consumption illustrates that this opposition does not hold up. Consumption itself is a productive activity, not one that produces places and things, but one that produces ways of using things and ways of operating in the world that may or may not be in line with socially prescribed norms. Playing on this false dichotomy, de Certeau refers to the act of consumption as consumer production.

In "Walking in the City," the first chapter of his particularly influential section on spatial practices, de Certeau (1984: 92–111) defines the terms *voyeurs* and *walkers*. A voyeur stands on the top of the World Trade Center in New York City and looks down upon the city. From this high-up perspective the voyeur can see the whole of the city as a city planner, institution, government, or leader might see. But what the voyeur misses from this perch is the myriad goings-on and differences in everyday life on the street. This perspective, while allowing a total view of the city, puts the voyeur at a distance from and masks its actual operation. Walkers, in contrast, form the chorus of footsteps that give life and meaning to the concept of the city. While the spatial order constructed by planners, leaders, or institutions organizes what is possible, the walker actualizes some of these and also invents others.

The interrelated concepts of place and space develop from the concepts of voyeurs and walkers (de Certeau 1984: 115–30). Place refers to the ordered settings that people create and give meaning to, which subsequently influence people's lives. Space refers to the multifaceted experiences of being and doing in a place that may or may not conform to previously constructed and/or conceived meanings and that continue to constitute and reconstitute the meanings of places. Spaces are brought into being by the diverse walkers who work through the possibilities of place by following certain possibilities, disregarding others, and inventing new possibilities. Place and space are only extricable as analytical abstractions, because the two depend on each other for their operation. Space does not exist outside of place, nor does place have any meaning until activated by space. "Thus the street geometrically defined by urban planning is transformed into a space by walkers" (de Certeau 1984: 117).

Conceptual tools like de Certeau's place and space, which interrelate the ordered worlds that humans construct with their lived experiences of being in that world, provide a way out of the impasse of theoretical polarities between studies of society as structured and society as practiced (Robin 2002a). From a temporal perspective, if the places and meanings people constructed in the past influence people's subsequent actions (place/voyeurs/production), then it should also be that people's ongoing actions (use of space/walkers/consumers) continue to construct and reconstruct social meanings.

To forward an understanding of everyday life, de Certeau is particularly interested in finding ways to document and understand nondiscursive practices. Even as one who studies contemporary societies, he asks, "Of all the things everyone does, how much gets written down?" (1984: 42). He identifies the uses of space and ways of dwelling as paramount in his research (1984: xxii), and his approach to spatializing the practices of everyday life is one of the most significant contributions of his book (Robin 2002a). De Certeau (1984: xv) contends that all practices in the world are indeed spatial practices highlighting the utility of his approach for archaeological research. His focus on the contexts of practices (1984: 33) and the relationships between the traces of practices and the practices themselves (1984: 97) again makes his work particularly amenable to an archaeological endeavor that examines contexts and traces of practices.

The American political scientist and anthropologist James Scott is another scholar who has worked through ideas about how everyday life has the potential to transcend established norms. Particularly in his book *Weapons of the Weak: Everyday Forms of Peasant Resistance* (1985) he develops a concept of everyday forms of resistance—which explicates how resistance can happen every day through seemingly mundane acts that are not overtly defiant (also see Scott 1990). Scott combines a variety of intellectual traditions in his work, including phenomenology, ethnomethodology, critical theory, practice theory, feminist theory, and subaltern studies, but he does not explicitly draw upon the writing of everyday life thinkers such as Lefebvre and de Certeau, although there are interesting parallels in his writing, particularly with these two authors.

In *Weapons of the Weak*, Scott begins by questioning intellectual traditions of studying peasant rebellions, and like Lefebvre he questions why politicians, historians, and others privilege the study of such extraordinary political events. State records typically record the presence of peasants as statistics, and only document them as social actors when they rebel. Thus, an intellectual focus on rebellious peasants plays into a stereotype of passive peasants who only become active agents of change in society when they rebel (1985: xv–xvi, 28–29). Scott further notes what would be obvious to any historian: revolutions, by peasants or others, are in fact few and far between over the course of human history. Because revolutions alone cannot explain the political and regime changes that historians see in human history, Scott asks how and why resistance happens.

Subtle acts of resistance can happen without any overt and defiant confrontations with authority; thus, they go unnoticed in historical records, which are often written by elites. As well, these acts are typically unnamed (as in the naming of political movements and revolutions) by their practitioners. But in the end, everyday acts of resistance may be a significant and effective means of change (1985: 36). As individual acts they may not produce any significant or observable change, but as they multiply through repetition and time, their effects may be profound. Thus, any attempt to understand peasant politics must take seriously ordinary acts of resistance in everyday life.

Scott (1985: xvi, 29) identifies a set of ordinary weapons that relatively powerless groups can and do use in their daily lives to resist and effect change. These include "foot dragging, dissimulation, desertion, false compliance, pilfering, feigned ignorance, slander, arson, sabotage, and so on." He refers to these as tactics, and here his use of the term "tactic" is similar to that of de Certeau (1984: xviii–xx)—a tactic is a trick or a ruse that seems to comply with an existing order but in fact does not. Tactics may ultimately be effective because their apparent compliance leads them to go unnoticed and allows their further replication. But Scott is quick to point out that researchers should not overly romanticize these weapons of the weak (as scholars have already done for peasant rebellions) because although they are potentially powerful, they may in fact turn out to have a minimal effect, if any effect at all. At the same time, researchers should not trivialize them because they do not overtly confront authority, as over the long term some of these seemingly mundane acts turn out to have been effective means of generating political change. As an example of this, Scott draws attention to the role played by the desertion of poor Southern non-slave-owning whites in the collapse of the Confederate army in the American Civil War (1985: 30).

Scott's (1985: 314–50) work is a direct confrontation of Antonio Gramsci's notions of hegemony, ideological domination, and false consciousness, which Scott feels are dangerous for studies of class relations. To assume that dominant classes can and do impose their own visions of the social order on the consciousness of others who are mystified and passively comply with the means of their domination denies the existence of enforcement, coercion, and sanctions in legitimating class relations.

Particularly in this light, understanding everyday resistance is a critical endeavor.

Scott's work is focused on class relations and particularly the relations of dominated groups, so he explores how groups with relatively little power in society can effect change through seemingly unnoticed acts of everyday resistance. But he notes that the implications of his work can extend to all groups in society—powerful and powerless. Powerful people in society as well can contest and change state policies that are not to their advantage in subtle ways that do not betray their allegiance to the state (1985: 30). Scott's ideas can be expanded to encompass a more general understanding of change in human societies. In particular, they are useful for thinking about the changes that go on in societies in the absence of large-scale revolutions or other great events, changes that can occur through the day-to-day questioning, acceptance, rejection, understanding, and misunderstanding of existing ideas and norms.

Contradiction, conflict, diversity, and change are key aspects of society embraced by late twentieth-century feminists. These feminists, like their predecessors, identify the daily lives of ordinary individuals as key arenas for understanding society, its social differences, and potential for change (e.g., Abu-Lughod 1993; Scheper-Hughes 1992; Tsing 1993).

Post-Marxist feminist Susan Willis takes up this position most directly in *A Primer for Daily Life* (1991). Her goal is to take the distinctly French theorizing on everyday life by Lefebvre and de Certeau and place it in a contemporary U.S. context of consumer capitalism. Exploring taken-for-granted aspects of U.S. culture from Barbie dolls to plastic packaging, Willis demonstrates how important seemingly trivial things are for understanding contemporary capitalism and uses these understandings to ask provocative questions about the diverse society of the United States and its relationship to its commodity practices. These questions in turn lead her to imagine alternative practices and social formations that reveal the transformative capacity of everyday life.

Everyday life thinkers of the 1970s and early 1980s were critical of structuralist positions that envisioned people's everyday lives as overdetermined by sets of rules that were generated exterior to their lives, and their solution to this problem was to illustrate how everyday life itself produced the means of generating conformity to social norms. Later scholars were critical of this position, because although it located the production of so-cial norms within what people did, it still left people and society being constrained by tradition. There seemed to be little recourse for under-standing how things could change in these models. Particularly telling in Bourdieu's work, ruptures of doxa (what is taken for granted in society) that can lead to change because people are able to question their taken-for-granteds occur because of "political or economic crises correlative of class division" or "culture contact" (1977: 168–69). Thus, dramatic upheav-als or external forces are the catalysts for change. Next to Lefebvre, de Cer-teau can be seen as the most significant contributor to studies of everyday life because he enables a complete break with structuralism, by showing how everyday life is a source of creative and transformative potential in society. Along with other late twentieth-century postcolonial and feminist thinkers, he illustrates how the minutiae of everyday life allow for diverse, often conflicting, and sometimes entirely new interpretations of social life. Change does not have to happen in dramatic ways or from outside impetuses. It can happen every day as people accept and question the meaning of existing social relations.

The Constraining and Creative Potential of Everyday Life: Bridging Twentieth-Century Perspectives

Twentieth-century scholarship establishes everyday life as a core but over-looked aspect of human existence. It develops two strands of everyday life thinking that initially seem quite dissonant. While on the one hand scholars such as Bourdieu and Smith see everyday life as a fertile ground for people's socialization into existing social norms, on the other hand, scholars such as de Certeau, Scott, and Willis see everyday life as ripe with potential for creativity and the ability to challenge existing norms. Although my own work is more closely allied with the intellectual posi-tion of de Certeau (Robin 2002a), I do not believe that these two positions are as antithetical as they first appear (comparable to de Certeau's opposi-tions, production/consumption, voyeurs/walkers, place/space, which are not actually oppositions at all). Rather, I argue that constraint and creativ-ity are part of the same process of everyday life. If scholars wish to under-stand the role of everyday life in society, they must understand both how people are socialized into existing social relations across their everyday lives and how everyday life can produce new social forms. Socialization and the production of new social forms do not have to arise from distinct acts of everyday life; the same act may simultaneously replicate a social norm and produce a new understanding. For example, as I discuss in part 2 of this book, as Maya farmers at Chan worked their agricultural fields, they simultaneously created a tradition of agricultural work that respected the integrity of the forest and also innovated new technologies for agricultural production and enabled the production of new forms of political representation.

In a similar sense, combining the work of these twentieth-century theorists illustrates that stasis, as well as change, requires maintenance. While it is clear that change requires some form of action to compel it, stasis is often seen as a state of inaction: the automated replication of social norms. But the production of conformity itself is generated by what people do in their everyday lives, not by reflex automation.

Everyday Emancipation

While there are dissonances that run through the works of the twentieth-century everyday life thinkers, a common thread within much of this theorizing is that there are moral and political dimensions, not only an intellectual dimension, to studies of everyday life. This position is most personally illustrated by Dorothy Smith in "A Berkeley Education" (1994), in which she discusses how her work is shaped as much by her involvement in radical student activism and politics at Berkeley as by the intellectual environment of her graduate education (Gardiner 2000: 180–81). A sociology that replicates dominant structures is not only intellectually troubling but also morally and politically troubling for her. Smith ardently believes that researchers must engage with the moral and political dimensions of their work. Drawing on Foucault, she sees that knowledge of society is related to control of society, which implies that researchers must be attentive to the knowledge they create. Whimsically she writes, "Universities suck knowledge out of people" (Smith 1992: 130). Thus, for Smith, the project of studying everyday life must not simply be an academic one: from the perspective of everyday life, researchers can develop critical knowledge about power relations in society and how they relate to people. Her goal in creating a feminist sociology is not to do a sociology *about* women or *about* everyday life; it is to uncover critical knowledge about power relations in society that might be used not only *by* sociologists but also *by* people in their daily lives as well. Because people act in a world that is already socially organized but also one that is becoming organized again as they act, research (like action) can either play into existing structures or create new ones (Smith 1987: 126).

This moral and political prerogative for studies of everyday life is a unifying theme that links the French and Anglo-American traditions previously discussed with German, Hungarian, and Russian schools of everyday life thought. Philosopher, literary critic, and linguist Mikhail Bakhtin was the center of the Bakhtin Circle, a twentieth-century school of Russian thought. Presaging the work of the French everyday life theorists Lefebvre, Bourdieu, and de Certeau, Bakhtin felt that Western thought had shunned lived experience in favor of theoretical abstractions. Two early works central to his thought, *The Dialogic Imagination: Four Essays* ([1930] 1981) and *Rabelais and His World* ([1941] 1984) were not translated into French until the 1970s and thus were not known to Lefebvre when he began writing about everyday life, although they were available for Bourdieu and de Certeau (Merrifield 2006: 16). Morson and Emerson (1990) coined the term *prosaic imagination* to refer to Bakhtin's ideas about the centrality of everyday life in human existence (also see Gardiner 2000). Critical to Bakhtin's discussions of everyday life were the ethical concerns of such studies: because the values and meanings that are most deeply felt arise within everyday life, it is the site of the production of moral judgments. Thus, in order to create a moral philosophy, philosophers must pay attention to everyday life: "A philosophy of life can only be a moral philosophy" (Bakhtin 1993: 56).

Hungarian philosopher Agnes Heller was part of the Budapest School, a group of intellectuals surrounding Marxist philosopher György Lukács. Her central discussion of everyday life, *Everyday Life* ([1970] 1984), was influenced by the work of Lefebvre. In this book, drawing on Lefebvre's approach, she makes a critical break from Lukács' ideas about everyday life, which upheld an absolute distinction between the everyday (unexamined customs) and the non-everyday (higher forms of thought; Sheringham 2006: 34–39). In Heller's work there remains an unresolved tension between Lukács's and Lefebvre's perspectives on everyday life, but she makes it clear that everyday life is the ground for the formation of non-everyday knowledge (Heller [1970] 1984: 45–114). For Heller, studying everyday life is about trying to understand how people live their lives; thus, ethics are central to any analysis of everyday life. In the 1984 preface to the English translation of *Everyday Life* she states that "how to change everyday in a humanistic, democratic, socialist direction is the practical issue of the book" (1984: x). Like Scott she does not believe that social change arises from the macro scale alone. Everyday life is a critical domain for social change because people can test and question the norms and rules that appear to be taken for granted. The emancipatory potential of everyday life arises from this ability to question the status quo and the ways in which daily life includes not only what is learned but also new experiences and what gets taught. For Heller, theorizing everyday life is about developing a social theory animated by emancipatory interests.

The *Alltagsgeschichte* (or history of everyday life) school is a late twentieth-century German school of historiographic thought founded by Alf Lüdtke and Hans Medick. The goal of *Alltagsgeschichte* is to take history from the university and bring it into people's everyday lives (Eley 1995: viii). In this way *Alltagsgeschichte* historians were able to develop a political movement that moved beyond the academy and incorporated public history, museums, education, and government (Eley 1995: viii). The attempted reformulation of the discipline of history included focusing research on ordinary people's and workers' basic experiences (Lüdtke 1995) and developing more anthropological approaches to history (Medick 1995). But there was always an ethical dimension to this research: a focus on the details of ordinary housing could reveal information on homelessness, a study of eating habits could elucidate issues of hunger, and so on. Coming to terms with Germany's Nazi past was one of the stimuli for *Alltagsgeschichte*, which sought to bring to light the stories of the "hounded, exploited, and murdered millions" (Lüdtke 1995: 4).

A unifying theme that runs across the diverse body of work of the twentieth-century everyday life theorists is interest in and embracing of the ethical, moral, and political dimensions of research. In an attempt to bolster the objectivity of research, traditional social scientific inquiry shunned approaches with moral or political dimensions. But a critical study of everyday life is more than simply an academic exercise. It is a project that embraces the moral, ethical, and political dimensions of studying human societies and reveals the potential emancipatory capacities that studies of everyday life might have for people in society. Once theory—rather than replicating and reinforcing the perspectives of elites and institutions—uses everyday life studies to expose the structural constraints that exist for people in society and the avenues people might take to modify their conditions, emancipation becomes a possibility. Then theoretical work will be in the service of the people rather than in the service of dominant institutions. These are lofty aspirations, to be sure. But why shouldn't academic work on everyday life have a role to play in everyday life as well?

The Materials and Spaces of Everyday Life: Into the Twenty-First Century

Exploring the material and spatial dimensions of everyday life was certainly not insignificant for the twentieth-century everyday life thinkers, particularly of the French school, such as Lefebvre, Bourdieu, and de Certeau. As well, the 1990s marked the beginning of the "spatial turn," which was followed by the "material turn" in the first decade of the twenty-first century across the social sciences and humanities disciplines, which focused attention onto the spatial and material dimensions of social life. As a bridge to the next chapter on archaeological thinking about everyday life I focus my discussion of twenty-first-century social theories of everyday life on the work of two interdisciplinary, archaeologically trained anthropologists, Tim Ingold and Daniel Miller, who further the importance of understanding everyday spaces and materials.

Even within a group of eclectic and provocative thinkers, British anthropologist Tim Ingold could be considered a polymath. Drawing on wide-ranging theories from developmental biology to ecological psychology and phenomenology, he investigates a seemingly straightforward question: how do humans relate to their environment? In *The Perception of the Environment* (2000) he works through phenomenology, particularly Martin Heidegger's concept of dwelling, which was also important in the writings of de Certeau (de Certeau et al. 1998: xxxi), and practice theory, among other theories, to develop an understanding of how the world that people build arises from their practical engagement with their surroundings (Ingold 2000: 153–88). The world becomes a meaningful environment for people through being lived in—not through being constructed in a formal design. Dwelling, following Heidegger, refers not simply to domestic dwelling but to living all aspects of daily lives.

As a sequel to *Perception of the Environment* (2000), Ingold's *Being Alive*

(2011) provides his broadest critique of modern Western thought, by illustrating how across its history Western thought has sought to eliminate the experiences of life that produced culture (Ingold 2011: 3). He moves beyond Heideggerian notions of dwelling and being-in-the-world, to suggest that what must be central to studies of humans and their societies is understanding being alive to what is going on in the world. Researchers must explore "life as lived" (2011: 4).

In the personal preface and acknowledgments to *Being Alive,* Ingold indicates that one of his goals in challenging anthropology with provocative thoughts is to seek an anthropology that "not only observes and describes life, but is also open to changing it" (2011: xi). He questions the academic practice of acknowledging all of the textual sources that have inspired an author but not "the ground we walk, the ever-changing skies, mountains and rivers, rocks and trees, the houses we inhabit and the tools we use, not to mention the innumerable companions, both non-human and fellow humans, with which and with whom we share our lives" (2011: xii). Researchers' daily engagements with people, places, and things inspire their work as well. He further asks whether the truth about life is to be found in a library book or "'out there' in the world of lived experience" (2011: 15). Through his challenges to accepted intellectual and pragmatic disciplinary practices, Ingold's goal is to "bring anthropology back to life" (2011: 14).

Just as Ingold is critical of an anthropology that privileges the relationships between people over the relationships between people and their environment and people and animals, British anthropologist Daniel Miller is critical of an anthropology that privileges people's interrelationships over their relationships with things. Across his research Miller focuses on the things that circulate in everyday life, not as mundane objects made by people but as important mediators of value, meaning, and social life. In *A Theory of Shopping* (1998), Miller explores Londoners' daily shopping habits to reveal how shopping for ordinary things involves more than daily provisioning and defines love, caring, and values within families.

Drawing upon and moving beyond Bourdieu's and de Certeau's call for renewed interest in the topic of consumption, Miller explores the diversity of social relationships involved in the consumption and production of objects (Miller 1998: 2–7). A goal of his work is to transform traditional binary thinking about person/thing, animate/inanimate, and subject/object. Ultimately, for Miller (2010: 135), "things make people just as much as people make things."

As glib as titles such as *A Theory of Shopping* and *Stuff* might sound, there are significant political dimensions to Miller's analysis of ordinary things. In *Au Pair* (2010) by Zuzana Búriková and Daniel Miller, the authors explore the everyday lives of Slovakian au pairs and their middle-class London host families. Hopes, dreams, tensions, and misunderstandings surround these relationships. Búriková and Miller's ethnography does not stop at the level of theoretical discussion but also postulates ways in which the relationships between foreign au pairs and their middle-class hosts can be improved. The companion volume to Miller's recent *Stuff* (2010), *Consumption and Its Consequences* (2012), explores the politics and political economy of materialism, particularly in terms of its role in the future of the environment.

In Miller's most recent works, particularly *The Comfort of Things* (2008) and *Stuff* (2010), he consciously departs from an academic style of writing. He is critical of the process of theory-making that requires the utilization of obscure abstractions and language. Instead, to "re-ground theory in its application to everyday lives" (2010: 80), Miller promotes through his own work an accessible writing style. The majority of the everyday life theorists do not embrace this proposition: Lefebvre and de Certeau, among others, are among the most abstruse writers. But some everyday life thinkers have, comparably to Miller, appreciated a lucid and engaging style of writing to express the everyday. This is a position I certainly endorse.

Following the "spatial and material turns," theoretical work across the social sciences and humanities disciplines began to more vigorously embrace the importance of studying the spatial and material dimensions of everyday life. These turns bring archaeological and broader social theoretical projects into greater alignment.

Everyday Life: A General Sensibility

While the scholars discussed above would all agree on the importance of everyday life, they do not present a unified perspective. They bring a diverse range of perspectives to bear upon this topic, creating vitally interdisciplinary projects. Some of the scholars discussed here draw on each other's work, but others do not. As Gardiner puts it, an everyday life perspective is "less a unified 'theory' than a general sensibility or ethos connected by a series of overlapping themes" (2000: 207).

Everyday life thinkers do not self-identify as one might self-identify as a phenomenologist or Marxist. The identification of a diverse body of thinking on everyday life is one that has arisen post hoc as subsequent scholars have begun to explore the terrain of everyday life (Gardiner 2000; Highmore 2002a, 2002b; Lüdtke 1995; Sheringham 2006). I often wonder, if many of these scholars were around today, what would they think of later scholars' grouping of their works?

The theoreticians discussed above would certainly not agree on all aspects of each others' work (nor would I). Combining aspects of their work leads to a greater appreciation for the importance of everyday life in human societies. Everyday life can socialize people into existing social relations and produce new social forms. It illustrates that stasis and change alike require social maintenance. It highlights the pivotal role that ordinary spaces and objects play in human societies, developing a strong linkage to archaeological research. A critical study of everyday life is always more than simply an academic exercise. It is a project that embraces the moral, ethical, and political dimensions of studying human societies and reveals the potential emancipatory capacities that studies of everyday life might have for people in society.

I draw six framing points about the importance of a critical everyday life approach from the authors discussed in this chapter. First, everyday life is central to human existence. Second, the practices of everyday life are not simply mundane but encompass a complexity of actions and interactions that are both shaped by and allow people to shape their world. Third, ordinary objects and spatial arrangements formalize how people learn about themselves and their world. Fourth, social change (and stasis) happens across everyday life. Fifth, a focus on everyday life draws attention to the role that all people—regardless of their wealth, status, gender, or ethnicity—play in the development of human societies. Sixth, a critical analysis of everyday life implies a willingness to consider the ethical, moral, and political dimensions of studying people's daily lives.

3 ✳ Archaeology and Everyday Life

As seen in the social theoretical literature, there is no self-identified subfield of archaeology called "everyday life archaeology," yet there are a number of subfields that have long explored aspects of past everyday lives. This chapter discusses and relates four of these: household archaeology, feminist archaeology, spatial archaeology, and historical archaeology. Brought into dialogue, these approaches illustrate how powerful the material and spatial dimensions of the archaeological record are for furthering critical discussions of everyday life.

Household archaeology has shown how past peoples organized and made meaningful their domestic spaces. By focusing on the complexity of day-to-day life within the domestic domain and the diverse nature of its inhabitants, household studies have been important in demonstrating how people, their practices, and differences play a crucial role in the organization of past societies (e.g., Allison 1999; Hendon 2004, 2010; Hutson 2010; King 2006; Robb 2007; Robin 2003, 2004). Feminist and gender studies further illustrate the need to incorporate the lives of all social groups into archaeological analysis—not only gender but also class, ethnicity, age groups, and so on (e.g., Brumfiel 1992; Gilchrist 1999; R. Joyce 2000, 2004; Meskell 1999, 2002; Meskell and Joyce 2003; Pyburn 2004; Robin and Brumfiel 2008). Space, place, and landscape research extends these agendas by showing how all living spaces are meaningfully constructed and experienced by people during their daily lives (e.g., Ashmore 2002, 2004; Ashmore and Knapp 1999; David and Thomas 2008a; Johnson 2007; A. Joyce 2004, 2010; Robin and Rothschild 2002; A. Smith 2003; Tilley 1994, 2010).

Historical archaeology has been particularly attuned to furthering studies of the material remains of everyday life, which are often neglected in the documentary record (e.g., Cantwell and Wall 2001; Hall and Silliman 2006; Hauser 2008; Hicks and Beaudry 2006; Johnson 1996; Meskell 2002; Wilkie 2000, 2003). Deetz (1977: 4) defined historical archaeology as being concerned with the "small things forgotten." The material remains of daily life identifiable in the archaeological record provide a means to both complement and challenge the macro-narratives of powerful people that tend to consume documentary sources.

The colonial encounter, in particular, brought taken-for-granted assumptions about how life worked to the foreground for both indigenous peoples and colonizers (an example of what Bourdieu would refer to as a rupture of doxa). Thus, for archaeologists of the colonial period, studies of everyday life are particularly fruitful ways to learn about the struggles and strife of colonial encounters (e.g., Hauser 2008; Lightfoot 2005; Oland 2009, 2012; Voss 2008a). As Silliman (2004: xviii) discusses in relation to the hundreds if not a few thousand Native Americans who worked at Rancho Petaluma between 1834 and 1857, "'Practice' may involve the mundane and seemingly innocuous events of everyday life. . . . Sometimes daily practices implicated politics of resistance and subversion; at other times it demarcated individuals' attempts to live in and through the colonial rancho world and both to uphold and to make tradition." As seen in the Rancho Petaluma case, and discussed in chapter 2, in relation to the social theoretical literature: everyday life simultaneously enables socialization into existing social orders and creates new visions of society. The "new traditions" (Pauketat 2001) that emerge in the colonial period are not simply the result of accepting one or the other of two worldviews presented by two societies in conflict, as in a structuralist model; they involve the making of new traditions by people across their everyday lives within conflicted colonial worlds. They also relate as much to the long-term histories of indigenous lives as to new colonial situations linking the academically defined domains of historic and prehistoric archaeology (Lightfoot 1995; Oland 2009; Oland et al. 2012; Stahl 2001).

I see that prehistoric and historic archaeologists have more in common, because of their mutual focus on the material remains of the past, than they differ because of the presence or absence of written documents. Historic and prehistoric archaeology also can be difficult concepts to operationalize in particular temporal contexts, such as colonialism, as the aforementioned authors note. Another case in which historic and prehistoric archaeology are difficult to operationalize is Maya archaeology, long considered a prehistoric study, but for which recent advances in hieroglyphic decipherment have now illuminated a corpus of elite writing. In this chapter, rather than address the research of historic and prehistoric archaeologists separately, I explore their unique and overlapping investigations into households, gender, and space as they engage studies of past everyday lives.

Like the broader field of social theory, archaeology has a history of polarizing debates between macro and micro, materialist and idealist, and objective and subjective approaches, which was formalized in the processual and postprocessual archaeology debates of the 1980s and 1990s. The processual or New Archaeology of the 1960s, pioneered by Lewis Binford, identified archaeology as a positivistic science based in hypothesis testing. By focusing on quantifiable and material dimensions of the archaeological record, processualists hoped to elicit information about past social process, function, and ecology (e.g., Binford 1977, 1978, 1982; Flannery 1976). To counter the dominant functionalist and materialist position emerging within processual archaeology in the 1980s, both processualists and postprocessualists began to highlight the symbolic dimensions of the archaeological record (e.g., Flannery and Marcus 1976; Hodder 1982; Leone 1984). Rather than seeing the archaeological record as reflecting functional or ecological processes, symbolic approaches posited that the archaeological record could also express symbolic, ideological, or conceptual knowledge of past peoples. But whether the archaeological record reflected past ecological processes or conceptual knowledge, the archaeological record was still viewed as a passive record of the past. In the 1980s, postprocessual archaeology, pioneered by Ian Hodder, emerged to take up this critique and show how the archaeological record and its material remains were actively constructed and meaningfully constituted by people in the past—a notion that now has wide resonance across archaeology (Hodder 1987, 1999; Shanks and Tilley 1988, 1992).

Since the 1990s, archaeological scholars have been trying to find fruitful ways to further active approaches to the past and recognize the importance of both material and symbolic, objective and subjective, and macro and micro dimensions of past human experience (Hodder 1992; Johnson 2010a; Meskell and Preucel 2004; Preucel 1991; Renfrew and Bahn 1996; Robb 2007; Robin and Rothschild 2002). This is perhaps even more imperative for archaeological scholars than for scholars of the modern world, because many ancient societies such as the ancient Maya or ancient Egyptians did not have Cartesian or Platonic dualities as concepts (Meskell 2002: Meskell and Joyce 2003). While no consensus has emerged as to how to do this, I propose in this chapter that an archaeology that explores the past as lived across daily lives that are both materially constructed and socially experienced by people can help bridge these divides. Using archaeology to explore "situated experiences of material life" is an area where archaeology can make significant contributions to social theory (Preucel and Meskell 2004: 3–4).

The archaeological approaches discussed in this chapter emerge out of and go beyond interests in both processual and postprocessual archaeology. Processual archaeology's focus on social and ecological processes in part spurred the development of studies of human settlements, households, communities, and landscapes in archaeology. But these areas of research have equally been shaped by postprocessual archaeology's emphasis on people, ideas, and experiences and analysis of how people constructed and experienced the past as they lived in households and across landscapes.

Household Archaeology

Although the archaeology of ancient civilizations (and indeed the popular image of archaeology as a whole) can be characterized as the study of temples, tombs, and kings, a more recent academic descriptive triad identifies archaeology as the study of "the dead, the dross, and the domicile" (Samson 1990: 1). The latter description illustrates the ubiquitous nature of house remains in the archaeological record and the importance of understanding the everyday lives of the people who inhabited them. The material remains of domestic life are an important medium through which both ancient people in the past and archaeologists today create and understand memory, meaning, and identity (Hendon 2010). Although everyday life is not restricted to the domestic world, houses and domestic places are key arenas of everyday life where people learn about and transform their world.

Household archaeology takes as its domain the investigation of houses, households, and domestic activities and practices. Households are among the basic social units of human societies. Houses provide shelter, but they also "embody cultural values, commitment to places, and plans of action" (Robb 2007: 75). Houses and domestic spaces are places where people live, work, raise families, create memories, and communicate with others. They are an important nexus of diverse activities and interactions between household members and through which household members relate to their broader world—their local communities, regional polities, and broader societies.

Because the focus of household studies is micro-scale archaeological entities—houses or domestic activity areas—it brings archaeological analysis into engagement with past individuals and their daily domestic lives. Household archaeology places people and their practices and differences at the center of archaeological interpretations of the past, rather than subsuming them into the "noise" of passive and depersonalized depictions of ancient social systems (Robin 2003). A social archaeology of the household is one that is "embodied, agent-centered, [and] concerned with understanding social identity and difference through the analysis of the lived experiences of social groups" (Hendon 2004: 272). It is as much about understanding the meaning of houses and households as it is about understanding their function (Hendon 2004).

The monuments and inscriptions that have been the focus of a traditional archaeology provide insight into past *public transcripts* (sensu stricto James Scott), but it is archaeological studies of households—whether those of the humblest farmer or the most expansive royal court—that are exposing *hidden transcripts* (the lived experience of all members of society). In this way, investigating households—of the rich and the poor—can provide a more comprehensive understanding of the inner workings of past societies. By focusing on three dimensions of households (the diversity of actors within any household, the differences among households, and the linkages between households and society), household research can expose the varied roles and relations of *all* social groups in society (Robin 2003).

A focus on the people of past households highlights how households—through the internal and external interactions of their members—were simultaneously socially, economically, politically, and symbolically meaningful entities. Domestic places in the past could be important locations of political meetings and events, economic production, and religious and ritual activity. They were places where memories and traditions were established—the home was a place imbued with meaning and significance for those who lived there. Households were not isolated from society; they were affected by broader social changes in society. Conversely, the activities of their members could affect the world beyond their borders. Given the multiple foci of household archaeology research, it is not surprising that many of its practitioners have adapted and advanced a practice approach to looking at how people's core ideas are rooted in their daily practices within their homes (e.g., Hutson 2010; A. Joyce 2010; Lightfoot 2005; Lightfoot et al. 1998; Pauketat 2001; Robb 2007; Silliman 2004; Voss 2008a; Wilkie 2000; Wilson 2008).

Household members can be involved in a range of productive, consumptive, and/or reproductive activities, enabling household archaeologists to potentially investigate any of these areas. Households are not simply passive recipients of goods and ideas from elsewhere but are also active in the production of goods and ideas. Household archaeologists have shown that understanding what households produced for themselves (food, clothing, and so forth) is as important as understanding what households produced for the villages, towns, communities, regions, and societies beyond them (e.g., Brumfiel 1991; Gero and Scattolin 2002; Hendon 1996). But equally important has been household archaeologists' analysis of household consumption (Monica Smith 1999).

Just as Michel de Certeau describes for scholarship more broadly, within archaeology, the focus of analysis has been on production rather than consumption, because of the mistaken association of production with action and consumption with passivity. Household archaeologists have shown how consumption in the past is not simply a passive phenomenon but is implicated in how households reproduce and produce ideas, information, and goods. Members of households make choices in terms of consumption, and these choices resonate not only within the household but beyond it as well.

As the domestic world is both materially constructed and socially experienced, studies of past households help to bridge divides between material and social analyses. The material form of the dwelling encodes and expresses broader societal expectations through which residents learn traditional values and expectations. But dwelling spaces can also be used in new and unexpected ways by their inhabitants and can also serve, because of their oftentimes enclosed form, as protected spaces from the outside world that can foster counternormative behaviors or be havens from popular culture. Wood (2002) shows how leading up to Colorado's

Ludlow massacre, women's housework was a subversive politics through which they struggled for social change. In the aftermath of the collapse of the Zapotec state, Joyce and Weller (2007) identified a household where residents reused a piece of a monument depicting the face of a king to grind corn. Through living in a house, learning what is acceptable, reproducing traditional behaviors, and formulating and testing new ideas, the material and the social, the micro and the macro levels of social life intersect in people's daily domestic lives.

As a named subfield within archaeology, household archaeology emerged in the 1980s most prominently in the Americas through pioneering volumes such as Richard Wilk and William Rathje's (1982) special issue of the *American Behavioral Scientist* on household archaeology and Richard Wilk and Wendy Ashmore's (1988) *Household and Community in the Mesoamerican Past* (see discussions by European and historic archaeologists on the prehistoric and Mesoamerican origins of household archaeology: Allison 1999; King 2006; Monica Smith 2010: 15). Household archaeology was proposed to enable archaeologists to move beyond formal spatial analyses and functional studies of human settlement patterns to expose "the human behavior behind the material remains of settlement" (Ashmore and Wilk 1988: 11). Challenging normative models of households as simply by-products of larger social structures, Ashmore and Wilk demonstrated that what people did as part of households was crucial for understanding the operation of ancient societies. After the publication of their volume, household studies expanded across American archaeology in the 1990s. This is not to say that European archaeologists at the time were not also exploring the role of ancient houses—they were (e.g., Bailey 1990; Clarke 1977; Hodder 1990; Samson 1990). Some scholars have referred to such 1990s European approaches as "house archaeology" (Hendon 2004: 275) to emphasize how these approaches focused on analyses of houses as material expressions of social relations rather than focusing on households as social groups. Today the term *household archaeology* has expanded to encompass a range of theoretical orientations and is an important conceptual perspective within archaeology regardless of a researcher's region or temporal interests.

The field of household archaeology's early beginnings in Mesoamerican studies have implications for how this subfield has developed within archaeology and its orientation toward exploring how micro-scale phenomena have far-reaching impacts in human societies (Robin 2003: 309–16).

In the 1890s, when most Mesoamerican archaeologists were investigating temples and monuments, Mayanist Edward H. Thompson (1892) was one of the first archaeologists to study ancient houses (Ashmore and Willey 1981; Hammond 1994). Combining archaeological excavation and ethnographic analogy, Thompson determined that the small mounds that surrounded Maya centers consisted of the remains of ancient houses. But this documentation and description of houses was not the end of Thompson's analysis. He used this data to evaluate anthropologist Lewis H. Morgan's (1878) unilinear evolutionary model of the development of civilization from savagery. While Morgan (1879, 1881) had argued that the ancient Maya did not have true cities, because ancient Maya centers did not have urban residential areas, Thompson's documentation of ancient houses in Maya centers used Morgan's criterion of the presence of urban residential areas to illustrate that the ancient Maya, contrary to their evolutionary placement in the unilinear model, did indeed have cities. Thus, for Thompson, explorations at the micro-scale, and the archaeological identifications of houses, had broader implications for how researchers understand the development of human societies. Certainly this remains one of the important lessons of a household archaeology perspective—that micro and macro, social and material issues are not opposed to one another but are mutually implicated in one another.

Far from degraded domestic domains, households are active locales of everyday life where people formulate and transform their understandings of the world. Through living in a house, people learn what is acceptable and can reproduce traditional behaviors and formulate and test new ideas. Because what people do in their households is deeply implicated in what is going on in the broader world around them, a household approach illustrates how micro and macro, social and material aspects of social life are entwined.

Feminist and Gender Archaeology

Feminist and gender archaeology questions assumptions about women and gender relations in past societies and explores how understanding gender relations in any society can lead to a more productive understanding of the operation of that society. There has been a long history of cross-pollination between the work of gender and household archaeologists (Battle-Baptiste 2011; Hendon 1996; Robin and Brumfiel 2008; Tringham 1991). On the one hand, the lives of women that had long been missing from archaeological interpretations could be reached through a study of the domestic domain, where they (and others) would certainly be present (Tringham 1991). On the other hand, gender studies have shown the extent to which women's roles in society extend beyond the domestic sphere (e.g., Bell 2002; Bruhns and Stothert 1999; Hollimon 1997; R. Joyce 2000; Marcus 2001; Nelson 2003).

Like feminists from other disciplines, feminist archaeologists questioned the assumption that women and domestic life were passive elements in human societies. Because of their access to a record of human history that extends long before the development of capitalism, feminist archaeologists were also able to interrogate the long-term history of the domestic sphere and its association with women. Feminist household archaeologists were among the first to show that the contemporary Western division between "domestic/house/private/female/consumption/passive" and the active public world of male politics and production was not universal. Domestic and public spheres are constructs of particular historical scenarios, such as certain contexts in the development of Western capitalism (e.g., Gilchrist 1999; Hendon 1996, 2004; R. Joyce 2000; Robin 2002a, 2002b; Robin and Brumfiel 2008; Tringham 1991; Wall 1994). But there is no unilinear evolutionary theory posited here, because in precapitalist societies, such as ancient Egypt, houses and the domestic sphere were the bedrock of private relations in society, bearing many similarities to contemporary Western notions of private (Meskell 2002). Notions of private and public are culturally defined, not transcultural types, and researchers must endeavor to investigate, not assume, their meanings. Domestic places cannot always be defined as nonpublic places, because "public" ritual performances and political meetings may occur in these places. Even when "public" acts are not performed in domestic places, seemingly simple acts such as serving food can take on broader political meanings. People can modify their domestic routines in response to changes in the public sphere; similarly, people's decisions and modifications in the domestic sphere can impact the public sphere. Either through their effect upon one another or through their lack of separation from one another, public and private spheres can be closely interrelated.

Within Western capitalism, the divide between the public and private spheres was not inevitable—it had to be constructed. On both sides of the Atlantic, archaeologists have documented this construction from feminist, household, and postprocessual perspectives: for upper- and middle-class New Yorkers between 1790 and 1840 (Wall 1994) and middling classes in medieval and early modern England (Johnson 1996). Even at the height of the Victorian period, Victorian etiquette with its stark delineation of male and female roles and relations was more prominent among upper classes. Even for middle-class Americans, the content and boundary of male/public and female/private spheres was continually negotiated and changing (Spencer-Wood 1991, 1999). As this variability indicates, the separation of public and private spheres was not simply an outcome of capitalism. It was "located in everyday social and cultural practices as much as in large-scale economic transformations" (Johnson 1996: 155).

The historical dynamism of the domestic domain forces researchers to see it not simply as a passive and devalued version of a male public domain but as an integral part of the public and political life. Relating gender and household studies, archaeologists can develop a view of the past as it was lived and can consider how day-to-day practices and meanings are embedded in larger socioeconomic and political processes (Robin and Brumfiel 2008).

Feminist and gender research, which did not begin in archaeology until the 1980s, has followed three stages. The first is a critique of an androcentric bias in archaeological research, the second is new interest in studies of ancient women to fill knowledge gaps, and the third (which requires the first two) seeks to understand gender relations and gender identities and their implications for furthering understandings of human societies.

In the first two stages, the focus of research is on women. In the third stage, the focus is on gender (women, men, and other genders)—on how people understand, how they define, and what significance they place on gender in a society. By making gender relations and gender identities the focus of analyses, feminists brought the lives and interactions of all people—men, women, and other genders—to the fore of archaeological analysis. Exposing variation and difference in gender relations and gender identities through time led feminists to recognize the importance of studying difference more broadly in human societies (Gilchrist 1999; Hendon 1996, 2004; R. Joyce 2000, 2004; Meskell 1999; Meskell and Joyce 2003; Voss 2008a; Wilkie 2003). Gender could be a starting point, but studying different class, ethnic, age groups, and so on, in society was equally important. As succinctly stated by Brumfiel (1992: 553) in a passage that is frequently quoted,

> When archaeologists fail to assign specific activities to these groups [women, peasants, and ethnic groups], dominant groups in contemporary society are free to depict them in any way they please. Most often, dominant groups will overstate the historical importance of their own group and undervalue the contributions of others, legitimating inequalities. In addition, when women, peasants, and ethnic groups are assigned no specific activities in the past, professional archaeologists make implicit assumptions about their roles and capabilities, resulting in the widespread acceptance of untested, and possibly erroneous, interpretations of archaeological data.

Feminist archaeology highlights the importance of studying difference and recognizing the relevance and interrelatedness of the multiple types of social differences that exist in human societies, not just gender differences but also age, class, and ethnic differences, and so on. Feminist archaeology illustrates the importance of incorporating the lives of all past people and all past social groups into analyses of everyday life.

Space, Place, and Landscape Research

While the domestic domain may be an important location of everyday life, people do not check their everyday lives at the door when they leave home. Everyday life has myriad locations, from homes to yards, pathways, streets, work spaces, markets, stores, parks, fields, and forests—in fact, whole landscapes. Everyday life arises as much in the spaces in between the primary sites of contemporary archaeological analysis (buildings and built spaces such as houses or temples) as it does within those spaces. Whereas household archaeology takes past domestic spaces as its focus, space, place, and landscape research, in contrast, expands investigation to all past living spaces.

Unlike household, feminist, and gender studies in archaeology, which are recent additions to the archaeological program, spatial analysis is as old as archaeology itself (Robin and Rothschild 2002). For the culture historians, space was a neutral backdrop upon which the sites and artifacts of archaeological inquiry were situated (e.g., Kidder 1924, 1961). Processualists realized that there was much more to space than this—by quantifying the spatial distribution of archaeological sites, buildings, or materials, archaeologists could explain the human behaviors that led to those distributional patterns (e.g., Clarke 1977; Flannery 1976; Hodder and Orton 1976). In both of these approaches, space remains an inactive phenomenon, a platform for human activity. Postprocessualists introduced the idea that space was an active phenomenon (a social space versus an abstract space). Human involvement distinguishes social space from abstract space as social space is constructed, perceived, and lived by people. In this way, human space is both actively constructed by people and provides frameworks for their ongoing social relations. As people use, experience, move through, and interact with space and with others in space, they continue to influence the subsequent meanings of space. The meanings that spaces hold for people vary across gender, class, age, ethnic, and other lines of difference. Understanding space in these ways is what Ashmore has referred to as socializing spatial archaeology. As she states, "The still-growing appreciation that space is actively inhabited, and that social relations and spatial structure are linked recursively, has transformed our anthropological—and our human—understanding of the past" (Ashmore 2002: 1172).

In archaeology, and indeed across all disciplines that deal with space, the terms *space* and *place* are often evoked, often with quite different definitions (Ashmore 2002; Preucel and Meskell 2004; A. Smith 2003; Thomas 2008). Sometimes archaeologists use the term *space* to refer to a natural physical setting or an abstract Cartesian space. Places, then, by way of contrast, are spaces imbued with human action and social meaning—they are social space. Other scholars (such as de Certeau [see chapter 2]) refer to the social nature of both abstract physical space (which must be made or perceived as abstract or physical in a social world) and place (also see Casey 1996; Robin 2002a). Other scholars suggest that researchers should refrain from using the term *space* when referring to the inhabited world, because of its historical association with a notion of abstract Cartesian space (Ingold 2011).

Building upon similar lines of inquiry, some landscape archaeologists have embraced the social nature of landscape to distinguish between the notions of a physical landscape and a human landscape (e.g., Ashmore 2002, 2004; Ashmore and Knapp 1999; Bender 1993, 1998; David and Thomas 2008a; Head et al. 2002; A. Joyce 2004, 2010; A. Smith 2003; Snead 2008; Tilley 1994, 2010). Landscapes are not simply passive natural domains that form the contexts for artifacts and buildings; they are cultural domains defined by uses and perceptions of land. Landscape studies have drawn attention to the social meaning of built and unbuilt aspects of landscape. Natural landscape features such as mountains, caves, rivers, and lakes, as well as constructed aspects of landscapes, often have salient social meanings for inhabitants. Landscape research draws attention to the importance of studying whole domains of human action, which is allied with an approach that considers the myriad spaces of everyday life. Human landscapes are imbued with and express powerful meanings for the people who construct and live in them. By living out daily lives in landscapes, "we come to know the world, and ourselves in the world, by moving through it" (David and Thomas 2008b: 245). Similarly, Johnson (2007: 145) has proposed a practice-based approach to the archaeology of historic landscapes that explores landscapes as "the effects of real people leading real lives" (also see A. Joyce 2004, 2010 for practice approaches to ancient landscapes).

More influential than practice theory in landscape archaeology are phenomenological perspectives from Heidegger's and Ingold's work on dwelling (living all aspects of daily lives). Thomas (1996, 2001, 2008) and Tilley (1994) illustrate how the landscape is not an objective topography but rather the context of human dwelling, a "context within which everyday activities are performed that enables specific places to reveal themselves in ways that are readily intelligible" (Thomas 2008: 303). Hutson (2010) brings together a dwelling approach and household archaeology to explore how people derive their identity from their everyday engagement with others, things, and the world around them.

Spaces and landscapes may also embody and express political processes and power relations (e.g., Ashmore 2000; A. Joyce 2010; A. Smith 2003). Exploring the constitution of political authority in space through the making and remaking of landscapes, Adam T. Smith identified three dimensions of landscapes—experience, perception, and imagination (2003: 73–77). Experience defines how people move through landscapes. Perception defines the sensual interaction between people and landscapes. Experience and perception are closely related to the material forms of landscape, whereas imagination refers to discourses about landscapes— the way people represent their landscapes often through textual media.

Together these three dimensions inform the ways people understand the landscapes of their lives.

※

A concept of lived space, which encompasses all of the spaces that people construct, use, and perceive across their lives, brings together the multiple social meanings of space, place, and landscape (Robin 2002a; Robin and Rothschild 2002). This concept draws upon archaeological ideas as well as insights from the work of de Certeau and other work in time-space geography. Lived spaces are human creations that embody all aspects of people's lives—social, political, economic, and ritual. They bring together the material and social dimensions of human life as they are materially constructed and socially experienced. By constructing a spatial world and interacting with others in space, people integrate local and personal knowledge with larger political-economic processes. Lived space encompasses both monumental spaces and ordinary spaces. A notion of lived space is quite applicable to the study of everyday life, because all spaces are encountered and perceived across people's everyday lives.

The Politics of Household, Feminist, and Spatial Archaeology

Feminist archaeology, like feminisms elsewhere, is based in a critique of inequality, initially critiquing inequity for women and later questioning inequality for any group considered "other" in a society (e.g., Brumfiel 1992; Conkey and Gero 1997; Geller and Stockett 2006; Voss 2008b; Wylie 1992, 2007). This critique is not just a critique of inequality in the past, but a critical inquiry into how inequality operates in human societies and its implications for inequality in the modern world. For Brumfiel (n.d.: 1), an important dimension of feminist and gender archaeologies is to "help design more effective strategies for attaining gender equality in contemporary Western societies and elsewhere." In developing a black feminist archaeology, Battle-Baptiste (2011: 31) attempts not only to further a historical archaeology attentive to issues of race, class, and gender but also to produce an archaeology "relevant to contemporary struggles for social justice and liberation." For some of its practitioners, feminist archaeology is also a pedagogy, a way of teaching and involving students in learning and research, that promotes critical thinking and attempts to break down hierarchies between professor and student (Nelson 2006; Pyburn 2004; Robin and Brumfiel 2008).

To say that all feminist and gender archaeologists embrace or advocate political interests would be a misnomer, and inaccurate. In fact, since the inception of the field to today, there has been significant debate as to the extent to which an overt concern with politics advances or detracts from gender research in archaeology (see discussions in Wylie 1992, 2007). Some scholars seek to develop a gender archaeology, as distinct from a feminist archaeology, which would distance the study of gender in the past from political interests in the present so as to make gender studies more credible within the field of archaeology (Sørensen 2000). Concerns with the corruption of research by political interests is a legacy of traditional social scientific inquiry that attempted to bolster the objectivity of research by eschewing such seemingly subjective dimensions of research, as discussed in chapter 2. But as Wylie (1992: 15) has long argued, and I develop further in chapter 4, being explicit about one's political interests in fact enhances the "conceptual integrity and empirical adequacy" of research. A politically engaged science enables a "more rigorous, self-critical, responsive to the facts" approach than do supposedly neutral approaches to science, in which personal bias can remain unexplored in the research (Wylie 1992: 30).

Although perhaps not as obviously political, the development of landscape archaeology attracted attention to the contemporary social and political dimensions of studying past landscapes among its practitioners (David and Thomas 2008a). The notion that a landscape as defined in a contemporary Western sensibility was a purely natural, physical environment was significantly challenged by indigenous conceptions of landscapes that imbued them with wide-ranging meanings beyond nature (e.g., Head et al. 2002; Lane 2008; Langford 1983; McNiven 2008). For archaeologists studying ancient landscapes, taking into account contemporary indigenous conceptions of landscapes seriously transformed the field. In a related vein, Johnson (2007: 162–92) notes that the move from a romantic vision of a landscape as a natural place to a notion of a social landscape in the British landscape tradition was not just an intellectual exercise; it was a political one as well.

Taking the multiple stakeholders in archaeological research seriously was as critical for Hutson's (2010: 153–83) application of household archaeology and "dwelling" to his ancient Maya studies as it was for his understanding of the past. He asks whether genealogy (direct descent from ancient residents) is the only valid connection that indigenous people can have to the ancient past or whether dwelling (situated everyday practices in the modern world) in and around ruins can also constitute a valid connection for indigenous people and the past. His conclusion that living among ruins provides indigenous peoples a valid connection to the past regardless of their ability to trace a direct genealogical line of descent from the original builders of the ruins has important implications for identity politics and cultural heritage management alike.

For historical archaeologists who have taken on studies of topics such as colonialism, slavery, the development of capitalism, and so on, which have in part precipitated contemporary world events, political and academic interests often elide. As Silliman (2004: xi) notes in relation to colonial archaeology, "The consequences of these colonial encounters are lived daily by those whose ancestors suffered and those whose ancestors imposed colonial worlds, labor regimes, and social inequality. This legacy informs or perhaps fuels many of the politics surrounding ethnic identities, rights to human burial remains, land claims, economic development, and government power." For Lightfoot (2005: xi), studying the archaeology of culture contact in California is not just about understanding the relationship between native people and European colonists but also about asking, "Why are some California Indian tribes recognized by the United States government, although others remain unacknowledged?"

Oland, Hart, and Frink develop an archaeology of transition, which explores how long-term indigenous histories were influential in colonialism, turning traditional models of colonialism that see colonizers as the principal agents of change on their head. But this turn is not simply an academic one; it develops alternative approaches that "address Indigenous concerns, are shaped by Indigenous values, and engage with Indigenous peoples in the present" (Oland et al. 2012: 2).

Archaeology Matters is the title of a recent book by Sabloff (2008) that highlights the relevance of archaeological research to issues of contemporary concern. Archaeology has the potential to create a "more humane world" (McGuire 2008: 4). Contemporary archaeological theory and practice is pragmatic, even if not always overtly so (Preucel and Mrozowski 2010). Archaeologists demonstrate through their research that "current social relations are neither natural nor inevitable, but rather the creation of particular cultural traditions that have developed in specific ways over a long period of time" (Preucel and Mrozowski 2010: 34). A political archaeology of everyday life is about the past and about the present, but it is also about the future. "If we acknowledge that life in the past, even for 'our ancestors,' was different, the implication is that life can be different in the future" (Johnson 2007: 190).

Archaeology matters and everyday life matters, in the past, present, and future. Attending to everyday life in the past has a role to play in addressing social issues in the present and future because it is across everyday life that people address, accept, and transform society. With the growing recognition of the profound impact of Western and capitalist penetration in the world today (Wolf 1982), scholars are aware that the range of living situations represented in contemporary society is a limited set of what might be possible for human societies. In this way, the importance of archaeological discussions drawing upon data from past everyday life grows for all scholars interested in understanding human diversity. As I discuss further in chapter 4, when archaeologists are overt about their ethical, political, and moral interests, they can be more rigorous in their research than are so-called neutral scientists for whom bias remains unexplored.

Archaeology and Everyday Life: A General Sensibility

There are vibrant traditions of thought within archaeology that highlight the critical role played by everyday life in human societies. Still, in 2005, Lightfoot noted that popular concepts of "'real' archaeology, such as working on temple sites in Mexico, finding lost cities in South American jungles, or recording Paleolithic cave art paintings in France" still overshadow the digging of everyday rubbish that so many actual archaeologists do (2005: 14). Why should this be, when the material and spatial remains of everyday life are the means through which people in the past as well as archaeologists today come to understand and question ways of life?

Household, gender, and space and place research in archaeology illustrate the important contributions that archaeological approaches have for furthering critical studies of everyday life. Initial archaeological attention was on the grand monuments of the past, which provided archaeologists with an institutional and elite-centric perspective on past societies. But the analytical questions of the approaches highlighted in this chapter reveal that the myriad spaces and objects of daily life are ubiquitous in the archaeological record. The ubiquity of ordinary spaces and objects is not what makes them so consequential. That they provide a significant source of information through which people learn about themselves and the world around them makes them consequential.

Household, gender, and space and place research in archaeology, at least in part, all grew out of researchers' drive to question dominant discourses in archaeology: questioning the domestic/public divide, questioning the roles and status of women (and other understudied groups) in antiquity, questioning the seeming naturalness of the landscape. This in turn has led to new ways of thinking about framing research questions in archaeology with studies of everyday life emerging as a critical means to answer archaeological questions. For instance, instead of asking how presumed aspiring elites impose hierarchy on their societies, Arthur A. Joyce (2010) working in Formative Oaxaca, Gregory Wilson (2008) working at the Mississippian site of Moundville, and Monica Smith (2010) working from a prehistoric cross-cultural perspective ask how changes in the everyday lives and social and economic relations of people living in small social groups made it possible for leaders to emerge. In a similar vein, rather than asking why centralization, sedentism, and agglomeration occur in the Neolithic, Ian Hodder and Craig Cessford (2004) ask how changes in everyday life enabled these institutions and practices to develop. Rather than asking how colonialism affected indigenous populations, researchers who bridge historic and prehistoric archaeology are asking how the long-term histories of daily life for indigenous peoples also had an effect on colonial relations (Hart et al. 2012). In the Chan work, rather than asking how farmers and their farming communities were affected by the rise of polities and their leaders, I ask how the daily lives of farmers in their farming communities may also have had implications for rising polities and how aspiring leaders may have had to accommodate to these ways of life (chapters 6 and 7).

Although not a named subfield within archaeology, an explicit everyday life approach is emerging as more and more archaeologists are incorporating analyses of everyday life into their research, as seen in the research discussed in this chapter. The term *everyday life* is certainly one that a reader might encounter frequently in contemporary archaeological literature, although used in a much more wide-ranging manner than in the research discussed in this book. Within archaeological literature in general, the term *everyday life* is often used in an uncritical, undertheorized, or colloquial manner. Exploring these colloquial uses, and the misconceptions they entail about everyday life, provides interesting insight into the meanings and misunderstandings of *everyday life.*

There are three common uncritical usages of the term *everyday life* in the archaeological literature. First, *everyday life* often becomes a synonym for the house or the domestic domain. For example, in the edited volume *Secular Buildings and the Archaeology of Everyday Life in the Byzantine Empire,* the archaeology of everyday life is equated with the archaeology of secular domestic architecture (Dark 2004). In this usage, *everyday life* becomes a term that could be used interchangeably with the term *household archaeology.* While the domestic domain may be an important arena of everyday life, and as I have argued in this chapter, household archaeology has played a critical role in the development of archaeological studies of everyday life, the two are not equivalents. The spaces and places of everyday life are vast, and doing household archaeology does not necessarily entail doing an archaeology of everyday life.

Second, the use of the term *everyday life* often designates studies involving meticulous and detailed descriptions of seemingly mundane objects and practices. The book *Craft, Industry, and Everyday Life: Leather and Leatherworking in Anglo-Scandinavian and Medieval York* provides detailed descriptions, photographs, and drawings of leather small finds from York and documents methods of shoe making and sheath and scabbard making (Mould et al. 2003). At an analytical level, in this usage, a study of everyday life ends once the detailed description of ordinary objects and practices is accomplished. However, a critical archaeology of everyday life steps beyond describing daily life and enables broader discussions about people and their social world.

The third colloquial usage of the term *everyday life* is quite distinct from the first two. In this usage, *everyday life* becomes a synonym for the totality of a past society. Greenwood Press's Daily Life through History textbook series now has ninety-five titles. The series web page states that the purpose of the books is to answer the question "What was life really like for ordinary people in other cultures throughout history?" (http://www .greenwood.com/catalog/series/The%2bGreenwood%2bPress%2bDaily% 2bLife%2bThrough%2bHistory%2bSeries.aspx). Looking at the table of contents for one title, *Daily Life of the Ancient Egyptians* (Brier and Hobbs 2008), one finds the following chapters: (1) History, (2) Government and Society, (3) Work and Play, (4) Food, (5) Clothes and Other Adornments, (6) Architecture, (7) Arts and Crafts, (8) Warfare, and (9) Medicine and Mathematics. Here daily life designates the totality of an ancient society.

In this third colloquial usage, it is clear that writers are just as comfortable using the term *everyday life* as a way to characterize the nature of entire societies as they are in using it to refer to particular and mundane aspects of those societies. The proliferation and inconsistent colloquial uses of the term *everyday life* within archaeology might suggest that this term lacks the specificity to be useful as a robust theoretical concept. But the assumptions behind the three primary colloquial usages of the term *everyday life* provide a glimpse into what is specific and theoretically robust about the concept. On the one hand, there are the micro usages of the term "everyday life" (as house, mundane object, or act), and on the other hand, there are the macro usages (as a window into the nature of a society). Analytically, the micro usage of the term *everyday life* is associated with meticulous attention to ordinary details, but analysis is halted once those details are thoroughly catalogued and presented. In its macro usage, an analysis of everyday life would entail studies of all aspects of past societies. What is hinted at in these three usages (but not realized in any single usage) is that studying everyday life enables researchers to understand how the micro (people, interactions) and macro (institutions, power relations, societies) aspects of social life intersect. This is what a critical archaeology of everyday life attempts to do.

A critical archaeology of everyday life examines the ordinary practices, materials, and spaces of past daily lives to develop a critical understanding of human societies. Taking everyday life seriously in archaeology involves five overlapping themes. First, daily life is a complex phenomenon that involves the myriad spaces, objects, people, and interactions that make up the social world. Second, ordinary spaces and objects of daily life are not simply mundane; they form the means through which people create, learn about, and transform their world. Third, everyday practices are profoundly implicated in what is going on in the world and thus are critical both for understanding local experiences and interpersonal interactions and for interpreting broader social, political, and power relations as well as change. Fourth, focusing on everyday life highlights the importance of studying social differences and identities in the past, as all people—regardless of wealth, status, age, gender, ethnicity, or other lines of difference—play roles in the constitution of their societies through their everyday lives. Fifth, attending to everyday life in the past has a role to play in addressing social issues in the present and future because it is across everyday life that people address, accept, and transform society.

To these five, I would also add one more that might be less easily embraced by the widest of archaeological audiences. Sixth, effective academic writing about past everyday lives invokes a writing style about everyday life that makes it intelligible to the everyday life it attempts to capture through the written word.

In terms of my last point, it would be disingenuous for me to insinuate that there was anything like a move away from strict academic style of writing about everyday life in archaeology; the work discussed in this chapter is typical of academic writing in the field of archaeology. But certain practitioners craft archaeological writing in which clarity is an intentional vehicle for communicating information about everyday life (e.g., Ashmore 2004; Battle-Baptiste 2011; Deetz 1977; Hodder 2006; Johnson 2010b; A. Joyce 2010; Lightfoot 2005; Robin 2003). Writing about everyday life in a way that is intelligible to everyday life promotes and advances its analysis and interpretation.

The social theoretical literature discussed in chapter 2 establishes the centrality of everyday life in studies of human existence and points to the importance of material and spatial analyses in the pursuit of understanding everyday life. Archaeology establishes the crucial role that material and spatial analyses play in studies of everyday life as the materials and spaces that people create give shape and meaning to their world and also give them the ability to shape their world and make it meaningful. The lived spaces that people inhabit are not simply domains of nature or passive backdrops for life. People actively construct, use, and modify the world around them. Through their material presence, these spaces encode and express social norms, expectations, and power relations and provide a means through which people can question these. As people use, experience, and perceive the material and spatial world during their everyday lives, they learn social expectations and challenge them. The material and spatial world can be constraining or enabling and even both simultaneously—it can inform and influence people's actions, but also the way people use, reuse, and reconstruct it can create and inscribe new meanings in the world. While the monuments and inscriptions of traditional archaeological inquiry evoke the history of elite classes of society, all people leave behind material and spatial traces of their everyday lives. Examining ordinary materials and spaces enables a focus on all people and social groups in society and allows better interpretations of organization, power relations, and change in society that necessarily involved all members of society.

Archaeologists, through their access to a deep record of human history that extends well beyond that of written records and contemporary societies, are uniquely equipped to study the long history of everyday life. Because everyday life is where people and societies, micro and micro, and material and social intersect, rather than seeing studies of everyday life as inconsequential, studies of everyday life should be increasingly central to informing critical understandings of the past, present, and future.

4 ✳ Methods for a Critical Archaeology of Everyday Life

For Lefebvre, as with all of the everyday life theorists discussed in this book, everyday life cannot be understood at an abstract theoretical level. Theoretical insights must complement a deep commitment to furthering empirical studies. Given the goal of confronting academics with life, everyday life scholarship pays particular attention to the relationship between theory, methods, and data. Theory does not stand alone as an abstraction but is deeply implicated in how researchers use theory and what data they bring to it. Because data and theory are mutually implicated, everyday life thinkers have always been as concerned with the development of methods as they have been with the development of theory. The same is true within the field of archaeology. A critical everyday life approach must be grounded as much in empirical work as in theory.

Postprocessual archaeologists initially made the point that archaeological data are theory laden: data are not neutral but informed by theoretical perspectives, the questions researchers do and do not bring to them, and what researchers decide does and does not constitute evidence (Hodder 1999; Johnson 2010a). De Certeau (1984: 43–77) makes the interesting corollary point that theory is also data laden: theoreticians create theory in the world within which they live and are influenced by what they see around them and what they know about the world. Thus, as much as data is influenced by theory, theory is also influenced by data. Wylie (1992) makes a similar point in her discussion of the "evidential constraints" on archaeological knowledge: while data are not neutral, they can and do constrain what archaeologists can say is possible about the past. While everyday life thinkers note that analyses cannot stop at simple (or complex) descriptions of everyday life, the absence of such descriptions is disabling, because without an evidential basis for what everyday life is like, theories will simply perpetuate prevailing understandings of the banality of everyday life or other prevailing understandings. Theory does not reside in some higher intellectual domain or exist subjectively locked inside researchers' heads; it arises from researchers' practical engagement with the world and others around them across their everyday lives. Just as data are both subjective and objective, theory too is both subjective and objective. Given the interpenetration of data and theory, subjectivity and objectivity, theory can guide what researchers choose to accept and look for as data, and data can place constraints on what researchers might say is theoretically possible.

This chapter develops archaeological methods and research design to further a critical archaeology of everyday life. I focus largely on insights from the Chan project but also draw upon complementary examples from other archaeological projects. A critical archaeology of everyday life involves an intensive archaeological process from the beginning (designing research) to the end (publication) of that process. It involves long-term research projects and extended field seasons whereby researchers can immerse themselves in the archaeological record of past everyday lives (as well as present everyday lives). It involves collaborative research in which insights beyond those of the primary researchers' field(s) can enhance the "conceptual integrity and empirical adequacy" of research (Wylie 1992: 15). It involves a deep and detailed engagement with the archaeological record through archaeological methods such as horizontal (open area) excavation and engagement with new scientific methods that provide extended insights into past everyday life.

In ethnographic terms, this intensive archaeology of everyday life opposes Lévi-Strauss's structuralist position, critiqued by Lefebvre (see chapter 2), that "just a quarter of an hour alone" with someone from another culture is a sufficient basis for interpreting culture. Such a short-term engagement is insufficient to understand the complexities of everyday life. An intensive archaeology of everyday life is akin to undertaking an archaeological "thick description" (sensu stricto Geertz 1973): a deep and elaborate study of the meaning of what people do, which illustrates that simple actions are much larger than they appear (Robb 2007: 23; Robin 2012b). Archaeologists who focus on everyday life call for a type of archaeological research that is extensive, multiscalar, and often diachronic, and includes as many types of data as possible and fine-grained inquiries into those data (e.g., Robin 2002a, 2003, 2012a; Hodder and Cessford 2004; Lightfoot et al. 1998: 202; Özbal 2006; Robb 2007: 22–24; Silliman 2004: xv: Voss 2008a: 117–43). A critical archaeology of everyday life explores the fullest range of archaeological evidence afforded by the archaeological record, details that often are not visible from a traditional macroscopic archaeological perspective alone (Robin 2001).

While a critical archaeology of everyday life is an intensive archaeology, this does not imply that researchers need to collect ever vaster amounts of detailed data on past daily lives. A "selective rather than encyclopedic" data set on past daily lives should be the goal (Robb 2007: 23). It is, for better or for worse, an impossible task to collect all the details of the daily life of even a single individual. This dilemma is wonderfully illustrated in Robb's (2007: 22) summary of Tor Age Bringsvaerd's fantasy science fiction short story "The Man Who Collected the First of September, 1973"— "a man who, in fear of losing his grip on reality, decides to collect all the information available on his everyday world. Quickly overwhelmed by the size of the task, he limits himself to learning all possible facts about one day. Even this quickly takes over his life; there is so much to know. His apartment fills up with boxes and files, its walls shaggy with papers. He becomes increasingly myopic, fixated, and unable to communicate. Finally, verging on solipsism, madness, and disease, he dies."

Processual archaeologists were the first to critique the process of the accumulation of archaeological data as a means and an end in and of itself because more data does not necessarily lead to a better analysis (Binford 1989; Clarke 1968; Johnson 2007: 61–63). Thus, developing appropriate methods for data collection and analysis is critical for understanding the details of everyday life, since the important thing is not simply how many details researchers accumulate but how significant those details are to the questions they ask. Because data are theory laden, and theory is data laden, techniques must develop in concert with theoretical interests so that researchers are not making the false pretense of collecting value-free empirical evidence and so that they are collecting robust empirical evidence to provide constraints on their interpretations (e.g., Hodder 1999; Johnson 2007, 2010a; Wylie 1985, 1992, 2002).

This chapter proceeds by developing three important methodological implications for everyday life research. First, I highlight the critical role that collaboration plays in everyday life research, both collaboration with local communities that can challenge and transform existing research frameworks and multidisciplinary research collaboration that develops robust and independent multiple lines of evidence about past everyday life. Second, I explore the importance of methodological issues such as horizontal (open area) excavations of the contexts of everyday life and investigation of the vast expanses of open spaces that are locales for daily interactions. Finally, I engage new scientific analyses that are revealing ever more detailed information on past daily life, to illustrate how an everyday life approach can bridge long-standing disciplinary divides between scientific and humanistic research.

Research Design:
A Collaborative Archaeology of Everyday Life

An important part of Dorothy Smith's critique of established academic sociology in the 1980s (see chapter 2) is that as researchers stand outside of everyday life their research reinscribes dominant ideologies in society back onto its research subjects. A way to move beyond society's and sociology's hidden assumptions is to engage with everyday life and generate new questions about the world from people's everyday lives, which may present new sets of questions that are not being posed in academic research. As I discuss in the prologue, I initially came to the study of everyday life not through academic work but because of my experiences as an undergraduate archaeology researcher in Belize in the 1980s and my conversations with Belizeans, many of whom were strangers, at archaeological sites and on the streets of Belize. These conversations often turned on a similar question: What was daily life like in ancient times for an ordinary person like me? This question struck me, because my undergraduate education in archaeology was filled with topics such as the rise and fall of civilizations, not the everyday lives of ordinary people. Only later did I learn that the 1980s was also a time when philosophers of science and feminist theorists were promoting a critical engagement with everyday life as a stimulus for research such as that which made my experiences with people in Belize more than personal experiences, instead serving as important challenges to and reformulations of academic knowledge (e.g., D. Smith 1987; Wylie 2008).

Turning more specifically to archaeological practice, Alison Wylie (1992, 2002, 2008) argues from an epistemological perspective that intellectual and practical collaboration with nonacademics, particularly descendant and nondescendant communities living around archaeological sites, epistemic advantage on the margins, can counteract insularity and provide corrective insights for science. I certainly observed this to be the case over and over again in the Chan research.

I initiated the Chan project in 2002 after sixteen years of working in Belize, including working with the Belize Institute of Archaeology, the government organization that oversees archaeological research in Belize, as a United States Peace Corps volunteer, and working as an archaeologist in communities in northern and western Belize. I had worked in Succotz, the modern town nearest to Chan, for eight years and spent the two years prior to establishing the project speaking with people in Succotz and the Belize Institute of Archaeology about the project and getting their permission for the research (forty-nine landowners have land in what used to be the Chan community and provided permission for the Chan work). Derric Chan, one of the co-owners of the central portion of the Chan site, and after whose family the site is named, had initially approached me in 1996, while I was still a graduate student, to conduct research at Chan. But as a graduate student, I could not command the financial resources necessary to mount a community-scale project even at a smaller community such as Chan.

Derric is an environmentalist, and along with Rafael Manzanero, he cofounded Friends for Conservation and Development (FDC; www .fdcbelize.org), a nongovernment co-management agency that works to protect Belize's natural heritage and educate the public about conservation. Derric and his father, Ismael Chan Sr., have been the custodians of the Chan site, protecting it from looting and destruction. Derric always believed there was a significance to Chan, despite its small size, in part because of the numerous agricultural terraces found throughout the community, a type of agriculture not practiced in Belize today; he wanted to know more about this ancient practice and whether it held any information for contemporary conservation efforts. Working with Derric and listening to his insights on designing an archaeological project at Chan, I found an intellectual kinship for my academic inquiry into the importance of an ancient farming community. He helped me remember that there was a potential for a much broader audience for my work than archaeologists. During the course of the Chan project, Derric also consulted with the Field Museum of Natural History in Chicago to help them guide their new Ancient Americas exhibit to be conscious of the interests and concerns of local communities across the Americas.

I initiated the Chan project first with smaller grants from the National Geographic Society and Heinz Foundation for Latin American Studies and later with larger grants from the National Science Foundation and the National Endowment for the Humanities, among other awards. In addition, Northwestern University was always a strong supporter of the project. Ultimately, I received as much of the project funding from grants devoted to fostering collaborative research as I received from grants devoted to archaeological research. The collaborative research grants highlighted the importance of two aspects of multinational research collaboration: (1) the ways in which bringing together an international multidisciplinary research team with a range of scientific expertise both in and beyond archaeology could enhance the empirical foundations of the project by developing multiple lines of evidence on ancient every-day life, a topic to which I turn later in this chapter, and (2) the ways in which binational collaboration between U.S. and Belizean archaeology professionals and laypeople and the training of U.S. and Belizean students could promote research interests. The grants spelled out in detail the first aspect of the collaboration, but only in retrospect did I come to realize that some of the most profound challenges and transformations to my research design arose from unanticipated outcomes of the second aspect of the collaboration.

Succotz was the community where J. Eric Thompson, the foremost early twentieth-century Mayanist, came to recruit Belizean workers for his archaeological excavations at major Maya centers across Belize. Since the 1920s, foreign archaeologists in Belize have followed suit, coming to Succotz to acquire their archaeology work forces. The current residents of Succotz are the grandchildren and great-grandchildren of the workers on these early archaeological projects, the most skilled and sought-after archaeological workers in Belize. I always felt fortunate to work alongside the talented archaeologists from Succotz (for many of whom, by comparison, my sixteen years of archaeological research in Belize was a drop in the bucket). Training archaeological workers in excavation techniques was never something I had to do on the Chan project, but learning new ideas about archaeological excavation was always possible. Archaeology workers from Succotz took on roles within the Chan project that are typically assigned to foreign archaeology professionals and students, such as archaeological illustration, field data recording, directing the Chan project laboratory, computer database management, and project accounting. Some Belizean members of the Chan project moved on to supervisory roles on other projects or within the tourism industry and have been able to maintain archaeology as their sole source of income and advancement.

But for most residents of Succotz, archaeology is only a part-year job. For the other part of the year, many residents are farmers. While the Chan project lasted for four to six months a year across its eight years and employed up to forty archaeological workers per year, archaeological projects in Belize often last for only one or two months per year. The length of the Chan project field seasons was related to developing an intensive engagement both with the archaeological record of everyday life at ancient Chan and with contemporary everyday life.

The first phase of the Chan research focused on the mapping of a 3.2-square-kilometer area around Chan's community center (Robin, Wyatt et al. 2012). This work was conducted by the entire Chan team in 2002 and a smaller team directed by Andrew Wyatt in 2003. The survey team members included U.S. graduate students, undergraduate students, and archaeology professionals, as well as Belizean archaeology workers from Succotz and archaeologists from the Belize Institute of Archaeology. Surveying the ancient farming community of Chan alongside contemporary Belizean farmers created a dynamic intellectual environment for studying ancient Maya farming. There were constant discussions during the survey work about the nature of ancient Maya farming, particularly as it related to contemporary farming practices. Each day, the survey work revealed a vast array of agricultural terraces, the most ubiquitous and substantial constructions at Chan (figures 4.1 and 4.2). The hilly locations that ancient farmers chose as their agricultural lands were not the flat and alluvial areas that contemporary farmers choose for farming. The dissonance between ancient and contemporary farming practices was abundantly clear to farmers from Succotz.

Not until I heard Wylie's distinguished lecture to the American Anthropological Association in 2008, "Legacies of Collaboration: Transformative Criticism in Archaeology," and later heard her talk on a similar subject at Northwestern while I was writing this book, did I realize the impact that those daily conversations about the differences between modern and ancient farming had on my thinking. As cultural outsiders, archaeologists

Figure 4.1. Surveyors Ethan Kalosky and Bernabe Camal Sr. stand along the uppermost of a series of cross-channel terraces set along a seasonal drainage area where two hill-slopes meet. This photograph was taken in a clear pasture area at Chan north of the community center (excavation area c on figure 6.1). From this vantage point the viewer can see the rolling upland terrain in which Chan is situated in the background. Pastures are uncommon at Chan.

are often impressed by the continuities in traditions between the ancient people they study and modern residents. But as cultural insiders, for the farmers of Succotz, the differences between the past and the present were paramount.

In Maya and Americanist archaeology there is a long tradition of a direct historical approach in archaeology, which builds upon the notion that people in a given culture share similar ideas about the world, so that archaeologists can use the more detailed data sets about a modern culture to develop models for understanding people of an antecedent culture (e.g., Kidder 1924; Lyman and O'Brien 2001; Marcus 1993: Rice 2004; Strong 1933; Wedel 1938). The benefit of using direct historical analogies is that they potentially allow greater insight into cultural concepts that have been uniquely developed through time by groups of people. The main criticism of direct historical analogy is that it assumes that cultures broadly stay the same though time. Wobst (1978: 303) refers to this problem as the "tyranny of the ethnographic record," in which the present colors the past, and history and change are erased (also see Robin 2006; Robin and Brumfiel 2008; Stahl 2001). To help alleviate this problem, Wylie (1985) suggests that it is as important to evaluate dissimilarities as it is similarities when making historical comparisons (also see Marcus 1995; Robin 2006; Stahl 2001). Differences are as important as similarities in understanding cultural and historical change and continuity. The latter point is the point that the Belizean farmers working on the Chan survey were making to me.

In 2006 I published an article in *Current Anthropology* entitled "Gender, Farming, and Long-Term Change: Maya Historical and Archaeological Perspectives." This article explored how Maya farming practices changed through time, particularly in terms of the gender relations of farming. It exposed the research assumptions that led to images of timeless farming relations among the Maya. My academic inspiration for this piece was research by Guyer (1988) and Stahl (2001) critiquing timeless notions of

Figure 4.2. Surveyors Ethan Kalosky and Bernabe Camal Sr. stand along a set of contour terraces set along a hillslope. The terraces are clear along a *picado*, a survey line the surveyors cut with machetes through the dense brush that is typical of the Chan forests. The terraces are located 0.8 kilometers north of Chan's community center (excavation area b on figure 6.1).

farming in Africa, which left contemporary Africa and its peoples as the primitive remnants of an ancient past, theoretical work by Wylie (1985) on the appropriate uses of ethnographic analogy in archaeology, and archaeological work in the Maya area that exposed a long history of technological changes in Maya farming practices (Fedick 1995, 1996; Hammond 1978). But only more recently have I become consciously aware of the ways in which my conversations with Belizean farmers over their concerns about understanding ancient Maya farming demanded that I take seriously the problems associated with imposing the ethnographic record on the archaeological past, which has been a centerpiece of my research perspective (Robin 2006; Robin and Brumfiel 2008). For an archaeology of everyday life in the past to have an impact on the present and future, researchers must be able to distinguish between the past, present, and future.

Other engagements with Belizean archaeological workers on the Chan project led to immediately obvious reformulations of project research design in ways that strengthened the project's ability to evaluate evidence for ancient everyday life. I will provide two potent examples. In 1996, I undertook my dissertation research at a neighboring cluster of small farming households south of Chan's community center, referred to as Chan Nòohol (*nòohol* is Yucatec Maya for "south"). Bernabe Camal Jr., then a teenager, was excavating along the centerline of a small farmer's house, immediately behind the house. The centerline of buildings is a typical location where ancient Maya placed ritual caches. Having cleaned his discovery for photography, Bernabe called me over and wanted to know whether I wanted him to draw it as well as photograph it. I looked down but saw no archaeological evidence—certainly nothing worthy of either a photograph or a drawing (figure 4.3 upper). So I asked Bernabe what he had found. He pointed to four ordinary river cobbles, the kind anyone could find in a stream or river in the vicinity of Chan. These were located around a broken fragment of a greenstone axe. I had not initially noted the dirt-covered fragment of the greenstone axe, but as soon as I did, I registered it as an artifact, albeit a broken one, which might have been discarded behind the house because of its broken and fragmentary nature. Bernabe asked why I thought the greenstone fragment might have been discarded. Broken things, he said, can be very useful. Bernabe noted further that the four ordinary river cobbles were oriented to the cardinal directions around the greenstone fragment and that each river cobble had a different coloration: yellow, white, black, and red (figure 4.3 lower). Could this have some symbolic meaning, he asked. The stones did not look ritual or symbolic to me; they were too ordinary or too broken. I doubted at the time that he had actually found an ancient ritual deposit, but because he had already cleaned the find for photography and was one of the best illustrators on the crew, I let him go ahead and photograph and draw the find. He asked me whether I would look into his idea that the stones had a ritual significance. I said that I would, but I promptly forgot.

Some weeks later, an undergraduate on the project was reading Schele and Freidel's (1992) *A Forest of Kings: The Untold Story of the Ancient Maya*. The book was open to a page that had an image of the Maya cosmogram, which is schematically represented as a quincunx pattern oriented to the cardinal directions with particular colors associated with particular cardinal directions. I looked down and realized that the color and directional associations of the Maya cosmogram were the same as those of Bernabe's river cobbles. I realized that Bernabe had made what might well be a very important find: humble Maya farmers were using ordinary and broken objects to represent the Maya cosmogram to ritually sanctify their home in similar ways to what Maya royals did to sanctify their palaces and temples with a rich array of elaborate objects. Subsequent finds similar to Bernabe's made by members of the Chan project further indicated that the development of complex religious ideas by farmers at Chan predated the adoption of these ideas by Maya royalty. Farmers created a wealth of religious knowledge in their homes and communities, and only later was this "popular religion" elevated by Maya royalty into a state religion (chapter 6). This finding reverses conventional archaeological thinking that when commoners and elites do the same things, it is the commoners who are emulating the ideas of the elites.

Bernabe's find required a reevaluation of what I considered archaeological evidence and how I recorded that evidence. I had to create new categories in the Chan coding sheets for unmodified natural objects and highlight to the archaeological team the potential importance of these objects. I also had to reevaluate the in-field interpretation of broken or fragmentary items and how excavators would define archaeological contexts such as refuse deposits and ritual deposits. Discarded debris was certainly a possible interpretation for broken items, but as Bernabe was aware from his own everyday life, broken objects could be quite meaningful and useful. Rethinking the context and meaning of broken and

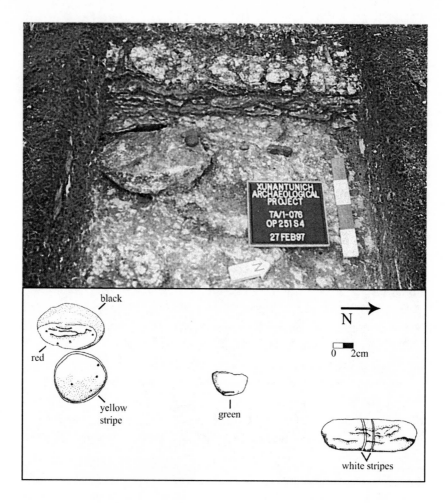

Figure 4.3. River cobble cache behind eastern house at household CN5. CN5 is located south of Chan's community center (excavation area h on figure 6.1). The upper image shows the original field photograph. The photograph illustrates how difficult it is, from a conventional archaeological perspective, to identify the river cobbles as a significant archaeological find. The two southernmost cobbles of the cache are located on a capstone covering a miniature *chultun*—a small bell-shaped subterranean chamber that residents excavated into the ground in this location. *Chultuns* are both underground storage chambers and portals to the underworld. This chultun was empty upon excavation but may have originally held perishable items. Given the small size of the chultun, it is unlikely to have functioned as a significant storage facility for the residents of CN5. Its association with the river cobble cache suggests that it was part of the ritual deposit CN5 residents created to consecrate their home as the center of the world. The lower image is an illustration of the river cobble cache by Bernabe Camal, with colors marked.

fragmentary objects found across the Chan project led to understanding both the practical utility of broken objects for farmers and the ritual practice of breaking important items, burying a part of them and retaining another part within the living community for future interment sometimes hundreds of years later (chapter 6).

In a second example, during the 2003 excavation season at Chan's community center, excavation foreman Everaldo Chi and excavator Ciro Hernandez noticed that large fragments of hard limestone were scattered across the Central Plaza at the community center (figure 4.4). They identified these as fragments of a stela, a standing stone monument usually about two meters in height, often found at major Maya centers. When carved, stelae tend to depict royalty. The Chan hard limestone fragments had no carvings. It did not entirely make sense to me that there would be a stela at Chan, given the small size of the community coupled with the fact that stelae had been found in the upper Belize Valley at only two sites: the polity capital of Xunantunich, and Actuncan, a site north of Xunantunich

Figure 4.4. Early Postclassic shrine (Structure 1) at Chan's Central Group. The top of Stela 1 is located on the west edge of the shrine. Other fragments of the stela were dispersed across the plaza. *Inset:* Stela 1 as reconstructed by Everaldo Chi and Ciro Hernandez. (Photographs by Michael Latsch.)

that may have been the ancestral home of Xunantunich's rulers (LeCount and Yaeger 2010). None of the numerous other major centers in the upper Belize Valley, which were much larger than Chan, had stelae. Why would Chan?

Everaldo and Ciro wanted to map the location of the possible stela fragments and then move them to a central location and try to fit them together. I was unconvinced about the project but did not have a problem with their doing it, especially since they were willing to carry all of the heavy stones. A few days later Everaldo and Ciro had put together Stela 1 from Chan (figure 4.4). In 2006 Bernadette Cap's team identified Stela 2 in the West Plaza of Chan's community center (Cap 2012). There are potentially two other stelae represented by stone fragments at Chan. Chan's multiple stelae date to the Terminal Classic period (AD 800/830–900), a time when royal political power was declining across the Maya area and major centers of the Classic period were declining or being abandoned. In the Terminal Classic period, based on the inscriptions on carved stelae at major centers, as the power and authority of the Classic Maya kings waned, lesser groups of royalty and nobility and smaller seats of royal power usurped the ability to erect stelae, once reserved for only the mightiest of kings and the largest of centers. Chan's at least two late uncarved stelae seem to represent the furthest extension of this process of appropriation and emulation, as even smaller nonroyal centers were able to usurp the original symbols of the divine kings for their own purposes (chapter 6).

Just as Stela 1 visibly marked the sacred importance of Chan to ancient residents, so too did it serve as a daily reminder of this importance for the entire Chan project team. When the project reburied the Chan site after excavations were complete, Everaldo, on behalf of the excavation team, asked whether the broken Stela 1 could remain reassembled in the center of Chan's Central Plaza to mark the importance of that place. Similarly, excavations in 2004 in the east structure of Chan's E-Group, the tallest building of the Central Plaza, uncovered an altar (Altar 3) carved out of a single piece of stone, the only one of Chan's altars to be carved out of a single piece of stone. Everaldo likewise asked whether rather than reinterring that altar the project could leave it exposed so that contemporary residents could "see" the importance of Chan's 5.6-meter-high temple. Graduate student excavation supervisor Caleb Kestle made a replica of a Postclassic spiked incense burner and left it on the exposed altar after the last season of major excavations in 2007 (see cover image). Two years later, in 2009, upon returning to the site, the Chan team discovered that modern residents had used the incense burner and altar: there were remains of burned incense in the incense burner and a book on the altar. The book could not be opened or read, because it had been repeatedly rained upon since the time of its deposition. Once again, modern residents in the vicinity of Chan are reentering a place of ancient ritual significance and reformulating a new type of ritual knowledge that leaves new material traces.

Community collaboration was a key aspect of the Chan research that led to new understandings of the nature of archaeological evidence, new insights into the application of archaeological theory, and reworkings of the Chan project research design that provided for better insights into the nature of past everyday life at Chan. This community collaboration was also always part of a dialogue, and it created new understandings of farming and the nature of sacred sites in the lives of contemporary residents as well.

Excavating Everyday Life: Horizontal (Open Area) Exposures and the Investigation of Outdoor Spaces

Another significant aspect of an intensive archaeology of everyday life at Chan is the project's focus on conducting full-scale horizontal (open area) exposures of the spaces and places of everyday life: houses, agricultural terraces, outdoor activity areas, and any other place that was a part of residents' daily lives. An intensive archaeology of everyday life requires full exposure of the archaeological contexts of past daily lives. Test pits and trenches, which are appropriate for understanding chronology and stratigraphy, stop short of exposing daily living.

In Kent Flannery's (1976: 13–15) now-classic tale of the Real Mesoamerican Archaeologist (R.M.A.) and the Skeptical Graduate Student (S.G.S.), one of the confrontations between the two was the question of whether horizontal contextual excavations were necessary for archaeological interpretation or not. The R.M.A. was solely interested in excavating trenches in arbitrary 20-centimeter levels to collect ceramics for seriation. The S.G.S., in contrast, worked meticulously to expose a house floor and associated hearth and identified the postmolds that penetrated the clay house floor and the wattle-and-daub walls that collapsed upon it subsequent to its abandonment. Flannery's goal in presenting this particular confrontation was to demonstrate that the R.M.A.'s arbitrary 20-centimeter levels dissected a single house and its wall collapse, floor and fill, and postmolds into three arbitrary levels that he presumed to be chronologically distinct and to represent three different types of house construction (houses constructed with wattle-and-daub, houses constructed with clay floors, and houses constructed with postmolds), whereas the S.G.S.'s meticulous horizontal and contextual excavations showed all of these to be part of the construction and abandonment of a single house. While Flannery's discussion of the importance of full-scale versus trench excavations stopped with documenting how horizontal exposures can in fact enhance an archaeologist's understanding of chronological and stratigraphic relations, I take the significance of horizontal excavations one step further. Horizontal excavations define the contexts of past daily life. They are what allow archaeologists to expose the spaces, places, and contexts of everyday life so that they can evaluate the nature and variability of daily practices in the past and determine what these may have said about beliefs and values and conformity with and confrontation with broader social norms.

Household archaeologists have long advocated an excavation focus on full-scale horizontal exposures of households, because only through such broad and contextually focused exposures can archaeologists explore the range of activities that make up a household (e.g., Flannery 1976; Hodder and Cessford 2004; Hutson 2010: 61; Lightfoot et al. 1998; Robb 2007; Robin 2003; Sheets 2002). Horizontal exposures are less common in agricultural archaeology, for which researchers typically use test pits and trenching to determine the chronology and construction techniques of agricultural features. Andrew Wyatt's (2008a, 2008b, 2012) dissertation work on Chan's agricultural terraces recognized that terraces are much more than their construction techniques: they constitute complex systems for soil and water management and are places where people perform daily work and socialize with one another. Because Wyatt conducted horizontal exposures of terraces rather than trenches and test pits, he was able to explore terraces as complex agricultural systems that formed daily contexts for the production and sharing of social and economic strategies and knowledge about the local environment (chapter 6). In a similar vein, Caleb Kestle's (2012) research on Chan's limestone quarries opened horizontal exposures across quarry areas in order to ascertain that quarries were not simply passive locations for the extraction of stone but "were active locales where people labored and interacted, developing economic strategies for their households."

The spaces and places of past daily life are vast and are not limited to houses, agricultural areas, quarries, or other features of the archaeological record that are marked by visible constructions. While archaeologists tend to focus their excavations on visible constructions, which are typically architecture, the oftentimes-larger portions of the archaeological record that are situated between buildings and other constructions are active locales of daily life (Robin 2002a; Robin and Rothschild 2002). Because these parts of the archaeological record are devoid of the physical surface traces that can help guide archaeologists in placing their excavations, they are often ignored. But to fully examine everyday life in the past, these spaces must be explored as well. Prospective techniques suited to identifying subsurface remains within the large expanses of seemingly "empty" spaces in the archaeological record are a requisite step for identifying how open spaces were used in past daily life.

At Chan, given the shallow depositions of soil, a posthole testing technique provided a rapid and effective means of identifying the past uses of open spaces and isolating areas for further horizontal excavation (Robin, Meierhoff, and Kosakowsky 2012). The Chan researchers excavated postholes at four- to five-meter intervals across thirty- to fifty-meter-square blocks around all architectural groups investigated at Chan and sometimes across whole neighborhoods (Blackmore 2012; Robin 1999). They collected artifacts, stone, and soil samples for chemical testing from each posthole. The types, form, and condition of subsurface artifacts; size, shape, and density of stone; and chemical signatures provided a means to evaluate the use and meaning of spaces that lack visible architectural constructions. Across Chan's porous soil surfaces, working, walking, cleaning, interacting, the rhythms of everyday life were inscribed in material and chemical ways that were not visible on the surface of the site but were identifiable archaeologically through subsurface prospection. The posthole testing research at Chan even identified the pathways of heavy foot traffic as people moved across their daily lives. These insights into how residents organized and used space were critical for assessing shared understandings of home and community that rooted people in place as well as the different and conflicting understandings of life and society that led to changing dynamics within the community (chapter 6).

Microanalysis and Everyday Life

In archaeology, as well as across academia more generally, there is a divide between scientists and humanists: the "two cultures" of academia (Hodder 1999; Jones 2002). An archaeological approach to everyday life develops a healthy union between scientific inquiry, which allows ever more fine-grained analysis of the ancient activities and activity areas of daily life, and social and archaeological theory on everyday life, practice, and experience (Robin 2001). From scientific analyses of soil chemistry, micromorphology, microartifact analysis, paleoethnobotany, phytolith studies, pollen analysis, stable-isotope analysis, petrography, and the sourcing of objects and people, among other analyses, archaeologists are gaining more comprehensive understandings of ancient day-to-day life (e.g., Cap 2012; Fladmark 1982; Hastorf 1991, 1999; Hauser 2008; Hodder 2006; Hodder and Cessford 2004; Hutson 2010; A. Jones 2002; Lentz 2000; Manzanilla and Barba 1990; Matthews et al. 1997; Middleton 2004; Middleton and Price 1996; Özbal 2006; Robin 2001, 2002a; Wells and Terry 2007). While traditional analyses of architecture and macroartifacts provide critical information about the past, because people sweep their floors clean or remove their belongings when they abandon their living places, it has often been difficult for archaeologists to identify activity patterning, what people did in particular spaces, within architecture based on in-situ or secondary macro remains. Although the macro remains of human activities may be gone, most human activities leave behind some types of material or physical remains that are not visible to the naked eye but can be observed through microscopic analyses, such as the chemical residues of phosphorus, calcium, and wood ash from cooking areas or the microscopic flake debris from a chert or shell worker's workshop. Through the detail orientation of an everyday life approach, the scientific and the postmodern find a common ground.

Conducting a microanalysis of ancient everyday life involves engaging in a collaborative multidisciplinary research endeavor, because many of the scientific techniques useful in identifying the micro traces of past daily lives have been developed outside of archaeology. This is the aspect of collaborative research that I was able to elaborate most fully in my grant applications. Microanalyses yield multiple independent lines of evidence from archaeological data that allow for a robust "evidential reasoning" (sensu stricto Wylie 2002) about the past.

Some of the most significant lines of evidence about past everyday life at Chan were revealed by microanalyses. I will mention two of these here as examples, more of which can be found in chapter 6. Because of Chan's contemporary tropical environment, organic remains are not preserved. Even the preservation of carbonized remains is quite poor. But by taking substantial ten-liter soil samples for flotation from excavation contexts, the Chan researchers documented a significant array of micro carbonized plant remains that revealed a diverse range of forest species. Lentz and colleagues (2012), working out of the Department of Biological Sciences at the University of Cincinnati, identified that Chan's farmers maintained the mature tropical forest canopy across the community's two thousand years of expanding agricultural production. This is a key insight into the environmentally sustainable practices that enabled the longevity of the Chan community, insight that would have been lost had preservation of macro organic and carbonized remains been considered a hindrance for paleoethnobotanical research.

In a completely different vein, Meierhoff and colleagues (2012) used a portable X-ray fluorescence (XRF) device at the Field Museum of Natural History in Chicago to source all of the obsidian objects from Chan. This research identified a small number of obsidian objects from quite distant sources (up to 1,070 kilometers away from Chan). Although Meierhoff and colleagues identified Central Mexican Pachuca obsidian at Chan, this highly valued green obsidian was not identified at the polity capital of Xunantunich, which provides an interesting commentary on the control of long-distance trade in Maya society and power relations between a farming community and a polity capital (discussed further in chapter 6).

Conclusion

The most detailed excavations of farmers' everyday lives to date in the Maya area were conducted by Payson Sheets (1992, 2000, 2002) at the Cerén site in El Salvador, located 350 kilometers to the south of Chan. A UNESCO World Heritage Site, Cerén was buried under the ash of a volcanic eruption around AD 590. The organic remains of perishable buildings and foodstuffs in fields and homes were preserved at Cerén. Cerén provides an intimate glimpse into daily life in a farming community: the crops are still standing in the fields, people's finger swipes are visible on dirty dishes, the occasional mouse or ant had found its way into a storage vessel, and other unique findings.

The details of everyday life revealed at Cerén were quite surprising, because although its farmers lived in simple perishable structures with thatch roofs, Sheets (2002) identifies that their lives were quite rich. Beautiful polychrome vessels, chocolate (thought to be a royal drink), and jade and greenstone were all found in farmers' humble homes (Sheets 1992). Workshops and work areas surrounded houses, demonstrating a wide range of craft specialization that operated beyond the reach of the ruling elite class: every household produced some item in excess of what it needed to participate in community-level exchanges (Sheets 2000).

Why did the everyday lives of Cerén's farmers seem so much more affluent than that which Mayanists had identified for farmers living at sites of regular archaeological preservation? Was it simply an issue of preservation, that is, Cerén's unique deposition preserved a host of remains that would not otherwise have been preserved? Or could it have been environmental issues? Cerén's farmers farmed volcanic soils, arguably some of the richest agricultural lands, and this may have afforded them opportunities in the Maya world.

The research at Chan argues that neither preservation nor environment can fully account for the richness of farmers' lives at Cerén. Chan is a site of regular, or perhaps poor, archaeological preservation. Chan's hilly terrain and Vaca suite Cuxu subsuite soils are considered marginal under modern mechanized agricultural regimes (King et al. 1992). But as I discuss in chapter 6, compared with farmers living in other Belize Valley communities, Chan's farmers' lives, like those of Cerén's farmers, are quite rich. There are also striking parallels between Chan and Cerén, including divination areas at each site that are nearly mirror images of each other. The richness of Chan's and Cerén's farmers' lives appears to have been generated not by the environmental conditions they inherited or the depositional processes that interred their communities but by the communities they created.

As significant as Cerén's unique preservation is, the reason why archaeologists have access to the range of details about everyday life at Cerén is because of the excavation methods employed by Sheets (2002). Sheets conducted full-scale horizontal excavations, not just on buildings but also in fields, gardens, and the areas around buildings (extramural spaces where substantial amounts of daily life occur). He engaged in a collaborative research process that involved a host of scientists engaged in a wide range of microanalytical methods and drew insights from the knowledge of local famers.

An intensive, collaborative archaeology of everyday life that pays as much attention to horizontal excavation and developing multiple lines of evidence from microanalytical techniques as it does to developing new insights from engagement with the communities living around archaeological sites provides a productive methodology for furthering a critical archaeology of everyday life. Bringing together scientific and humanistic research, as well as academic and nonacademic thought, a critical archaeology of everyday life is a fruitful means of ameliorating long-standing disciplinary divides and divisions between humanistic, scientific, and other forms of knowledge.

II ☀ Everyday Life at Chan

5 ✳ Situating Chan

Although this book is divided into two sections—the first being more "theoretical" and the second being more "empirical"—the two sections are not isolated entities. As critical everyday life scholarship argues, theoretical and empirical research are dependent upon one another. There is a constant interplay between theoretical issues that develop from empirical studies and empirical problems that relate to theoretical arguments. The interrelatedness of theoretical and empirical work is a central aspect of an everyday life approach. If people create and are constrained by the material and spatial practices of day-to-day life, then an academic understanding of people cannot be found at the abstract level but must be located in the practice of studying people's everyday lives. This is precisely what I set out to achieve in this section of the book.

About Chan: A Summary

Chan is a farming community with a two-thousand-year history (800 BC–AD 1200). The community is located in the upper Belize Valley region of west-central Belize, a peripheral part of the ancient Maya world (figure 5.1). Its two-thousand-year occupation spans the major periods of political-economic change in Maya society (the Preclassic, Classic, and Postclassic periods), making it an ideal place to explore how everyday life intersects with broader transformations in society.

Unremarkable in terms of community size or architecture, the farming community of Chan nonetheless flourished for two millennia while the fortunes of nearby major Maya civic-centers waxed and waned. The Chan research into farmers' everyday lives reveals innovations in human-environment practices, religious knowledge, and political strategies and

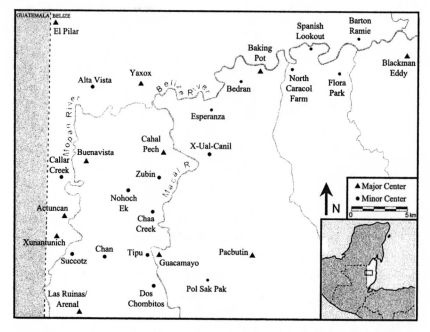

Figure 5.1. Map of the Belize River valley and Maya area showing the location of Chan. (Map by Elizabeth Schiffman.)

yields new insights into the operation of power in ancient Maya society. The archaeological record of everyday life at Chan belies traditional notions of peasants as a passive, backwards, and simple folk.

The majority of Chan's residents were farmers, and their agricultural terraces were the most ubiquitous and substantial constructions at Chan. Farmers constructed terraces up and down hillslopes and across channels. Chan's farmers lived in the midst of their agricultural terraces. Thus, rather than being a densely nucleated community, the Chan community consisted of clustered farmsteads around a community center. There were also many others who lived at Chan: craft workers, diviners, and political leaders. All of Chan's residents, from its humblest farmer to its community leaders, lived in perishable buildings with thatch roofs constructed on stone substructures. The Chan settlement survey documented the remains of 274 households and 1,223 agricultural terraces in a 3.2-square-kilometer area surrounding Chan's community center.

Chan's residents constructed their community around a community center, which they situated at the spatial and geographical center of the community on a local high point in the topography. The community

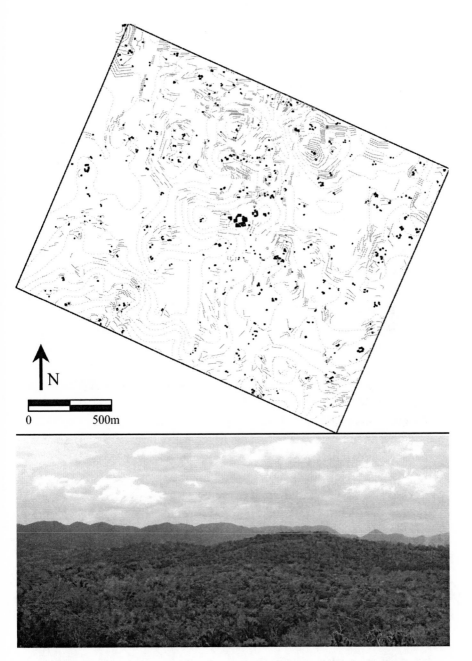

Figure 5.2. *Top*: Topography, settlement, and agricultural terraces at Chan. Black squares are mounds; gray linear features are agricultural terraces. Ten-meter contour interval. *Bottom*: Chan's hilly terrain. Photograph taken from the Central Group looking south. (Photograph by James Meierhoff.)

center consists of two adjoining plazas: the plaza of the Central Group and the West Plaza (figure 5.3). The Central Group is the largest architectural complex and plaza at Chan and its main location for community-level ceremony, administration, and adjudication. It also houses a residence and associated ancillary structures for Chan's leading family. On the east and west sides of the Central Group are an E-Group, a distinctive type of paired east and west ritual structures in which the east structure is a tripartite construction and the west structure is a single construction. These distinctive architectural complexes are common throughout the Maya area, and their particular architectural configuration was inspired by agricultural rituals (Aimers and Rice 2006). The east structure of the E-Group is the tallest structure at Chan, rising to a height of 5.6 meters. Chan's community center met all the functions of large Maya civic-centers, albeit at a smaller scale, with the exclusion of a ball court.

Chan's landscape was heavily terraced—in fact, more so than other areas of the Belize Valley, itself known for high agricultural productivity—making Chan an important center of agricultural production in this agriculturally productive region. Terraces were more numerous and often larger than residences at Chan, making them a key element of construction activity for farmers. Farmers constructed terraces up and down hillslopes and across ravines, producing a landscape that would have looked like green stepped pyramids across the community.

Rather than beginning with a dispersed set of farmsteads whose residents may not have envisioned themselves as living within a single community, as people initially began to build the place of Chan in the Middle Preclassic (circa 650 BC) they constructed a focal community center and situated their homes clustered around this central place. Chan's community center held an enduring meaning for residents across its history, even after most community members had left. Across the subsequent 1,500 years of Chan's history, more and more people moved into the community, building new houses and expanding community lands. Across its history, Chan's residents interacted with those of numerous neighboring civic-centers in the upper Belize River area and beyond. In the late Late Classic period (AD 670–800/830), when the community reached its largest extent and peak in construction, the nearby late-rising polity capital of Xunantunich asserted its authority over the complex provincial landscape of the upper Belize Valley. Xunantunich's rise to power was rapid, and so was its decline.

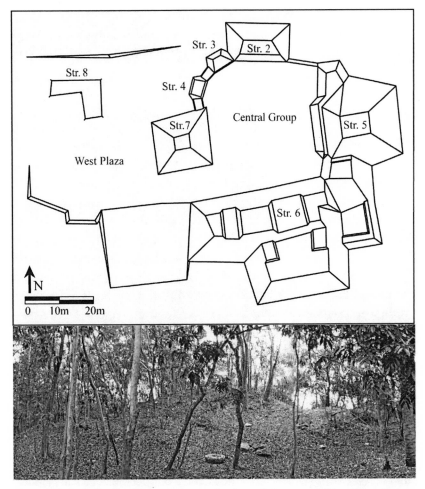

Figure 5.3. *Top*: Chan's community center, the Central Group and West Plaza. *Bottom*: East structure of E-Group (Structure 5), Chan's tallest building. (Photograph by James Meierhoff.)

Although it never became a large center, Chan had an enduring occupation history spanning two millennia. Through time the Chan community weathered the rise and fall of numerous neighboring civic-centers, including the polity capital of Xunantunich, and broader political-economic changes in Maya society. In the Terminal Classic period (AD 800/830–900), Chan's last major period of occupation, many people left the community, as people had done all across the Belize Valley. Still the spatial organization of the community and its focus on its community center remained intact. In the Early Postclassic period (AD 900–1150/1200), while few people remained at Chan, its community center remained an important ritual focus for the dispersed farming families that dotted the Belize Valley.

Initial Investigations: The Chan Settlement Survey

The upper Belize Valley area where Chan is located is defined as the region where the Belize River branches into the Mopan and Macal River branches (see figure 5.1). In the 1950s, Gordon Willey selected the site of Barton Ramie for his pioneering settlement survey research, the first formal settlement research in the Maya area (Willey et al. 1965). Barton Ramie is located in the lower Belize Valley to the east of the upper Belize Valley along the Belize River prior to its branching. Since then, the entire Belize Valley region has been a hub of settlement survey research and site excavation projects. The Belize Valley is one of a few areas in the Maya world where settlement patterns are understood at a regional level. Across most of its pre-Columbian history, numerous midsized centers jockeyed for power across the valley. These centers were organized as competitive peers, but none became a paramount center until the late and short-lived florescence of the Xunantunich polity capital (Ashmore 2010; Ball 1993; Ball and Taschek 1991; Houston et al. 1992; Leventhal and Ashmore 2004; Taschek and Ball 1992). With over half a century of archaeological research in the Belize Valley since Gordon Willey's, many of these midsized centers have been the subject of extensive archaeological excavations or are currently under investigation, so their political histories are understood (e.g., Ashmore 2010; Awe 1992; Ball and Taschek 1991, 2001; Driver and Garber 2004; Garber 2004; LeCount 2004; Leventhal and Ashmore 2004; Neff et al. 1995; Yaeger et al. 2009). It is safe to say that there are more archaeological projects ongoing in the Belize Valley than in all other parts of Belize taken together. This is one of the reasons why I selected Chan for research: I knew that if I wanted to understand how everyday life in a farming community related to broader goings-on in the Maya world, the region that surrounded the farming community would have to already be well understood archaeologically.

Prior to establishing the Chan project, in 1996 and 1997, I conducted dissertation research at seven small neighboring late Late Classic (AD 670–800/830) farmsteads at Chan that were located just south of the community center (Robin 1999, 2002a, 2002b, 2006). I called this area Chan Nòohol, in reference to its southern location in relation to Chan's community center (*nòohol* is Yucatec Maya for "south"). Yucatec Maya is the indigenous language spoken in Succotz, the nearest contemporary community to Chan (although by the 1990s, few people in Succotz, and mostly the oldest generations in the community, spoke Yucatec Maya). I undertook my dissertation research as part of the Xunantunich Settlement Survey, directed by Wendy Ashmore, and the Xunantunich Archaeological Project, directed by Richard Leventhal. These joint projects sought to explore the polity capital of Xunantunich, its surrounding settlement, and neighboring communities (Leventhal and Ashmore 2004; LeCount and Yaeger 2010).

The Chan Nòohol research, which I discuss in more detail in the next chapter, provided a textured understanding of the daily lives of residents of some of Chan's humblest households during the community's largest period of expansion during the heyday of Xunantunich. But it also generated even more questions about how these farmers related to Chan's diverse residents and how they became part of a community that existed for over a millennia before them and hundreds of years after them. How were residents of the Chan Nòohol households part of a community? How did Chan as a community with a deep history relate to other communities in the Belize Valley and Maya world? These questions, among others, generated the Chan project.

In this chapter I focus on the results of the initial phase of research at Chan, the 2002 and 2003 Chan settlement survey seasons (Robin, Wyatt et al. 2012). In the next chapter I will draw upon the results of the next two phases of project research, excavations and laboratory analyses, which ran from 2003 to 2009. By starting with the settlement survey, I use this chapter to provide the background information on Chan, its settlement, chronology, and regional setting. I do this also to illustrate how across the project's initial encounters with the archaeological remains of Chan as many new questions were opened up about Chan as were answered, highlighting the continual interplay of empirical research and theoretical problems.

During the 2002 and 2003 settlement survey work, project investigators mapped a 3.2-square-kilometer area and documented 274 households, 1,223 agricultural terraces, and Chan's community center (see figure 5.2). The fifteen-member 2002 survey team and the four-member 2003 survey team spent long days in the field systematically walking the Chan community. As with the excavation and lab work schedule, surveyors worked a six-day week for the four- to six-month duration of the field season, with a week break toward the end of the season to attend the annual Belizean Archaeology Symposium sponsored by the Belize Institute of Archaeology, which brings together foreign and local archaeologists, tour guides, students, and other laypeople interested in Belizean archaeology. Fieldwork began at 6:30 and ended at 3:30 so that project members could avoid the hottest afternoon suns. The survey work was full coverage. Surveyors both walked along and between *brechas* and *picados*, survey lines cut largely by Belizean team members skilled in machete work, through the mosaic farmland, dense secondary growth, and tropical forest canopy that now covers the site. The brechas and picados gridded the site spaced 20 meters apart from each other (see figure 4.2). Chan's karstic upland terrain is a rolling landscape of high rounded limestone hills with peaks over 160 meters. A day spent surveying could be physically challenging.

The Chan settlement survey combined standard and new survey techniques of topographic mapping, archaeological reconnaissance, surface collections, and Geographical Information Systems (GIS) to develop an understanding of Chan's changing cultural landscape. Surveyors digitally recorded topography and natural and cultural features using a Topcon GTS 605 laser theodolite. They collected qualitative and quantitative information on natural features (for example, land formations, vegetation, and environment) and cultural features (for example, architecture, agricultural fields, and other human constructions) to begin to document the nature of the community. They collected ceramic surface collections from all identified cultural features to identify a relative chronology of Chan's occupation. After the survey was complete, Elise Docster (2008) developed a GIS bringing together the cultural, natural, and chronological data from the settlement survey to model Chan's changing cultural and natural landscape.

Throughout this intensive archaeological process, surveyors had a chance to encounter and experience the Chan landscape. For surveyors, aspects of Chan's history became visible as they paid attention to the material details of the landscape. This material visibility of history embedded in a landscape was also important for Lefebvre's approach to everyday life (chapter 2). It is worth noting here that many of the details of the spatial ordering of the community that I discuss later in this chapter as being quantifiably significant were intuitively visible and discussed by surveyors during the survey work: the ubiquity and location of terraces, the relatively small size of house mounds compared to the relatively larger size of terraces, the dispersal rather than nucleation of larger residential groups within the community, and the visibility of the community center from across the community. But other aspects of Chan's history were impenetrable to surveyors as they walked around Chan, particularly the chronological ordering of the elements of the community that they identified. Chan's deep temporal history was only knowable after detailed analysis of the ceramic surface collections. Ultimately the landscape that the surveyors came to know through their walking was a palimpsest of the community that wove together its two-thousand-year history and the subsequent history of land use after Chan's abandonment. It was a landscape most similar to the late Late Classic (AD 670–800/830) community when Chan reached its maximum size. But as a palimpsest it was a landscape that was never experienced by any of Chan's ancient residents who lived at Chan at particular times in the past.

As important as topographic mapping or GIS, experience (walking the landscape) was a dimension of knowledge production on the Chan survey. On the face of it, this method shares important parallels with the work of the British school of phenomenological studies (e.g., Tilley 1994) in the following way: both approaches share the idea that archaeologists can use their sensory experiences (walking, seeing, and so on) within the landscapes they study to ascertain cultural meaning. However, I would argue on closer analysis that this parallel conceals deeper differences: the Neolithic landscapes that are the subject of much of the British school research are ritual landscapes, and the walking experience that Tilley and others attempt is one of processional walking, whereas at Chan surveyors were engaging with mundane landscapes of everyday life. Experience was one of multiple lines of evidence, not the sole line of evidence that shaped the Chan project's understanding of the landscape. Perhaps even more significantly, the British school work assumes the possibility of a unitary experience shared by archaeologists and ancient residents that inserts contemporary agents into the archaeological past (many have pointed to this as a weakness of the approach; e.g., Meskell 1996; Robin 2006; A. Smith 2003), something that was impossible to assume at Chan given researchers' awareness of the temporal palimpsest of the archaeological remains.

Identifying the Chan Community

Chan has long been known to the nearby residents of the contemporary community of San Jose Succotz, Belize. The Xunantunich settlement survey team, directed by Wendy Ashmore, first documented the site for the archaeological community in 1994 (Ashmore et al. 1994, 2004). The members of the Xunantunich settlement survey team named the site after its landowners—dons Ismael and Derric Chan, a customary naming practice in Maya archaeology for nonroyal sites that have no textually recorded name. I always thought the name Chan was quite suitable for the community, as *chan* can mean "small" in Yucatec Maya.

The Xunantunich settlement survey work extended a survey transect, transect archaeological 1, measuring 400 meters wide and 8 kilometers long southeast from the polity capital of Xunantunich along the Mopan branch of the Belize River to the minor center of Dos Chombitos along the Macal branch of the Belize River. A settlement concentration is intuitively visible in the center of this transect equidistant (4 kilometers) between Xunantunich and Dos Chombitos (figure 5.4). Surveyors also identified and mapped a small community center just north of the transect and north of the settlement concentration. This settlement concentration and small community center, now known as Chan, are not only intuitively visible but also identifiable based upon nearest neighbor and stem-and-leaf analysis (VandenBosch in Ashmore et al. 1994).

The Xunantunich settlement survey's transect archaeological 1 identified the east and west boundaries of Chan, which are located approximately 1 kilometer from its community center. Rather than being a continuation of survey transect work to precisely identify Chan's north and south boundaries, the Chan settlement survey was focused on undertaking a full-coverage survey of the settlement within the site itself, defined by a 3.2-square-kilometer survey area surrounding the community center (see figures 5.2 and 5.4).

The initial survey work of both the Xunantunich settlement survey and the Chan settlement survey provided some interesting questions by which to frame future research. The survey work identified that Chan was a site (a discrete settlement cluster). But was it an emically defined community

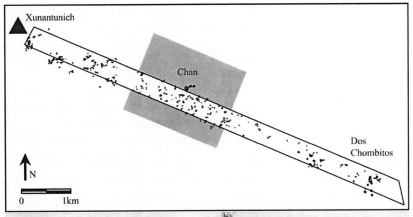

Figure 5.4. *Top*: Transect archaeological 1 of the Xunantunich settlement survey showing the settlement cluster identified as Chan. Gray square shows the location of the Chan settlement survey work. *Bottom*: Surveyors Bernabe Camal Sr., Andrew Wyatt, and Ethan Kalosky inspect the remains of low rubble mounds in an area burned for milpa farming.

for its ancient residents? Yaeger and Canuto (2000) define a community as both a place and a group of people who create a salient social identity based upon that place. What salient identities were created at Chan? If indeed Chan was a community for its residents, was it a community across its two-thousand-year history, or was it at some earlier point in time separate farmsteads that lacked any community identity?

Chan's Cultural Landscape

Across Chan's hilly terrain, surveyors identified a total of 562 mounds (the remains of stone structures that were often houses) and 1,223 terraces (shelf-like slope modification features that often have agricultural functions). These included 275 mound groups (274 residential mound groups and Chan's community center) and 396 terrace sets. Surveyors gave a sequential number beginning with C-001 (which designates Chan's community center, the Central Group) to each mound group they encountered on the survey. Likewise, they gave terrace sets a sequential number beginning with TC-001.

The majority of Chan's mounds are quite low and would have supported perishable buildings. Only one mound at Chan, its central administrative building (located in the Central Group), is a masonry building with a vaulted stone roof. Residential mounds at Chan have an average elevation of 0.55 meters, ranging between 0.05 and 2.15 meters (based on survey data). Of the residential mounds, 59 percent have an average elevation of less than 0.50 meters and 91 percent have an average elevation of less than 1 meter. By way of contrast, terraces had an average elevation of 0.90 meters, ranging between 0.1 and 3.15 meters. Terraces ranged in length from 53 to 85 meters, making them not only more ubiquitous than mounds at Chan but also more substantial in their construction (Wyatt 2008a: 102–18). Chan's residents constructed terraces along hillslopes (contour terraces [see figure 4.2]) and across seasonal drainage channels (cross-channel terraces [see figure 4.1]). In terms of their construction efforts, farmers at Chan expended more energy building terraces for agriculture than they did in house construction.

Although sites across the upper Belize Valley are heavily terraced, with a density of 382 terraces per square kilometer, there is a greater density of terraces recorded at Chan than has been reported from settlement surveys conducted in the surrounding Xunantunich region, where surveyors have identified densities of between 164 and 227 terraces per square kilometer based on comparable survey methods (Ashmore et al. 1994; Neff et al. 1995; Yaeger and Connell 1993). Chan's undulating limestone uplands make it particularly well suited and adapted for terrace agriculture (Juarez

2003; Wyatt 2008a, 2012). While Chan's Vaca suite, Cuxu subsuite soils are considered marginal under modern mechanized agricultural regimes (King et al. 1992), they have a rich potential for nonmechanized and terrace agriculture, a potential that Chan's farmers drew upon to create a productive agricultural landscape that supported the community during its long occupation. While Mayanists have long identified this part of the Belize Valley as an important area for agricultural production in Maya society (Ashmore et al. 2004; Ford and Fedick 1992; Willey et al. 1965), Chan's residents made particular use of their local environment in terrace construction to develop agricultural production.

The late Jennifer Ehret on the Xunantunich settlement survey developed a seven-tiered mound group typology that investigators for the Chan project used to provisionally assess socioeconomic variability in Chan's settlement (table 5.1; Ehret in Ashmore et al. 1994). Four criteria—number of mounds and platforms, height of mounds and platforms, formality of mound arrangement, and presence or absence of a focal mound—classify

Table 5.1. Mound group typology for Chan

Type	Description	Total identified		Total excavated	
		N	%	N	%
1	1 mound, <1 m in height	134	48.7	12	9.0
2	>2 mounds, <1 m in height, informal layout	66	24.0	4	6.1
3	>2 mounds, <1 m in height, formal layout	42	15.3	4	9.5
4	>2 mounds or platforms, 1–2 m in height, mixed layout	21	7.6	3	14.3
5	>4 mounds or platforms, 1–2 m in height, formal layout	9	3.3	2	22.2
6	>4 mounds or platforms, 2–5 m in height, formal layout	2	0.7	1	50.0
7	>4 mounds or platforms, >5 m in height, formal layout	1	0.4	1	100.0
Total		275	100	27	9.8

differences in mound groups. The smallest and least formal type 1 mound group consists of isolated mounds and associated features that are one meter or less in height. The largest and most formal type 7 mound group consists of a platform group with four or more mounds, at least one of which is five meters in height. Type 2 to 6 mound groups represent variation in terms of size and formality between these two extremes.

There is only one type 7 mound group, Chan's community center, the Central Group (C-001). Residents built the Central Group on a hilltop at the center of the community (see figure 5.2). From the Central Group the majority of Chan's settlement was visible, and Chan's residents would have likewise been able to see the Central Group. The main temples at both Xunantunich and Dos Chombitos are visible from the Central Group. The leaders of the farming community of Chan situated the center of their community in a locally prominent position from which they could see and be seen, just as the royals of the Xunantunich polity capital did later in time as they constructed their civic-center on a hilltop location with a commanding view of their polity (Ashmore 2010). This (among other examples that I discuss in the next chapter) illustrates how many of the state-level political practices of Classic Maya royalty have their origins in ideas and practices initially developed in the homes and communities of farmers. Typically when archaeologists identify that commoners and elites were doing the same thing, they argue that commoners were emulating the ideas and practices of elites. But the Chan research, through many examples, challenges this general expectation and shows that commoners can and do create complex ideas and practices that elites then emulate.

The Central Group is one of two mound groups at Chan with predominantly nonresidential architecture. The other is C-039, a type 1 group consisting of a single L-shaped mound in a large open plaza. C-039 is adjacent to and adjoins the Central Group to the west; hence, it is known as the West Plaza (Cap 2012). The adjoining Central Group and West Plaza form Chan's community center (see figure 5.3).

Type 5 and 6 mound groups represent Chan's largest residential platform groups. They consist of formally arranged platform groups with four or more mounds where at least one mound is 1–2 meters in height or more than 2 meters, respectively. There are two type 6 mound groups and nine type 5 mound groups at Chan. A type 6 and a type 5 mound group are located just east of and adjacent to Chan's Central Group (C-002 and

C-003). These mound groups are the locations of the residential compounds of the extended families of Chan's leaders. The remaining type 6 mound group and eight type 5 mound groups are dispersed across the site, located roughly 700 meters to 1 kilometer from the Central Group, rather than nucleated around it. These larger residential mound groups are the households of head families of subgroups or neighborhoods across Chan, as demonstrated by Chelsea Blackmore's research at Chan's Northeast Group, a neighborhood located 1 kilometer east of the Central Group (discussed in the next chapter; Blackmore 2007, 2011, 2012).

Type 1 and 2 mound groups are the most common mound groups at Chan. They are located across the entirety of the site and make up 48.7 percent and 24.0 percent of mound groups, respectively (see table 5.1). Type 1 and 2 mound groups generally correspond to humble farming households. The proportions of mound group types at Chan is comparable to those seen across settlements in the Xunantunich polity (compare Neff et al. 1995), except that at Chan smaller mound groups are more prevalent and larger mound groups are less prevalent. Type 1 groups make up 48.7 percent of Chan's settlement and 41.0 percent of the broader polity settlement. Type 5 to 7 groups make up 4.4 percent of Chan's settlement and 8.0 percent of the broader polity settlement (Wyatt 2008a: 110).

The Chan settlement survey revealed a diverse populace—diverse in terms of occupation (farmers, craft workers, community leaders) and diverse in terms of socioeconomic status (with seven status groups provisionally identified). This diversity led me to ask certain questions about the community. What was daily life like for Chan's diverse residents? To what extent did they share understandings of home and community that rooted people in place? To what extent did they hold different and conflicting understandings of life and society that led to changing dynamics within the community?

Chan's Two-Thousand-Year History: Chronology and Population

Laura Kosakowsky (2012) established Chan's chronology through relative ceramic dating of approximately 321,000 sherds, as well as whole and partial vessels, largely from excavation contexts, based upon well-established sequences in the area, in conjunction with twenty-four radiocarbon dates from carbonized wood and human teeth (table 5.2). People inhabited Chan from the early Middle Preclassic (800 BC) until the Early Postclassic

(AD 1200). Major occupation falls between the Middle Preclassic (650 BC) and Terminal Classic (AD 900), with the community being abandoned in the Early Postclassic. The early Middle Preclassic period is the first period of Maya occupation in the Belize Valley (Garber et al. 2004; Healy et al. 2004; LeCount et al. 2002). At that time, people were living in scattered homesteads as well as organized communities. Some ephemeral activities are likely to have been going on at Chan during the early Middle Preclassic period, because excavation research identified redeposited ceramics from this period at Chan's Central Group in later mixed deposits (Kosakowsky 2012). But given that the intensive excavation work of the project identified no primary early Middle Preclassic occupation, it seems unlikely that a significant settlement existed at Chan at this time.

During the Chan settlement survey, surveyors collected diagnostic ceramics from the ground surface, looters' trenches, and any other disturbed area at each identified mound group to develop a settlement chronology. They identified diagnostic ceramics at 45 percent of mound groups (123 of 275 mound groups). Thirty-three of these were originally collected during the Xunantunich settlement survey and analyzed by Jennifer Ehret

Table 5.2. Chronology chart for the Chan site

	Calendar years[a]	Chan ceramic complexes[b]
Early Postclassic	AD 900–1150/1200	(Not a complete complex)
Terminal Classic	AD 800/830–900	Vieras
Late Late Classic	AD 670–800/830	Pesoro
Early Late Classic	AD 600–670	Jalacte
Early Classic	AD 250–600	Burrell
Terminal Preclassic	AD 100/150–250	Potts
Late Preclassic	350 BC–AD 100/150	Cadle
Middle Preclassic	650–350 BC	Boden
Late Early Preclassic / Early Middle Preclassic	1000/800–650 BC	(Not a complete complex)

[a] Calendar years are approximate dates based on ceramic seriation in conjunction with twenty-four radiocarbon dates from Chan and correlation with other sites in the Maya lowlands.

[b] Chan ceramic complexes are named for geographic bodies of water in and around the Belize Valley.

(Ashmore et al. 1994). Ninety collections were made during the Chan settlement survey and analyzed by Laura Kosakowsky (2007, 2012). Elise Docster (2008) incorporated this temporal data into the Chan GIS to develop a spatial model of temporal changes in Chan's settlement.

For each major period of occupation at Chan, I developed minimum and maximum population estimates for an area with a one-kilometer radius around the Central Group—corresponding to the intuitively and statistically identifiable settlement concentration around that group (Robin, Wyatt et al. 2012). This area includes the core of the community and surrounding subgroups. The population estimates should be considered heuristics for understanding how population changed through time at Chan and for comparing Chan's population to that of other communities in the Maya area. In calculating population estimates, I considered several variables: number of structures, percentage of structures determined to be residential, percentage of structures dated to the phase in question, percentage of structures inhabited contemporaneously, and number of individuals living in each structure (e.g., Beekman 1998; Culbert and Rice 1990).[1] Depending on how a researcher estimates any one of these variables, the projected population estimate can vary widely. Thus, I see generating ancient population estimates not as a means of getting at absolute population levels but as a means of identifying relative population levels for comparative purposes. I used excavation data to determine what percentage of mounds were residential. (This and other implications of the estimating procedures I used and how these affect the resultant population estimates are discussed in note 1.)

Middle Preclassic Settlement (650–350 BC)

The Middle Preclassic is the first major period of occupation at Chan. During this period, residents established farmsteads at 19 percent of Chan's mound groups and began constructing the Central Group (figure 5.5a). In terms of spatial organization, Middle Preclassic farmsteads cluster around the Central Group. Excavation data (discussed in chapter 6) indicate that the plaza of the Central Group was a center for community-level ritual even as Chan's earliest residents began to build their community. Rather than beginning with scattered farmsteads that later developed into a community, as people established Chan they defined the Central Group as the spatial and social focus of the community.

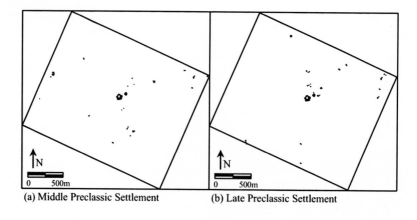

(a) Middle Preclassic Settlement   (b) Late Preclassic Settlement

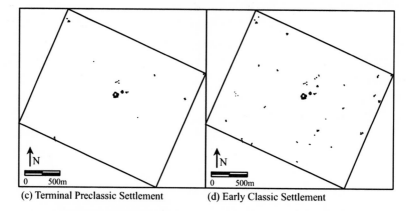

(c) Terminal Preclassic Settlement   (d) Early Classic Settlement

Figure 5.5. Changing settlement patterns at Chan: Middle Preclassic to Early Classic.

Between 249 and 418 people may have lived at Chan at this time, but Chan's Middle Preclassic occupation may be overrepresented by the project's surface collection sampling strategy (Kosakowsky 2007, 2012). Surveyors collected diagnostic ceramics in their surface collections. In the Maya area, collecting only diagnostic ceramics can result in a bias toward time periods that have particularly distinctive diagnostic ceramics. In the Belize Valley, Mars Orange Ware ceramics account for a significant portion of Middle Preclassic ceramics. These are easily identifiable because of their orange paste, which is distinct from the dull gray to tan pastes that make up the majority of later ceramic assemblages. Thus, it is likely that the population estimates for Chan in the Middle Preclassic are too high. Excavations did reveal less Middle Preclassic occupation than in the subsequent Late Preclassic period, although the population estimates for these periods would indicate the reverse situation.

Late Preclassic Settlement (350 BC–AD 100/150)

During the Late Preclassic period, occupation remained fairly constant. During this period, residents built and inhabited farmsteads at 15 percent of Chan's mound groups (figure 5.5b). Between 196 and 330 people may have lived at Chan at this time. Chan's settlement continued to be spatially clustered around the Central Group, and people lived in similar parts of the community as they had in the preceding Middle Preclassic period. Residents constructed the first ceremonial architecture at the Central Group at this time.

Terminal Preclassic Settlement (AD 100/150–250)

During the Terminal Preclassic period, residents built and inhabited farmsteads at 11 percent of Chan's mound groups (figure 5.5c). Between 144 and 242 people may have lived at Chan at this time. Farmsteads continued to cluster around the Central Group, and people lived in similar parts of the community as they had in the preceding Middle and Late Preclassic periods.

The apparent slight decline in the Terminal Preclassic occupation at Chan may be an artifact of the ceramic analysis (Kosakowsky 2007, 2012). Many Late Preclassic ceramic types continued in use in the Terminal Preclassic, and in the absence of formal characteristics, or types that are present only in the Terminal Preclassic (for example, mammiform supports or San Antonio Golden Brown), some material that is included in the Late Preclassic ceramic counts may in fact represent slightly later occupation. Terminal Preclassic architecture is not underrepresented in excavations at Chan relative to Late Preclassic architecture.

Early Classic Settlement (AD 250–600)

During the Early Classic period, Chan's settlement expanded. Residents built and inhabited farmsteads at 28 percent of Chan's mound groups (figure 5.5d). Excavations yielded comparable evidence for expansion of ceremonial and domestic contexts in the Early Classic. Between 366 and 615 people may have lived at Chan at this time. Farmsteads continued to cluster around the Central Group, and Chan's expanding populace constructed new farmsteads. This is the first period in which Chan's residents constructed farmsteads across what would become the full spatial extent of the community at its population maximum in late Late Classic times.

Early Late Classic Settlement (AD 600–670)

During the early Late Classic period, settlement continued to expand across the entirety of the community. Residents built and inhabited farmsteads at 37 percent of Chan's mound groups (figure 5.6a). Between 484 and 813 people may have lived at Chan at this time.

Late Late Classic Settlement (AD 670–800/830)

During the late Late Classic period, more and more people were moving to Chan; the community reached its period of maximum expansion as residents built and inhabited farmsteads at 76 percent of Chan's mound groups (figure 5.6b). Between 994 and 1,670 people may have lived at Chan at this time. The end of the Late Classic period is not only when the community expanded to its maximum size but also the period in which residents constructed the largest ceremonial and administrative architecture and expanded agricultural terracing to its fullest extent.

Terminal Classic Settlement (AD 800/830–900)

During the Terminal Classic period, people began leaving Chan, as people did all across the Belize Valley. The remaining inhabitants built and inhabited farmsteads at only 29 percent of mound groups at Chan (figure 5.6c). Between 379 and 637 people may have lived at Chan at this time. In terms of both population density and spatial distribution of farmsteads, Chan's Terminal Classic settlement pattern is most similar to its Early Classic settlement pattern. Although the number of farmsteads occupied in the Terminal Classic declined significantly from the preceding period, there was no contraction of Chan's settlement in terms of the spatial extent of its settlement, as the full spatial extent of the community remained occupied. The similarities between Chan's Terminal Classic and Early Classic settlement patterns suggest that although there was a significant decline in the number of people living at Chan in the Terminal Classic,

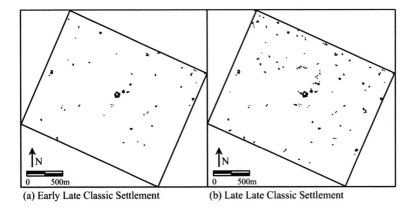

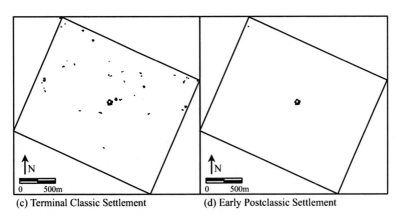

Figure 5.6. Changing settlement patterns at Chan: early Late Classic to Early Postclassic.

some aspects of community organization may have endured. The Central Group remained the spatial and social focus of community life in this period.

Early Postclassic Settlement (AD 900–1150/1200)

Surface collections identified only one farmstead inhabited in the Early Postclassic period: mound group C-301, a small type 1 single mound located 1 kilometer to the northwest of the Central Group (figure 5.6d). Excavators subsequently identified an additional Early Postclassic ceremonial complex in the Central Group and adjacent West Plaza. It is unlikely that Chan was a full-scale community at this time. A few farming families remained in the Chan area and indeed across the upper Belize Valley area in the Early Postclassic. Chan's community center continued to be an important locus of ritual activity for the scattered farmsteads that occupied this part of the broadly abandoned upper Belize Valley.

The settlement survey research exposed certain dimensions of change and continuity across Chan's two-thousand-year history, but these data led me to ask more probing questions about the nature and meaning of change and continuity across these millennia in subsequent excavation work. Given that two thousand years is a long period of time, what did Chan's residents do to help make sure their community endured?

Chan in a Regional Context

In terms of the size and scale of Chan's settlement and architecture, Mayanists would classify Chan at the smaller end of minor centers in the Maya area. In the 1960s, Gordon Willey and William Bullard defined three levels of settlement in the Maya area: major centers from which paramount rulers governed, minor centers with minor leaders, and house mounds (Bullard 1960; Willey et al. 1955, 1965). Minor centers are smaller than major centers but have the same range of architectural components. They are types of communities, as these centers are often found surrounded by house mounds (Willey et al. 1955). Their complexity in conjunction with their small size initially suggested to scholars that they were a quite variable community type that served a wide variety of functions (Willey et al. 1955; also see Hammond 1975; Iannone and Connell 2003).

The major center, minor center, house mound typology is a gross typology for classifying Maya settlement (Hammond 1975). One comparative measure that Mayanists use to judge site size is the height of the largest pyramidal structure at a site. At Tikal, the largest Classic Maya regal center and capital of an expansive long-lived regional state, located in the Petén area of Guatemala, the tallest temple (Temple IV) is 60 meters high. At Xunantunich, the capital of the short-lived Late Classic polity that included Chan, which is considered a midsized major Maya center, the tallest temple (El Castillo) is 43 meters in height. Xunantunich itself dwarfed other midsized major centers in the upper Belize Valley area, such as Buenavista and Cahal Pech, which had 24-meter-high temple pyramids (see figure 5.1 for location of Belize Valley sites). Chan, with its

5.6-meter-high east temple, is comparable to other upper Belize Valley minor centers, which have main temples between 5 and 6.5 meters high, such as Callar Creek, Chaa Creek, Nohoch Ek, X-Ual-Canil, and Zubin. These are not the smallest centers in the Belize Valley or Maya area: at Bedran in the adjoining central Belize Valley there is an E-Group with an east structure 2 meters high (for structure size data, see Conlon and Powis 2004; Connell 2003; Driver and Garber 2004; Leventhal and Ashmore 2004). Chan represents the smaller end of the spectrum of sites in the Maya area.

The upper Belize Valley region where Chan is located was a peripheral and provincial part of the Maya world throughout most of its history. During the 1,500-year period that spans the Preclassic, Early Classic, and early Late Classic periods (800 BC–AD 670), numerous midsized centers jockeyed for power across the region. These centers were organized as competitive peers, but none became a paramount center (Ashmore 2010; Ball 1993; Ball and Taschek 1991; Houston et al. 1992; Leventhal and Ashmore 2004; Taschek and Ball 1992).

Chan's interfluvial location between the Mopan and Macal Rivers in the upper Belize Valley situated it at the interstices of the six midsized upper Belize Valley major centers jockeying for power: Actuncan, Buenavista, Cahal Pech, Guacamayo, Las Ruinas, and Xunantunich (see figure 5.1). Xunantunich is located 4 kilometers to the west, Guacamayo is 4 kilometers to the east, Las Ruinas is 5 kilometers to the south, and Actuncan, Buenavista, and Cahal Pech are located to the north and northwest, with Cahal Pech (at the junction of the central and upper Belize Valleys) being the most distant at 9 kilometers away.

Not until the end of the late Late Classic (AD 670–800/830) did the short-lived and late-flourishing Xunantunich polity capital unify this well-developed landscape (LeCount and Yaeger 2010; Leventhal and Ashmore 2004). The timing of Xunantunich's political expansion in a provincial part of the Maya area is not surprising. Toward the end of the Classic period, the system of divine kingship that had dominated Classic period politics and led to the expansion of large and powerful polities was experiencing tumultuous times. Large polities were fragmenting and declining in power, and new smaller polities such as Xunantunich were arising in peripheries within this emergent power vacuum.

The hilltop center of Xunantunich that housed the late Late Classic polity capital had a shorter and dramatic developmental history, although the broader settlement of the Xunantunich site had a long history. In the early Late Classic period, Xunantunich was a relatively small hilltop center with less power than its political neighbors (LeCount and Yaeger 2010). In the early part of the late Late Classic period, there was dramatic and unprecedented civic and political expansion at Xunantunich, which became a powerful but subordinate polity incorporated into the larger Naranjo regional state (Naranjo is located 12 kilometers west of Xunantunich in the Petén area of Guatemala). By the end of the Late Classic period, as Naranjo declined, Xunantunich became a fully autonomous polity capital with its own emblem glyph (Ashmore 2010; Ashmore and Sabloff 2002; Helmke et al. 2010; LeCount 2010; LeCount et al. 2002; Leventhal and Ashmore 2004). Xunantunich's rulers erected three carved stelae (standing stone monuments) in the early part of the Terminal Classic period, but these royal statements were short lived, as only 150 years after its rapid expansion, Xunantunich was in decline (Helmke et al. 2010; Schortman 2010). Across the Belize Valley, and indeed across the entirety of the southern Maya lowlands, the Terminal Classic period was a period of widespread transformation that included population decline and site abandonment as well as the florescence of new regions. While LeCount and Yaeger (2010: 359) argue that the growth of Xunantunich transformed the political hierarchy of the Belize Valley, they also suggest that local populations with deep historical ties in the upper Belize Valley "must have presented a formidable front against top-down policies emanating from Xunantunich's provincial leaders."

Chan's settlement peak and height of architectural construction at the end of the Late Classic period is concurrent with the short-lived florescence of the polity capital of Xunantunich. Located only 4 kilometers northwest of Chan, Xunantunich is within a few hours' walk of Chan. The main temple (El Castillo) at Xunantunich could have been seen from most locales at Chan in the late Late Classic period and likely served as a regionally important ritual venue for at least certain members of Chan. That there would be some relationship between Chan and the polity capital of Xunantunich is perhaps unquestionable given the proximity of the two sites. The question that emerges is what was the nature of the relationship between the two? The generally accepted archaeological narrative would discuss how the emergent polity capital of Xunantunich affected life for Chan's residents. But another question can be asked as well: how did life at Chan affect the rise and decline of Xunantunich?

This regional history provides another set of interesting research questions through which to frame the Chan study. Through time, Chan interacted with numerous upper Belize River valley centers in complex and overlapping relations of influence and authority. The late intrusion of the polity capital of Xunantunich into the long history of Chan provides an opportunity to explore how everyday life in a farming community might be transformed by its interaction with a polity capital, but also to consider the less-explored corollary—how a polity capital may have had to accommodate to preexisting contexts of daily life within farming communities. How might life in a farming community be similar to or different from that in a large Maya center during the pre-Columbian period?

Implications of the Chan Settlement Survey Research

I learned a great deal about Chan from the settlement survey and preliminary research, but this research opened up as many new questions as it answered. Particularly, I wanted to gain information on everyday life at Chan, which the project investigated in subsequent excavation seasons. Was Chan an emically defined community for its ancient residents, or was it simply a site (a discrete settlement cluster)? What was daily life like for Chan's diverse residents? To what extent did they share understandings of home and community that rooted people in place? To what extent did they hold different and conflicting understandings of life and society that led to changing dynamics within the community? How did life change (and stay the same) across Chan's two-thousand-year history? Given that two thousand years is a long period of time, what did Chan's residents do to help make sure their community endured? What relationships did Chan's residents establish with the numerous midsized centers of the Belize Valley? How did the late-rising polity capital of Xunantunich have to accommodate preexisting contexts of daily life within farming communities such as Chan, and how might everyday life at Chan have been transformed by Xunantunich? How was life in a farming community similar to or different from that in a large Maya center during the pre-Columbian period? These are some of the many new questions generated by the project's initial encounters with the ancient material record of Chan that framed subsequent research.

6 ✳ Everyday Life at Chan

For two thousand years, farmers, crafts producers, diviners, and community leaders lived at Chan. In the previous chapter I use settlement survey data to open up questions about everyday life in the past that could be explored through horizontal (open area) excavations. Exploring Chan's residents' everyday lives opens the possibility to examine not only people's experiences and interactions but also social dynamics within the community and beyond, power relationships in society, and the very nature of Maya society itself. By exploring the homes, workplaces, and meeting places of Chan's varied community members, it is possible to identify shared understandings of home and community that rooted people in place as well as the different and conflicting understandings of life and society that led to changing dynamics within the community. Viewing everyday life across a two-thousand-year period reveals how people and society are shaped by the historical conditions produced by their ancestors across their daily lives, as well as how everyday life can open possibilities to construct new selves and society.

To examine variability in Chan's households, between 2003 and 2006 and in 2009, project members undertook excavations at a 10 percent sample of Chan's households (26 households; Blackmore 2008, 2011, 2012; Hearth 2012; Kestle 2012; Robin, Meierhoff, and Kosakowsky 2012; Wyatt 2008a, 2008b, 2012; figure 6.1). The project explored households of varying wealth and status, from humble farmers to community leaders, including all status groups in between these as discernible through the seven-tiered mound group typology. The project explored households with varying occupational foci, from farming households to stone tool producers, limestone quarriers, marine shell crafters, and obsidian blade producers. It explored households from different time periods across

Chan's two-thousand-year history as well as households located at varying distances from the community center. Given the small size of Chan's community center, project members also excavated all ritual, residential, and administrative buildings at the community center (Cap 2012; Robin, Meierhoff, Kestle, et al. 2012; Robin, Meierhoff, and Kosakowsky 2012). The Chan excavation not only focused on the mounds (architectural remains) that form the traditional corpus of Maya studies; excavators also conducted extensive posthole testing grids extending for thirty to fifty meters from visible architecture to identify and further excavate activity areas and places of daily life in the open spaces that surrounded people's homes (chapter 4). Across excavations, excavators collected samples for microanalysis to enhance the understanding of everyday life in the past. These included taking ten-gram soil and plaster samples for chemical analyses across all floor, occupation, and activity contexts to elucidate the signatures of ancient activities that are no longer visible in macroartifact and architectural remains and taking ten-liter flotation samples for paleoethnobotanical analysis and microartifact analysis from all contexts to determine food consumption and production and the micro debris remains of ancient activities that are otherwise swept away or removed at abandonment by ancient inhabitants.

Specialists in the analysis of particular artifact classes examined excavated materials from Chan in each field season (2003–2006, 2009) as excavations were ongoing. Because of the time-consuming nature of artifact analysis, two seasons (2007 and 2008) were devoted entirely to analytical work. The roughly half a million objects of everyday life at Chan form one of the largest archaeological samples of Maya farming life. The specialists who analyzed each artifact class worked collaboratively with each other and excavators across the field season, conducting their research largely within the field lab in Belize (excluding technical analyses that required instrumentation not available in Belize). This allowed specialists to produce contextual understandings of Chan's excavated materials in dialogue with each other's analyses and the work of excavators. The major classes of material remains identified at Chan include ceramics (Kosakowsky 2012; Kosakowsky et al. 2012), plant remains (Lentz et al. 2012), chert lithics (Hearth 2012), obsidian (Meierhoff et al. 2012), shell (Keller 2012), jade, serpentine, and greenstone (Keller 2008), animal bone (Blackmore 2007), ground stone (analysis ongoing by Belizean student Sylvia Batty), microartifacts (Cap 2012), and soils (Hetrick 2007). Human remains were also

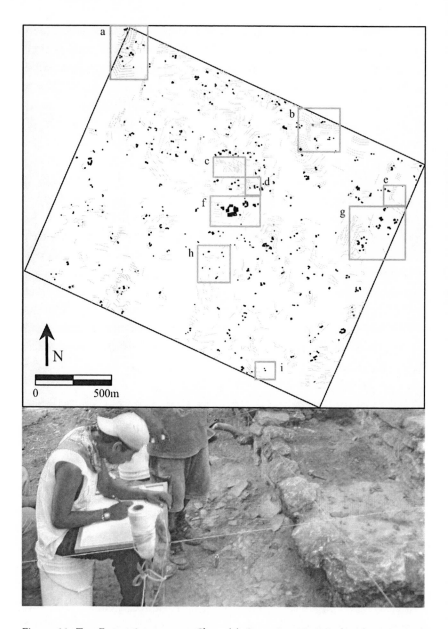

Figure 6.1. *Top*: Excavation areas at Chan: (a) Operation 15 agricultural terrace and household excavations; (b) Operation 4 agricultural terrace and household excavations; (c) Operation 20 agricultural terrace excavations; (d) Operation 28 limestone quarry and household excavations; (e) Operation 18 agricultural terrace excavations; (f) Central Group, West Plaza, and leading family household excavations; (g) Northeast Group midlevel neighborhood excavations; (h) small farming family household excavations (Chan Nòohol); and (i) chert biface production household excavations. *Bottom*: Illustrator Merle Alfaro draws a terminal deposit of ceramics in the front room of the east building of the E-Group.

identified (Novotny 2012). The furthest extension of the collaborative excavation and analytical work at Chan was the edited book I produced with the twenty lead Chan researchers: *Chan: An Ancient Maya Farming Community* (Robin 2012a). The synthesis of the Chan work that I present here is based upon the more detailed studies in this edited volume.

Farmers

I begin my discussion of everyday life at Chan with an exploration of farmers' lives. I will then turn to the lives of craft producers, leaders, and diviners. Farmers established Chan, they were Chan's most numerous residents in the Late Classic period when the community reached its peak in population, and they were among the community's final residents. Farmers' agricultural terraces dominate the landscape at Chan visually and in terms of labor investment (chapter 5). As a center for agricultural production, agricultural production framed the space and time of so many residents' daily lives. But farmers were not a homogeneous group; there were many types of farmers at Chan: humble farmers, high-status farmers, newly established farmers, long-established farmers.

Humble Farmers in the Late Classic

Humble farmers were the most numerous farmers at Chan, and the Late Classic is when the community reached its peak in population. The small farmsteads that I excavated as part of my dissertation research serve as my point of departure because these were the original excavations that led to the development of the Chan project, and following this discussion I incorporate the broader range of farming households excavated by Chan project participants.

In 1996 and 1997 I excavated a neighboring group of seven small farmsteads (Chan Nòohol) located just south of Chan's community center (figure 6.2; Robin 1999, 2002a, 2002b, 2006). At the center of each farmstead is a house lot, referred to as CN1 to CN7 (Chan Nòohol 1 to Chan Nòohol 7) on figure 6.2 and in this book for ease of reference (these correspond to mound group numbers C-251, C-252, C-342, C-250, C-256, C-268, and C-249, respectively). These farmsteads belong to the smaller-end, type 1 and 2, households at Chan. They were among the newly established households at Chan during its population peak at the end of the

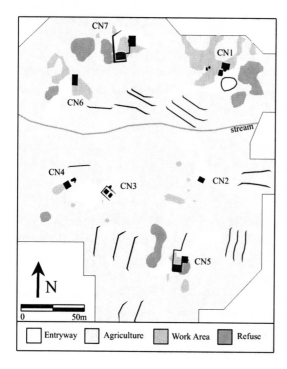

Figure 6.2. Chan Nòohol, a cluster of small farmsteads south of Chan's community center.

Late Classic period (670–800/830 AD). Small newly established family farms and other newly established craft-producing households comprised roughly half of Chan's population at that time.

Because farmers lived among their agricultural terraces, they situated their farmsteads at least 50 to 100 meters from one another, creating a mosaic of homes and fields in a dispersed but clustered (rather than nucleated) community. Within the farmstead there was a house lot and residential area, which consisted of houses, ancillary buildings, and outdoor workspaces for cooking, eating, crop processing, flake tool making, cloth making, storage, and ritual activities. Chan Nòohol's farmers constructed one or two residences at the center of their house lots within flat-lying terrain. In house lots with two residences, initially residents constructed a single residence and then added the second one later as their household grew. Farmers' homes were pole buildings with thatch roofs, on low stone substructures that ranged in height between 0.3 and 0.8 meters (figure 6.3). Around their homes, farmers terraced intervening sloping terrain and planted level areas for agricultural production and additionally enhanced these areas by incorporating household waste and amending the soils to enhance levels of phosphorus, zinc, and barium (Robin 1999, 2006; Wyatt 2008a, 2008b).

In figure 6.2, the placement and organization of the seven farmsteads may seem haphazard at first glance. But looking beyond geometric design or a Cartesian coordinate system reveals a cultural logic, based on an understanding of land and agriculture that informed farmers' construction of their homes and fields. Farm families oriented all house compounds except CN7 to face the now-intermittent stream running through that area. A small *aguada* (waterhole) within household CN1 was the location chosen by residents of this neighboring group for feasts, further highlighting the significance that water held for them. In a similar way, Maya farmers living at Cerén, 350 kilometers to the south in El Salvador, oriented their homes facing a nearby waterway (Sheets 2006). Water held both a practical and a symbolic importance in farmers' lives. Water was essential for agriculture and life; perhaps because of this importance, water was a part of farmers' sacred landscapes, providing sites for ritual events and feasting.

Within Chan's rolling hills, farmers identified, selected, and cleared the relatively flat plateaus in the underlying bedrock, and in one case a previously abandoned Preclassic house, for constructing their house lots and

Figure 6.3. To-scale reconstruction drawing of an ordinary farmer's house, household CN1. (Illustration by Jack Scott.)

surrounding yards. The stone retaining walls they built to construct terraces followed the contours of the topography, creating broad flat steps up and down hillslopes. As farmers constructed their homes and fields, they molded and extended a preexisting form that comprised both the natural topography and elements of earlier settlements. In this way, "natural" and "cultural" were blurred at Chan in a fashion distinct from a Cartesian binary division between the two.

In most residences, a large part of the interior of the house was taken up by a low bench (not more than 0.2 meters in height), a seating or sleeping area; thus, much of people's daytime living and working happened outside of houses in outdoor spaces. As people walked, worked, and cleaned around their homes and fields in repetitive ways across their daily lives, these actions and activities left traces in porous soil surfaces in terms of soil chemistry and trampled artifacts that allowed me to document routines of daily life (Robin 2002a). The general types of activity areas I identified through microanalyses around house lots include work areas, pathways, refuse areas, and agricultural areas (table 6.1; see figure 6.2). Even the paths engraved through residents' foot traffic were inscribed into the ancient ground surface, as walking can leave micro material and chemical traces in the archaeological record (for other examples, see Barba and Ortiz 1992; Middleton 1998; Stahl and Zeidler 1990). The pathways that feet inscribe into the ground through highly regimented movement are more archaeologically recoverable than are less-traveled or less-regular paths; thus, across Chan Nòohol, footpaths are visible where they led up to the fronts of houses and onto patios where people's walking synchronized as they moved in and out of their houses. The traces of pathways disappear as people moved farther away from their houses and their daily paths dispersed into the variable and multiple routines and uses of life.

On a day-to-day basis, farmers conducted a similar set of activities in their homes and fields: they cooked, ate, slept, farmed, processed crops, stored possessions, built and maintained houses and terraces, made expedient chert tools[1] and cloth for their daily domestic uses, and performed rituals. These activities were the basis for a set of common daily practices through which farmers would have seen themselves as belonging to a household, neighboring group, and community. These activities framed the space and time of life: the temporal rhythms of a day, the seasonal cycles of work, and the lived spaces of the land.

Farm families—men, women, and children—worked in house lots and

Table 6.1. Distinctive artifact and soil chemistry signatures for activity areas

Activity area	Average artifact frequency per m^3	Artifact diversity	Artifact condition	Soil chemistry
Entryway	3	n/a	n/a	low phosphorus and zinc, moderate manganese, high barium
Agriculture	39	low: largely ceramics and lithics	small and worn, some whole or broken tools	high phosphorus, barium, and zinc, moderate manganese
Work area	163	moderate: largely ceramics and lithics, but also may include all artifact types except shell	small and worn trampled fragments	high phosphorus, manganese, and barium, moderate zinc
Refuse	1,714	high: all artifact types	larger pieces, partial objects, whole objects	high phosphorus and barium, moderate manganese, low zinc

Note: Phosphorus is a robust indicator of enhanced human activity such as refuse disposal, food preparation, and fertilization. Manganese has been consistently identified as a component of wood ash in contemporary and archaeological contexts (Middleton 1998; Middleton and Price 1996). The presence of wood ash in work areas corresponds with the artifact signature of these areas as associated with food preparation and lithic production work. Barium, an element in bone, and zinc have also been linked to anthropogenic processes in the archaeological record (Middleton 1998).

agricultural fields that were not separated by great distances or physically constructed barriers (figure 6.4). Houses and fields were adjacent to one another, and in many cases (as discussed below), terrace and house walls actually adjoined, bringing domestic and agricultural spheres into direct physical engagement. Because people undertook domestic and agricultural activities largely in outside areas in spaces that were adjoining and interdigitating, daily experiences of work and life facilitated interaction in a number of ways. Through the day as people worked in open outdoor areas that were not separated by great distances or physical constructions, they had the ability to see or at least hear one another and possibly even

Figure 6.4. Idealized reconstruction drawing of farmsteads and agricultural terraces at Chan. (Illustration by Jack Scott.)

talk with one another (Robin 2002a). Household members shared in a midday meal of a warm soupy gruel cooked and served in large open bowls.

The collaborative nature of family farmwork was further enhanced by the pole-and-thatch houses that were partly light, sight, and sound permeable. As archaeologists and anthropologists have observed cross-culturally, the construction of pole-and-thatch houses enables a different set of possibilities in terms of visibility, audibility, and privacy for those inside and outside a house than when houses are constructed with solid walls (e.g., Helliwell 1992; Hendon 2010; Sweely 1998; Weiner 1991). In the case of pole-and-thatch houses, people immediately inside and outside of houses could have peered or at least talked through the pole walls, communicating and interacting with one another. There likely would have been social conventions, which are beyond the ability of the current archaeological evidence to reconstruct, that prohibited people, socially defined as outsiders by the household group, from walking right up and peering into a pole-and-thatch house, thereby creating privacy for its residents.

The type of collaborative family farmwork inscribed into the spaces of Chan Nòohol is different from that seen in the spatial, gender, and age relations of farmwork in much of contemporary Maya society (Robin 2006). Just as the contemporary male farmers that I worked with on the Chan settlement survey noted the differences between the locations that contemporary and ancient Maya farmers chose for their agricultural fields, as I compared the daily life inscribed into the ground surface at Chan Nòohol (and later across the community), I could see differences between the spatial ordering and also between the gender and age relations of contemporary and ancient farmwork. In contemporary Yucatec Maya communities, the most extensively studied contemporary Maya communities, adult males are the primary agricultural workers (e.g., Palerm 1967; Re Cruz 1996; Redfield and Villa Rojas 1934; Steggerda 1941). During the day, children are away at school and mothers stay home to take care of babies and the domestic world, while men go, oftentimes overnight or for several nights, to work in fields that are located at great distances from their communities, typically four to nine kilometers away, but possibly as distant as twenty-five kilometers away. Male agricultural workers do not always share in midday meals with their families, because of the impossibility of returning home for this meal. Women, in turn, make a time-consuming meal that includes tortillas cooked on flat *comales* (items of cookware rarely found at Chan), as male agricultural workers need a portable dry midday meal to carry to their fields. Brumfiel (1991) has shown in the Aztec area, where both corn gruels and tortillas were important foods as in the Maya area, that women switched to the more laborious task of making tortilla-based meals as Aztec tribute demands increased and more and more household members worked in agricultural fields distant from their homes.

The spatial, gender, and age relations of farmwork in ethnographically documented contemporary Yucatec Maya communities certainly parallels what I observed among farmers in Succotz. Mexico's Yucatan peninsula is located north of and adjoining Belize. Traditional histories suggest that the contemporary residents of Succotz were refugees from the Caste War of Yucatan (1847–1901), in which native Maya people revolted against Spanish ruling groups. Revisionary archaeological research highlights that Belize was not an abandoned backwater to which people fled in the colonial and historical periods. Because the Spanish never conquered and only sparingly visited Belize, the notion of Belize as an abandoned landscape is largely a figment of Spanish writing (Graham 2011; G. Jones 1998; Oland 2009, 2012). Thus, contemporary residents of Succotz are likely to be descendants of native Maya people both from Yucatan and from more local communities in Belize.

Because of the quantity and quality of ethnographic work in Yucatan, Mayanists often take life in Yucatan as iconic of contemporary and even ancient Maya life (see Atran 1993; Fedick 1996; Hammond 1978; Robin 2006). The traces of everyday life at Chan reveal a different pattern of farm life, one in which farms and homes are not divided by great distances and are not overtly and materially gendered female and male, in which children are not away at school and farmwork becomes a collaborative family project involving men, women, and children.

The Chan Community in the Late Classic

The late Late Classic residents of Chan Nòohol, and other places like it at Chan, may have moved into a part of the community that was not being utilized for residency at the time, but they were not moving into an abandoned landscape. They were part of a vibrant community that had existed for 1,500 years before them, and desiring to understand the broader community is what led me to develop the Chan project. For the remainder of this chapter I turn to the results of Chan project research.

The end of the Late Classic period (AD 670–800/830) is when there was the largest population at Chan and the largest population growth rate, as populations doubled during that time. But a doubling of population across 130 to 160 years could be accounted for by a natural rate of increase (birth rate–death rate); thus, all of the residents of Chan's newly established late Late Classic households could have been the younger members of existing families who moved within the community to establish their own house compounds. Also during this period, settlement was leveling off or declining in some nearby areas of the Belize Valley such as the areas around the civic-center of Buenavista (see figure 5.1), which was losing power relative to the polity capital of Xunantunich (Ehret 1995; Yaeger 2008). Some of Chan's newest residents at the end of the Late Classic period may have been newcomers arriving from not-so-distant areas adjacent to the faltering center of Buenavista, just a few kilometers away. I have previously used the term "voting with their feet," an analogy to Nancy Farriss's (1984: 76) discussions of Maya farmers who made choices and decisions to move in and out of the Spanish colonial world, to emphasize the active way that farmers' choices about where to move affected broader power relations in Maya society (Robin 1999, 2012c; Robin et al. 2010). Newcomers who came from nearby communities may not have been strangers to the Chan community but instead family and friends joining other family and friends in a nearby community. As they settled at Chan, they would have come into mutual intercourse with others of Chan's residents, both old and new, as they worked the land and participated in community-wide ritual and ceremony and, as discussed below, developed agricultural systems that involved not only collaborative household work but also the labor of cooperating households.

Long-Established Farmers

Andrew Wyatt (2008a, 2008b, 2012), for his dissertation research on the Chan project, explored the homes and fields of some of Chan's long-established farmers in four different areas at Chan to examine the range and variation in Chan's terraces and agricultural life across the community (areas a, b, d, and e on figure 6.1). Whereas my earlier research focused on extensive horizontal excavations of house lots, Wyatt extended the domain to include extensive horizontal excavations of agricultural terraces. Broad horizontal exposures of terraces are fairly unique in the Maya area, where trenches are the common excavation technique that researchers use to expose terrace walls and their construction techniques (chapter 4). But agricultural terraces are much more than their construction techniques, for they are complex systems for soil and water management. Wyatt's more extensive terrace excavation techniques permitted him to explore these complex agricultural systems and the social strategies and knowledge of the local environment that enabled them.

Farmstead C-304, excavated by Wyatt, is a type 1 household associated with contour and cross-channel terraces (figure 6.5; see figure 4.2 for agricultural terraces). Initially, farmers built a springhouse at farmstead C-304, which they later converted into a residence. Farmstead C-304 is located 0.8 kilometers north/northeast of Chan's community center. This was one of the first agricultural areas established by farmers at Chan in the Middle Preclassic period (650–350 BC), and farmers continuously occupied this location until the Terminal Classic period (AD 800/830–900). Farmers built the single structure at farmstead C-304 directly on sloping terrain rather than placing it on a level area within sloping terrain; thus, the terraces that adjoin the structure form the level areas for outdoor activities and domestic refuse disposal as well as agricultural planting areas. As seen at C-304 and many other houses at Chan that farmers built along slopes, farmers did not build their terraces and houses as separate constructions, which even further extends the interpenetration of domestic and agricultural worlds. Because farmers built the structure at farmstead C-304 on a slope, in its final form, it was barely elevated above the ground surface on its south (upslope) side and was elevated 1.5 meters above the associated sloping terraced terrain on its north (downslope) side.

Farmers began to construct the first low ephemeral earthen and stone-walled terraces in the area around farmstead C-304 in the Middle Preclassic period. Through time, they expanded terrace construction, increasing the size of existing terraces and expanding terracing into new terrain until by the end of the Late Classic period the majority of sloping terrain was blanketed with terraces (see figures 6.5 and 5.2). Farmers' terrace construction followed an accretional process in which they built, slowly through time, the terrace system now visible across the landscape.

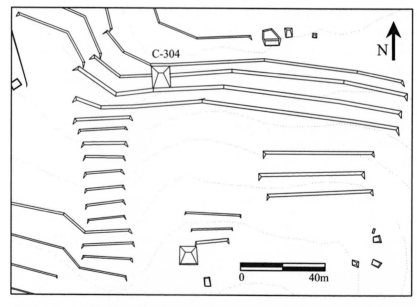

Figure 6.5. Farmstead C-304 and associated agricultural terraces. Four-meter contour interval. (Courtesy of Andrew Wyatt.)

Farmers' terraces were more than stone walls along hillslopes; they incorporated extensive and complex small-scale water management features. Farmers constructed small irrigation ditches at the junction of terrace walls to allow water to flow downhill through terrace beds. Uphill of the terraces, farmers constructed three contiguous aguadas, each one at a slightly lower elevation. Measuring three meters in diameter by one to two meters deep, these aguadas could have held a great deal of water. In addition to the larger aguadas (features commonly identified by archaeologists), there were small, stone-lined depressions on terraces which Wyatt called *aguaditas*; these measured one to two meters in diameter and thirty to forty centimeters deep and would have held smaller amounts of water located on individual terrace beds. The understanding of hydrology that farmers incorporated into their terraces included a detailed knowledge of the local microenvironments where they situated their terraces, as they also incorporated underground streams into their irrigation efforts.

Farmers built the first building identified at farmstead C-304 in the Late Preclassic period (350 BC to AD 100/150). This building was a springhouse, which they used to temporarily store water and house the course of a spring emanating fifteen meters above in the hillside (figure 6.6). The springhouse also supported a pole-and-thatch building. As with the expansion of the terraces, through time farmers expanded and eventually filled in the springhouse so that it could support a larger pole-and-thatch house, and they diverted the spring elsewhere. At each refurbishing of the stone house platform, residents gathered domestic garbage, incorporating it as well as quarried limestone and soil into the fill of the expanding house platform. Because farmers undertook no new construction projects at the house in the Terminal Classic period, domestic garbage from the end of the Classic period remained adjacent to the house in two areas at the junction of terrace and house walls.

As Wyatt notes, unlike heavily terraced parts of the Maya area such as the Río Bec region of Mexico's Yucatan peninsula (Turner 1983), there are no walls designating property division across Chan's terraces. Terrace walls that interlace with house platform walls often run through multiple households and their associated house platforms, suggesting that farming families did not work alone but worked cooperatively in multihousehold groups. The way in which farmers managed irrigation along sloping terrain required a level of cooperation between households sharing a hillside.

Figure 6.6. Stone-lined basin for collecting spring water from springhouse. (Courtesy of Andrew Wyatt.)

Agricultural Practices and Sustainability

Wyatt's research identifies several important features of the long-term agricultural strategies of Chan's farmers. Terrace agriculture at Chan was a local development by farmers to manage production in hilly terrain. Farmers' development of terrace agricultural systems avoided soil erosion and maximized water infiltration. Constructing more than simple terrace walls, farmers increased and maintained high levels of agricultural production through the development of complex small-scale irrigation and water storage systems. The engineering of these systems required a detailed local knowledge of the natural environment acquired through long-term residency and daily interaction with the land, as seen in the manipulation of underground streams. The extensive terrace systems that blanketed Chan's landscape by the end of the Classic period were the product of accretional, small-scale growth by cooperating farm families who developed knowledge of the landscape and agriculture through their daily practices and interactions with their environments that they established over centuries and passed down through generation after generation.

Forest Management Practices and Sustainability

David Lentz and colleagues' (2012) analysis of over 1,500 macro remains and micro flotation-extracted plant remains from across Chan revealed the botanical depth of farmers' agricultural and forest management practices. Farmers developed a complex, diversified agroforestry system that included annual crop species such as the triad of maize, beans, and squash; a variety of fruit trees such as cashew, *nance*, sapote, *coyol*, and avocado; and the manipulation of economically important wild species such as hardwood trees and palms (including poisonwood, *copal*, dogwood, *chico zapote*, mahogany, and *cohune* palm) used in construction and ritual, as well as weedy species that could have been used for food or other purposes such as making matting. Additionally, residents imported pine, an odoriferous wood that produces large amounts of smoke when burned, from seventeen kilometers to the south in the pine ridge area of the Maya Mountains.

Across Chan's history, residents had access to a large diversity of mature, closed-canopy, tropical forest hardwood trees (table 6.2). This was even the case as population expanded at Chan during the Classic period

Table 6.2. Hardwood species from Chan listed by time period

Time period	N	Genera and species
Late Preclassic	56	*Manilkara zapota, Pouteria* sp.
Terminal Preclassic	41	*Manilkara zapota*
Early Classic	18	*Anacardium occidentale, Manilkara zapota, Metropium brownei,* Sapotaceae
Early Late Classic	31	Amyris, Spermatophyta
Late Late Classic	123	Annonaceae, aquatic plant, *Manilkara zapota, Swietenia macrophylla*
Terminal Classic	102	Annonaceae, Flacouriaceae, *Guarea excelsa, Manilkara zapota, Swietenia macrophylla*
Building termination	38	*Albizia* sp., Annonaceae, *Astronium graveolens, Brosimum alicastrum, Byrsonima crassifolia, Colubrina arborescens, Grias cauliflora, Guarea excelsa, Licaria* cf. *campechiana, Manilkara zapota, Piscidia piscipula, Pouteria* sp., *Protium copal,* Sapotaceae, *Schefflera morototoi, Vitex gaumeri*
Early Postclassic	7	Spermatophyta

Source: Courtesy of David Lentz.

Table 6.3. Chan wood remains listed by time period and weight

Time period	Hardwood	Palm	Pine	
	(Percentage of weight in grams)			
	%	%	%	gr
Middle Preclassic	8.6	0.0	91.4	0.116
Late Preclassic	39.4	0.1	60.5	46.800
Terminal Preclassic	44.2	0.6	55.2	25.434
Early Classic	41.4	0.0	58.6	23.998
Early Late Classic	64.4	1.2	34.4	9.023
Late Late Classic	98.0	0.3	1.7	155.571
Terminal Classic	89.3	3.1	7.6	201.716
Early Postclassic	80.3	0.0	19.7	15.628

Source: Courtesy of David Lentz.

and farmers had a growing need for fuel, construction material, and agricultural land. As table 6.3 illustrates, unsurprisingly, residents' use of hardwood expanded at Chan in the Classic period.

More surprising is the large diversity of hardwood trees to which farmers had access even as population expanded and even in the final days of their inhabitation of the Chan community (see table 6.2). Chico zapote, a hardwood prized for its strength and favored in building construction across the Maya area, populated Chan's forests throughout the history of the community. Unlike at Tikal, one of the largest Maya civic-centers, where residents ran out of chico zapote in 741 AD (Lentz and Hockaday 2009), Chan's residents always had access to this wood. Other insights come from residents' incorporation of a diverse array of mature, closed-canopy, tropical forest hardwood trees in a series of terminal ritual deposits that they placed within the central ritual and administrative architecture at the community center as they stopped using it at the end of the Terminal Classic period (circa AD 900). These included chico zapote (*Manilkara zapota*), mahogany (*Swietenia macrophylla*), copal (*Protium copal*), and muskwood (*Guarea excelsa*), among others. Among these, mahogany is quite significant because its seedlings will flourish only in the shade of other tall trees, indicating that despite two millennia of occupation and agricultural production, residents maintained a mature, closed-canopy, tropical forest around Chan. The paleoethnobotanical evidence does not demonstrate what residents' forest management practices were, but whatever they were, residents established forest management practices across the centuries that allowed them to maintain the mature, closed-canopy, tropical forest while simultaneously building more houses and fields and expanding the community.

High-Status Farmers

Farmers did not constitute only the lower tiers of Chan's residents: the majority of residents regardless of wealth and status engaged in agricultural production. Chelsea Blackmore's (2007, 2011, 2012) dissertation research explored a neighborhood located one kilometer east of Chan's community center, called the Northeast Group, that residents occupied from the Early Classic to the Terminal Classic period (figure 6.7). This neighborhood consists of two type 5, two type 4, three type 3, and two type 1 households located in level terrain and surrounded by agricultural terraces that ringed the neighboring households. As seen at both Chan Nòohol and farmstead C-304, farming families at the Northeast Group molded and extended a preexisting topography to construct their homes and fields. In this case, a broad flat plateau in the sloping hillside provided a location for nine adjacent households, which were together surrounded by terraced fields. Blackmore refers to these household groups as NE-1 to NE-8 for ease of reference. (They correspond with Chan mound group numbers C-154, C-155, C-157, C-156, C-158, C-159, C-330, C-160, and C-163. NE-1 combines C-154 and C-155.)

The buildings Blackmore excavated within household groups NE-1, NE-3, and NE-6 ranged in height from 0.2 to 1.5 meters. The largest house

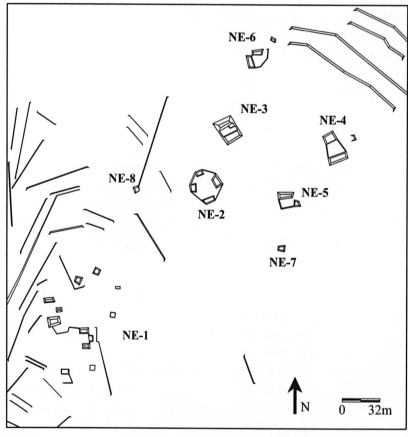

Figure 6.7. Northeast Group. (Courtesy of Chelsea Blackmore.)

platform she excavated was the northern building at NE-3. In its final form, residents elevated the stone platform of their house to a height of 1.5 meters. A southern stairway of seven steps led to the pole-and-thatch house. A bench, 30 centimeters in height, took up most of the interior space of the house. As with the smaller house platforms previously discussed, higher-status residents constructed their houses out of perishable materials but on taller stone platforms.

Beyond the leading family residences that are located just east of the community center, larger residential groups such as those located at the Northeast Group are dispersed across the community and, as at the Northeast group, are located roughly 700 meters to 1 kilometer from the community center. Blackmore identifies these midlevel farming families (in size, midway between the small farming households just discussed and the households of Chan's community leaders) as the head families of subgroups or neighborhoods across Chan. Like Chan's leading families and humble families alike, they hosted feasts within their house lots. At the end of the Late Classic period as the residents of household group NE-3 were reconstructing the patio area within their house lot, they interred a deposit that may be the remains of one such feast or a ritual deposition meant to represent a feast (figure 6.8). Residents placed ceramic vessels and the bones of consumed animals including white-tailed deer, brocket deer, white-lipped peccary, rabbit, bony fish, skunk, squirrel, and turtle around a hearth that faced onto their residential patio area and then buried this deposit in limestone rubble to resurface their patio. Residents buried the bone in a layer of ash, which aided in its preservation in a tropical climate. This deposit with its unusual preservation provides insight into the kinds of festival foods that people consumed at Chan.

Craft Producers

While farmers made up the majority of Chan's residents, they were not its only residents; craft producers, diviners, and community leaders also lived at Chan. As with farmers, craft-producing households were among the long-established households as well as later-established households during the community's Late Classic population peak. Craft workers produced *Strombus* marine shell beads and obsidian blades in the households of Chan's leading families beginning in the Preclassic period. The craft workers themselves either may have been members of the leading families

Figure 6.8. Northeast Group hearth deposit. (Courtesy of Chelsea Blackmore.)

who acquired and passed down through time the skill and knowledge of working these exotic and valuable materials or may have been itinerant specialists visiting the community and associating themselves with the leading families. These exotic raw materials were imported from long distances to Chan from the coast, 110 kilometers to the east, and from

Guatemala, 280 to 310 kilometers to the southwest. Engaging in the acquisition of the exotic materials from which to form marine shell beads and obsidian blades afforded Chan's leading families sets of long-distance connections to distant people and places that conferred prestige upon Chan's leading families. These connections to distant people and places also provided leading families with multiple external ties to people and centers beyond Chan, which they were able to build upon and develop across Chan's history. As I discuss below, particularly in relation to the acquisition of obsidian, these long-standing distant relationships may have even allowed Chan's leaders to play off more powerful places against one another, as they appear to have been able to do in the late Late Classic period when the newly emergent Xunantunich polity capital made its failed attempt at hegemonic control of the region.

Residents established households that made use of more local materials in craft production during the Late Classic period as more and more people were moving into the community. Like the leading family households, these local craft-producing households continued to be inhabited in the Terminal Classic period as many farmers were leaving Chan. Local craft workers produced cut limestone blocks and fill material that they quarried from the limestone bedrock underlying much of the community and also made chert tools from stone quarried from local or nearby sources.

Chert Biface Craft Workers

Lithic craft workers established a single chert biface production household, household C-199, at Chan in the late Late Classic to Terminal Classic periods. This production household was located 1 kilometer to the southeast of the community center (figure 6.9 upper). Craft workers there produced thick chert bifaces, the primary formal cutting and agricultural tool used by Chan's residents (figure 6.9 lower). Nick Hearth (2012) investigated this type 2 household, which included two domestic structures (one house and one ancillary structure) adjacent to a patio area that was also bounded by two narrow linear features. Household residents built a 40-centimeter-high stone platform to support their pole-and-thatch house. Adjacent to and north of the house within the house lot was a chert biface production workshop, measuring 2.5 meters by 2.5 meters, that consisted of a ground-level limestone cobble pavement associated with chert debitage and microdebitage. Adjacent and continuing downslope to the workshop was a production debris midden containing chert debitage and microdebitage that was 105 square meters in its densest portion. The dense portion of the midden contained 970,000 flakes per square meter—about 72 million total flakes.

Although no end products were identified at C-199, as is typical of chert production sites (Clark 1990), the flakes identified in the C-199 midden were predominantly biface production flakes, and these were found in consistently higher proportions than in domestic middens at Chan (see Hearth 2012: table 10.1). Multifaceted platform flakes, which are the result of thick biface production, were the most common of the identifiable flakes. The scale of production ongoing at C-199 was far greater than required for household-level provisioning and far less than regional-level provisioning, and thus likely provisioned the community.

In addition to the low-level occupational specialization in thick chert biface production at household C-199, residents across Chan, from its humblest farmers to its community leaders, made expedient flake tools in their homes from locally available chert within the community primarily using single-facet, single-direction flake core reduction (Hearth 2012). Hearth found no evidence for flake core production at any of Chan's households, suggesting that the cores residents used in flake and biface production were made elsewhere, potentially at a location yet to be identified at Chan (as chert is a local material), or were produced outside the community and brought into the community.

The nature of chert tool production at Chan suggests that there were complex economic relationships that promoted both household independence and household interdependency involving the production and distribution of this common tool type. Residents across Chan produced expedient flake tools for their own use in their homes, which they used in a range of daily cutting and scraping tasks. Residents also acquired thick chert bifaces, their primary formal domestic and agricultural tool, from producers at household C-199. All residents of the community acquired their flake cores either from an unknown location within the community or from outside of the community. Thus household members made some of their chert tools for themselves and acquired others from specialized producers within Chan, linking households across the community through exchange.

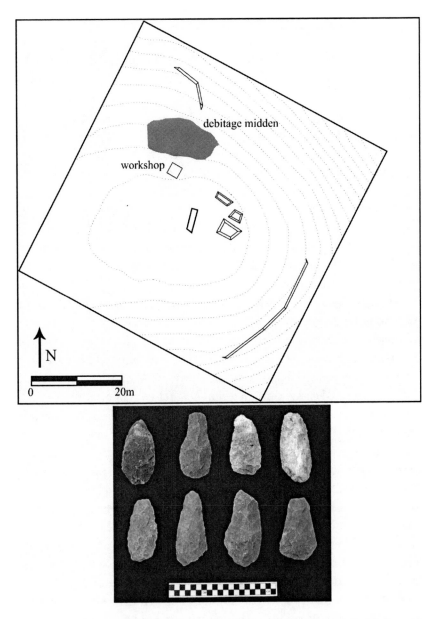

Figure 6.9. *Top*: Chert biface production household C-199 and associated workshop and debitage midden. One-meter contour interval. *Bottom*: Thick chert bifaces from agricultural excavations across Chan. (Photograph courtesy of Andrew Wyatt.)

Limestone Craft Workers

The Chan survey work identified eleven limestone quarry areas across the community, largely clustering around the center of the community and its largest architectural works. Caleb Kestle (2012) investigated a quarry area located seventy kilometers north of the community center (figure 6.10 upper). The quarry area consists of five quarry faces across a seventy-meter by forty-five-meter area. The quarries included both hilltop and hillslope quarries and quarries into hard tabular limestone and naturally eroding soft white limestone (figure 6.10 lower left and lower right). As with Wyatt's approach discussed above, Kestle (2012: 226) opened horizontal exposures across quarry areas in order to demonstrate that quarries were not simply passive locations for the extraction of stone but "were active locales where people labored and interacted, developing economic strategies for their households."

Kestle also excavated two households immediately adjacent to the quarries: household C-010 (a type 3 household) and household C-011 (a type 1 household). During the late Late Classic to Terminal Classic periods, residents of household C-010 built three low structures adjoining a patio area. Kestle excavated one of these structures, C-010.1, a low stone house platform elevated eighty centimeters in height that supported a pole-and-thatch house. Founded in the preceding early Late Classic period and inhabited into the Terminal Classic period, the adjacent household C-011 was built as a single structure (C-011.1), a low stone L-shaped house platform elevated fifty centimeters in height that supported a pole-and-thatch house. The wall of the L-shaped house platform extended to adjoin a set of terraces. Although architecturally speaking the two houses at households C-010 and C-011 are comparable, the residents of household C-010 maintained a larger inventory of thick chert bifaces that were in poor and broken conditions than did the residents of household C-011. These thick bifaces, such as those produced at household C-199, were general utility tools used in domestic and agricultural as well as quarrying tasks, but the quantity and condition of these tools at household C-011 suggest a specialized role for this household in relation to quarrying. The residents of household C-011 built agricultural terraces emanating from the walls of their house, materializing their connection with agricultural work.

The two different types of limestone, hard tabular and soft weathering stone, from these quarries were used for different purposes. Chan's

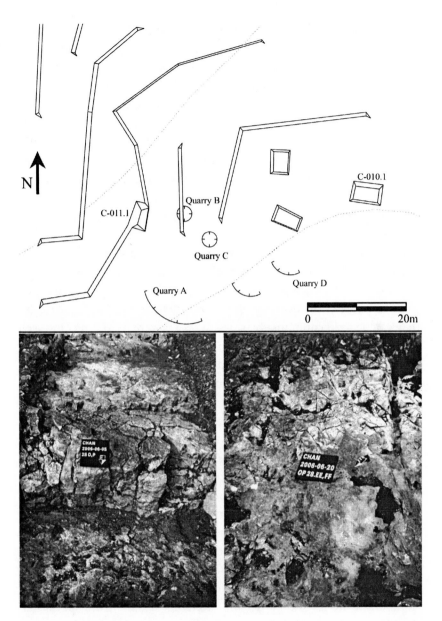

Figure 6.10. *Top*: Quarries, households, and agricultural terraces north of the Central Group. *Bottom left*: Hard tabular limestone, quarry A. *Bottom right*: Naturally eroding soft limestone, quarry C. (Photographs by Caleb Kestle.)

residents used hard tabular limestone as facing stone for buildings as well as for fill stone. Hard tabular limestone is more difficult to quarry than soft limestone is. Residents used the easier-to-quarry soft weathering limestone as fill material. Quarriers worked the two types of quarries differently. They used a fire-cracking technique (using fire to artificially weather stone) to quarry the hard tabular limestone, and the workers at hard limestone quarries removed their tools from the quarry locations. Soft weathering limestone did not require fire cracking to quarry, and workers on these quarries cached their tools (thick chert bifaces and informal limestone picks) on the quarry faces.

Ethnographic and ethnohistoric analogy to contemporary and historical quarrying in Mesoamerica indicates that soft, easily quarried, fill material is often quarried in communally held quarries by residents of nearby households to acquire their basic building materials (Kestle 2012: 218–20). In the contemporary and ethnohistoric cases, people working in communally held quarries often cache their tools at the quarries so they can be used communally by workers, a pattern of tool caching seen at Chan's soft limestone quarries. In contrast, specialized quarriers who work more difficult-to-quarry stone that they view as having intrinsic qualities necessary for their final product often store their tools at home rather than leaving them on quarry faces. The hard tabular limestone at Chan that naturally fractures in rectangular-ish pieces may have had intrinsic qualities related to the final form of a square or rectangular cut stone block used for facing buildings that was recognized by ancient residents and specially quarried by people living in household C-010.

These quarry and household excavations provide a tantalizing suggestion that stone quarrying at Chan may have been organized in complex economic ways that led to both household independence and interdependence, as seen for chert tool production. Household members used their own labor to quarry basic soft limestone fill material from quarries located near their homes, while at the same time they acquired cut limestone facing stones and harder limestone fill material from specialized quarriers at household C-010.

The nature of craft and agricultural production at Chan illustrates the operation of what Sheets (2000) refers to as three levels of the economy—the household economy, the village economy, and the regional economy. At

Chan, many households produced certain types of items—such as houses, agricultural terraces, food, cloth, and expedient chert tools—for their own use. A smaller number of households produced items in excess of what they needed for exchange across the community; these items include cut limestone block, thick chert bifaces, shell beads, and obsidian blades. Food was likely the only item that Chan's residents produced in excesses great enough for regional-level exchanges. Chan's residents (from humble farmers to community leaders) had a range of exotic items—shell, obsidian, jade, greenstone, and pine—in their homes that evidences the community's participation in regional-level exchanges. Through their daily work, household members produced some of what they needed on their own, developed intercommunity ties with households that developed certain specialized products for exchange within the community, and ultimately acquired goods from quite long distances through their excess production.

The Late Classic development of community-level production of local materials at Chan is intriguing. It illustrates how residents drew upon their internal labor and production to promote their economic viability at a time when political-economic relationships in the Belize Valley were being altered, particularly through the late rise of the Xunantunich polity capital. As Kestle (2012) notes, "When farming communities limit their dependence on centers for everyday items they are not only taking practical measures but are also engaging in political action." The late development of community-level production of local materials at Chan may not simply be coincidence but may indicate ways that community members were building upon their own labor and resources to buffer themselves against the vagaries of changing political-economic networks in the Belize Valley at the time. It was a strategy that residents maintained into the Terminal Classic, an equally turbulent time of overall political decline, population decrease, and community abandonment across the Belize Valley.

Community Leaders

Chan's leading families resided in the northern structure (Structure 2) of the Central Group (C-001) and two residential plaza groups (C-002 and C-003) located adjacent to and east of the Central Group (figure 6.11).

Structure 2 in the Central Group and Structure 17 in group C-002

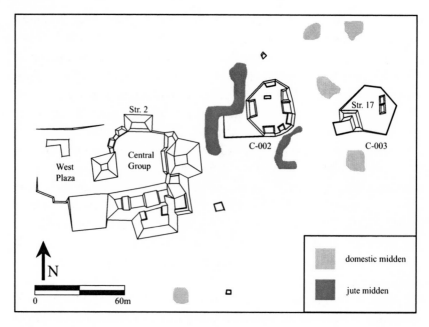

Figure 6.11. Chan's community center and adjacent leading family residences (C-002 and C-003). Structures marked on figure include leading family residence Structure 2 in the Central Group and leading family residence Structure 17 in C-003.

are the largest of the leading family residences at Chan. Structure 2 is a bilevel stone platform 1.5 meters in height with a front axial stairway that supported a perishable house with a thatch roof (figure 6.12). A low (20-centimeter-high) masonry bench took up most of the interior of the house. Structure 17 is a bilevel L-shaped stone platform 1.5 meters in height with a front axial stairway that supported a part masonry, part pole-and-thatch house. A 50-centimeter-high masonry bench took up most of the interior of the house. Structure 17 is the only residential structure at Chan that had low (50-centimeter-high) masonry foundation walls that supported full perishable walls and a thatch roof. The high status of Chan's leading families was not only visibly marked within the community through architectural distinction, it was also seen in their unique access to elaborate funerary rituals in the community center (Novotny 2012), certain exotic items such as non-Guatemalan obsidian (Meierhoff et al. 2012), and their involvement in the production of exotic luxury items such as marine shell beads and obsidian blades (Keller 2012; Meierhoff et al. 2012). They also orchestrated community-level ceremonies, held large-scale feasts, and presided over the administrative and adjudicative functions of the community.

While leading families lived in some of the most substantial residences at Chan, and this distinction was visible to any passerby or community member on a daily basis, like other residents at Chan, leaders lived in perishable houses, a commonality that was equally visible (compare figures 6.3 and 6.12). Although there are clear distinctions between Chan's leading families and other families living at Chan, there also are core similarities in how families across Chan organized the spaces and places of their daily living. As with the residents of Chan's humbler households, members of leading families built their homes at the center of house lots that they demarcated by depositing their garbage at the edges of their house lots (see figure 6.11).

Adjacent to Structure 2 in the Central Group are two low ancillary structures, Structures 3 and 4, low stone platforms that rose to sixty-five and seventy centimeters in height, respectively. Excavators identified higher quantities of ceramics on the surfaces of Structures 3 and 4 than on other structures at Chan (Latsch 2003), and ceramic analysis also identifies greater amounts of ceramics in Structure 3 and 4 fills than from other structures in the Central Group (Kosakowsky, personal communication, 2010). The higher quantities of ceramics at these ancillary structures suggest that at least one function of these buildings was the preparation of food—meals for the leading family and perhaps festival foods for the feasts that accompanied the ceremonies hosted by leading families in the Central Group.

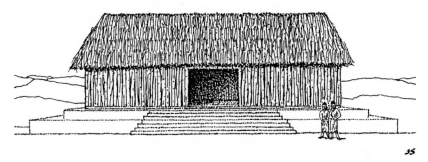

Figure 6.12. To-scale reconstruction drawing of leading family residence Structure 2 in the Central Group. (Illustration by Jack Scott.)

Craft production was another likely function of Structures 3 and 4. Excavators identified obsidian debitage related to core maintenance activities suggesting low-intensity pressure blade production in a fill episode in Structure 3 dating to the Early Classic period and a fill episode in Structure 4 dating to the Late Preclassic period (Hearth 2008; Kosakowsky 2009; Meierhoff et al. 2012). Structures 3 and 4 are the only places where excavators identified obsidian blade production debris at Chan. This suggests that the members of Chan's leading family either possessed the skills for obsidian blade production or associated themselves with attached specialists or itinerant specialists who may have worked at these ancillary structures (Hearth 2008; Meierhoff et al. 2012).

Angela Keller (2012) also identified that Chan's leading families were involved in small-scale *Strombus* shell ornament production in the Middle to Terminal Preclassic periods. She identified marine shell–working detritus from this production in fill episodes in Structure 2, Structure 3, Structure 7, the Central Plaza, and Structure 8 in the West Plaza. Preclassic shell workers produced relatively simple ornaments such as perforated shell fragments and disk beads for distribution within the community. By the Late Classic period, local shell working had diminished, and Chan's leaders were distributing fine worked-shell items produced elsewhere, including countersunk disks, rosettes, unperforated saucers, and an unusual toggle-bead type, all made of conch.

Chan's leading families had access to a single exotic item not found elsewhere in the community: non-Guatemalan obsidian (from Pachuca, Paredón, and La Esperanza; these Mexican and Honduran sources are located 320 to 1,070 kilometers from Chan). James Meierhoff and colleagues (2012) sourced a 100 percent sample of the obsidian from Chan using a portable X-ray fluorescence (XRF) device at the Field Museum of Natural History to determine geological sources for the entire obsidian assemblage. The four pieces of non-Guatemalan obsidian date to the late Late Classic period to Terminal Classic period. Because they do not occur in Chan's leading families' assemblages prior to the late Late Classic period (which is when Xunantunich rose to power) and are from the most distant location of any items found at Chan, one plausible interpretation for the presence of these items is that they might be political gifts from the more regionally connected rulers at Xunantunich, who may have had access to more distant trade networks than residents at Chan did. But there is another explanation: Chan's leaders played a historical role in obsidian production and exchange at Chan and may have built on these histori-cal ties to expand their regional networks in the late Late Classic period, and they may have done this drawing upon their long-term historical ties to distant places rather than through the emerging Xunantunich polity capital.

Understanding what political economic connections allowed Chan's leaders to procure distant non-Guatemalan obsidian requires the sourcing of obsidian at Xunantunich and other major centers in the Belize Valley, which unfortunately has not been undertaken to date. One of the pieces of non-Guatemalan obsidian found at Chan comes from the Pachuca source (located 1,070 kilometers distant from Chan, the most distant item found at Chan). Pachuca obsidian has a distinctive green coloration that allows it to be sourced visually, enabling investigators to explore how at least this one exotic item arrived at Chan. Kindon and Connell (1999) visually sourced the obsidian from the Xunantunich Archaeological Project col-lections, which include obsidian from Xunantunich and nearby smaller settlements. They identified no Pachuca obsidian at Xunantunich. Other than the Chan piece, the only Pachuca obsidian in the Xunantunich area comes from the minor center of Chaa Creek (three pieces) and the hamlet of San Lorenzo (one piece). Researchers have also visually identified Pa-chuca obsidian from recent excavations at the nearby Belize Valley major centers of Buenavista and Cahal Pech (Jaime Awe, personal communica-tion, 2011; Jason Yaeger, personal communication, 2011). Because Xunan-tunich's rulers did not possess Pachuca obsidian, they did not have any special claim on the distant trade networks that brought Pachuca obsid-ian into the Belize Valley. Conversely, major Belize Valley centers such as Buenavista and Cahal Pech, which were not as powerful as Xunantunich in the late Late Classic period, did have access to Pachuca obsidian, as did the residents of Chan. It is impossible to know exactly how Chan's leaders acquired Pachuca obsidian. (Through long-standing political economic relationships with Buenavista or Cahal Pech or some other center?) But clearly it was not through political gifting from Xunantunich. This sug-gests that the political and economic connections through which Chan's leaders acquired Pachuca obsidian in the Late and Terminal Classic peri-ods were those that they had historically constructed with other political centers with which they were already involved. Chan's long-term political and economic ties to a range of political centers in the Belize Valley and even beyond the Belize Valley seem to have been some of the resources that allowed Chan's leaders to develop some form of political constraint on the networks of power that the late-rising Xunantunich polity capital hoped to develop and ultimately dominated for only a short period of time (chapter 7).

Because the most distant objects (finished marine shell beads, non-Guatemalan obsidian) identified at Chan date to the Late to Terminal Classic period, this period was not only a time when the community turned inward to maximize its internal labor and resources through local craft production; it was also a time when the community turned outward to its greatest extent. Chan's leading families were turning outward and taking advantage of expanding regional networks to procure non-Guatemalan obsidian and finished marine shell ornaments, building upon their long-standing role in the procurement and small-scale production of these nonlocal items (Keller 2012; Meierhoff et al. 2012). In terms of Late Classic developments in Chan's internal production and external trade relations, residents variably drew on external ties and built up local production to buffer themselves and take advantage of expanding and contracting economic opportunities precipitated by the ebb and flow of broader political economies and the rising and falling of regional centers. The Chan community and its residents did not simply react to developments in the outside world; they strategically organized their internal production and external trade relations cognizant of the fact that broader regional economies fluctuated.

Understanding Chan's Social Diversity: Social Sustainability within the Community

The variable elevation of stone house platforms across the community was a visible way that residents perceived and signaled to one another, on a daily basis, social differences within the community. But equally visible each day were the social commonalities between residents that cross-cut these differences: every resident, from community leader to humble farmer, across 274 households in a 3.2-square-kilometer area, lived in a perishable house with a thatch roof. The latter point becomes even more striking in comparing Chan to neighboring communities.

Across the Maya area, housing types range from perishable constructions such as those seen at Chan, to residences that have low or partial stone foundation walls that supported higher perishable walls and thatch roofs (like Structure 17 at Chan), residences with full stone walls and thatch roofs, to the most elaborate residences completely made of stone, with stone walls and corbel vaulted roofs. That a full range of housing types is found at large civic-centers across the Maya area, but not at Chan, perhaps goes without saying. But the interesting points emerge through a comparison of housing types at Chan with nearby minor centers and even smaller settlements in the Belize Valley.

San Lorenzo, a hamlet, located 1.5 kilometers northeast of Xunantunich and 4 kilometers from Chan, consists of twenty household groups, a fraction of the number of household groups at Chan (Yaeger 2000a, 2000b, 2003). Type 1 to 6 household groups are found at San Lorenzo.[2] San Lorenzo's smallest residences, like Chan's, were perishable constructions on low stone platforms, but larger residences had low or partial stone foundation walls that supported higher perishable walls or had full stone walls, and at least one residence had a corbel vaulted roof. Despite being a smaller settlement in terms of residential architecture, San Lorenzo exhibited greater variability and more stratification of housing types. Between the San Lorenzo hamlet and its neighboring hamlet to the west, Yaeger identified SL-13, a unique construction with two patios, which he suggests was likely built by Xunantunich's rulers, indicating their direct role in affairs at San Lorenzo.

Although more distant from Xunantunich than either Chan or San Lorenzo, residents of the Chaa Creek area, located seven kilometers from Xunantunich and five kilometers from Chan, could see El Castillo at Xunantunich in the distance (Connell 2000, 2003, 2010). Type 1 to 7 household groups are found in the Chaa Creek area.[3] The Chaa Creek minor centers, CC1 (Stela Group) and CC18 (Tunchilen Group), are type 7 mound groups comparable to but smaller than Chan's Central Group and are surrounded by smaller settlement areas. Leaders of the Chaa Creek minor centers lived in corbel vaulted residences in the Late Classic period, reoriented architecture toward Xunantunich, displayed locally unprecedented wealth, and abandoned their ancestral ceremonial precincts, all of which indicate to Connell new and strong ties to Xunantunich's rulers.

Given this comparative data, it is more remarkable that at Chan, across 274 households in a 3.2-square-kilometer area, all residents lived in perishable houses. As much as this distinction is striking from a contemporary archaeological perspective, it would also have been as striking to residents of Chan and various nearby communities as they lived their daily lives.

The lesser degree of social stratification seen at Chan in terms of housing was also expressed in other visible ways across the community, in terms of people's belongings, particularly the luxury items they wore and other exotics they possessed. The only item that Chan's leaders possessed that others across the community did not was non-Guatemalan obsidian.

Chan's leading families had quantitatively more luxury items such as jade, shell, and Guatemalan obsidian than did other residents across the community, again marking their distinction in visible ways (Blackmore 2011, 2012; Keller 2012; Meierhoff et al. 2012). Still, all residents across the community had access to luxury items of comparable quality and style in their homes and for their bodily adornment, and this would have reinforced commonalities across the community. Residents of lower and higher status had comparable access to marine shell ornament types of similar quality and obsidian blades from the three primary Guatemalan sources: Ixtepeque, San Martin Jilotepeque, and El Chayal (figure 6.13; Keller 2012; Meierhoff et al. 2012). This differs from that seen at San Lorenzo, where higher-status residents had access to more elaborate shell ornament types than did lower-status residents (Yaeger and Robin 2004). At Chaa Creek, community leaders amassed locally unprecedented wealth including greenstone beads, polychrome vessels, chert and obsidian eccentrics, shell pendants, and high-quality tools and ground stone (Connell 2003).

The distribution of jade and serpentine at Chan, arguably the most valued objects in Maya society, shows a similar pattern between Chan and neighboring small communities. Excavators identified jade items at type 1 to type 7 groups at Chan, although they were more common at higher-status groups. Albeit small and few, jade and serpentine items were possessed by some of Chan's humblest farmers (as also was the case at Cerén). This differs from the pattern seen at San Lorenzo and Chaa Creek, where jade and serpentine were not identified in smaller residential groups. At Chaa Creek, only leading families living in corbel vaulted residences possessed jade (Connell 2000). At San Lorenzo, jade was found only in two larger patio groups, where residences had either full stone walls and thatch roofs or stone walls and corbel vaulted roofs (Yaeger 2000a). People living in perishable structures in these communities did not have access to jade, while they did at Chan and other farming communities such as Cerén.

Central Group

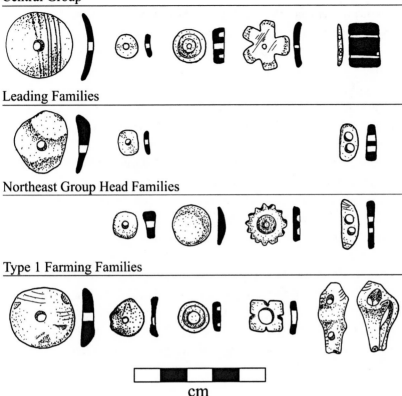

Leading Families

Northeast Group Head Families

Type 1 Farming Families

cm

Figure 6.13. Examples of shell ornaments distributed across the Chan community. (Illustrations by Carmen Ting.)

There were other differences between life at Chan and that in neighboring communities. Anna Novotny's (2012) osteological analysis from Chan suggests that levels of health remained comparable across the community's two-thousand-year history. The consistent presence of a low degree of biological stress in the Chan skeletal population seems to indicate the persistent good health of the community. This contrasts with evidence from major centers in the Belize Valley and across the Maya area that indicate that health declined across the Classic period (Haviland 1967; Healy 2004). As human health and the health of the forest often go hand in hand, it may not be surprising that both people and the forest were healthy at Chan.

In terms of the houses they lived in, Chan's residents could be classified at the lower end of the social spectrum in Maya society. Chan's residents certainly had less privilege and fewer possessions than did society's power brokers. But just as researchers were surprised at the richness of farmers' lives at Cerén, so too should we clarify that Chan's farmers do not seem "poor." Residents' everyday lives at Chan evidence a remarkable combination of possessions, personal health, and forest health, which suggests that at Chan there was something people might refer to today as "a quality of life" that was shared by residents across the community. While Chan's community leaders may not have amassed the opulence of leading families in nearby communities, the community's humblest residents seem to have been better off (in terms of health and possessions) than were other small-scale farmers studied in the region. Rather than indicating a failure of community leaders to achieve a certain level of status in society, as I discuss below, the more equitable distribution of wealth within the community seems to have been a conscious strategy employed by community leaders to promote a type of more communal, group-oriented, and heterarchically organized community. At Chan, all residents lived in perishable houses, goods were more equitably distributed, social stratification was less pronounced, health was consistent, and the forest was abundant—this attests to a quality of life and type of wealth that cannot be measured by access to goods or by type and size of houses.

Ritual and Politics at Chan's Community Center

I have just discussed what everyday life was like for Chan's diverse residents, and now I will turn to a discussion of ritual and politics at Chan, which illustrates how everyday life, ritual life, and political life were not isolated domains at Chan. Prior to the excavations at Chan, I queried (see chapter 5) whether Chan's ancient residents recognized it as a community, and if they did, whether Chan had been a community across its two-thousand-year history or had initially been farmsteads within a landscape that later coalesced into a community. There is precedent for both social formations in the Belize Valley. At what became the major Belize Valley center of Buenavista, Middle Preclassic residents lived in farmsteads in the area that would become Buenavista, but no community center existed as of yet (Ball and Taschek 2004). In other places, though, such as Blackman Eddy, Cahal Pech, and Xunantunich's Group E, communities developed around public and ceremonial architecture with attendant ritual deposits and feasting by the Middle Preclassic (Awe 1992; Brown 2010; Brown et al. 2009; Garber et al. 2004). Because Chan was a smaller community, I expected that there would be no Middle Preclassic community center. I was entirely wrong.

Beginning in the Middle Preclassic period, the Central Group was a center of community life for residents. Ritual deposits marking the center of the community, burial of ancestors, and distinctive architectural planning linking cardinal directions and religious and political beliefs originated with the founding of the community and residents' construction of its first farmsteads (Robin, Meierhoff, Kestle, et al. 2012). During the Middle Preclassic period, the Central Group was a largely open space. Its plaza was the focus of ritual activities that consecrated the center of the community through caches of objects chosen because they symbolically represented the concept of the "center" (center of the world, center of the cosmos, center of the community) in Maya thought, a practice that would last for another two thousand years. Located at the north and south ends of an open and accessible plaza space were two low stone residential platforms rising 25 and 20 centimeters in height, respectively, that supported perishable buildings with thatch roofs. As the community grew, so did the Central Group and adjacent West Plaza (see figures 5.3 and 6.11). Through time, residents constructed additional buildings at the Central Group, and these grew in size. At the height of its construction in the late Late Classic period, the Central Group consisted of six structures dominated by an E-Group with a 5.6-meter-high eastern temple surrounding a plaza that had an area of 1,154 square meters. By this time, community residents had restricted access to the Central Group, through only two entryways: one at the northeast corner and the other at the southwest corner of the group, the latter of which leads to the West Plaza. Through most of Chan's history, the Central Group was its sole community-level ceremonial space. But during the Late Classic period and through the Terminal Classic and Early Postclassic periods, the largely open West Plaza became an additional community-level ceremonial space for residents, which increased access to ceremonial life for the growing populace (Cap 2012). The West Plaza reached its maximum size in the late Late Classic period with an area of 1,928 square meters (including its broad south stair).

Drawing on ethnographic research on the number of people who can be accommodated in open spaces during public events, Inomata (2006, following Moore 1996) estimates that participants attending events in

Maya plazas would require between 0.46 m²/person and 3.6 m²/person of plaza space. The lower number corresponds to a tightly packed event, and the higher number corresponds to an event in which participants had substantial space in which to move around. Using these numbers to gauge a minimum and maximum number of people that could participate in events in Chan's plazas in the late Late Classic period suggests that between 857 and 6,700 people could have attended these events (Robin, Meierhoff, and Kosakowski 2012). The larger of these numbers is significantly more than the number of residents at Chan at its population peak, and the smaller of these numbers would have still included a broad spectrum of residents from across the community. Ritual events sponsored by Chan's leaders at its community center can correctly be referred to as community-wide festivals that involved the broad membership of the community. The community-wide nature of festivals at Chan diverges from what Inomata (2006: 811–14) identifies at the largest of Maya ceremonial centers, such as Tikal, where plazas could hold only a select portion of community residents. It is comparable to what he finds at small royal centers such as Aguateca, where, as at Chan, all residents of a community could have attended events in its central plazas.

The simultaneous presence of the entire Chan community for community-wide festivals furthers understandings of the power of these events in building community. Festivals were times when community members came into face-to-face contact with each other. Residents experienced together the convening with ancestors, the burning of incense, and the deposition of sacred objects that consecrated community. All of this would have given a physical and experiential reality to the Chan community.

Community-wide rituals would also have embodied the divisions and competition within the community (Blackmore 2011, 2012; Cap 2012). Social differences between community members would have been as visible at these events, through what people wore and where they were able to stand to view events, as was the shared community concept that they were constructing. As well, hidden in the crowded space of a public event in Chan's central plazas, a resident may have been able to find the privacy to voice concern or dissent (see Scott 1990).

Across its two-thousand-year history, Chan's community center was a place in which its residents came together for community-wide ceremony and political events. These were not daily events, nor were they devoid of or detached from everyday life. In the following sections I first describe the nature of community-level ceremonies ongoing in Chan's community center and then I follow this with discussions of how religion was implicated in everyday life at Chan.

Community-Level Ceremonies

Chan's Middle Preclassic residents manipulated cosmological principles in designing and building their community center (Robin, Meierhoff, Kestle, et al. 2012). Residents oriented the Central Group to the cardinal directions, not to features of the local landscape such as waterways and topography, as was prevalent in the organization and planning of farmsteads. On the east and west sides of the plaza of the Central Group sit the two pyramidal structures of its central religious buildings and ancestral shrine, its E-Group (Structures 5 and 7). To the north sits the leading family residence (Structure 2) and to the south is the administrative building (Structure 6). As Wendy Ashmore (1991) documents for larger civic-centers across the Maya area, in constructing their cities and placing particular types of buildings in north, south, east, and west locations, Maya royalty referenced cosmological understandings to make powerful political and ideological statements through the architecture of a city (Ashmore 1991; Ashmore and Sabloff 2002). East and west within a city spatially mark the path of the sun and the location of the rising and the setting of the sun as seen on the horizon. Maya royalty often marked the east and west sides of plazas with ritual structures that commemorate these significant natural cycles as well as agricultural cycles. Along the sun's daily path, north (up) marks the sun's height at midday, associating north with the heavens and a position of supreme power. South (down) is associated with a worldly and underworldly position, as the sun passes through the underworld at night. Across the Maya area, leaders of the largest Maya cities claimed the powerful north location for the construction of their residences or monuments commemorating their power to make a vivid and visual statement about their power. The worldly affairs of administrative buildings are often found in southern locations.

From a small Maya center such as Chan to the largest royal centers, residents employed similar directional principles and spatial layouts to define community centers and invest salient social meanings in spaces to define Maya places. When similar social ideals appear at small and large sites, archaeologists tend to argue that the small site is mimicking or emulating the ideas developed at the large site. But the historical depth of the planning principles employed in the construction and reconstruction of Chan's community center show that many of the ideas that later in time became part of a Maya noble and royal ideology and political strategy were in fact initially conceived by farmers in farming communities.

For two millennia, ritual practitioners sanctified the center of their community by placing caches in the plaza of Chan's Central Group, making this location the most sacred location in the community, if one measures sacred in terms of the length of time people use a location for ritual practices (Robin, Meierhoff, Kestle, et al. 2012). Ritual practitioners placed green objects, either of serpentine or of jade, more commonly in Central Plaza ritual deposits than in ritual deposits at other locations in the community center (Kosakowsky et al. 2012). Today (and in the past), Maya ritual specialists associate the color green with the "center," and Chan's residents used green objects in rituals to consecrate the center of their community (Blackmore 2003, 2011).

In the Middle Preclassic, in the Central Plaza, residents interred a single individual, an adult twenty to twenty-four years old of unknown sex (Burial 1). They placed the deceased in a shallow grave cut into the underlying limestone bedrock in an extended supine position with the deceased's "head" (which had been removed) at the northeast end of the grave (Novotny 2012). There were a few stones lining the grave (a simple cist grave). Reverents reentered the grave of this individual for centuries across the Middle Preclassic and Late Preclassic periods (650 BC–AD 100/150). At each reentry they deposited fragments of human bone, serpentine, jade, shell, and slate above the grave. These objects either were objects people had originally placed with the deceased and the later reverents removed and replaced during the reentries, or they were objects that later reverents deposited at the time of the reentries to commemorate the visitation of this individual. Regardless, the individual buried in this grave was revered through time with the most offerings of any ancestor or person buried at Chan. As reverents reentered the grave, they removed body parts of this ancestor from the grave and in some cases repositioned them in unusual ways. Although they removed the bones of the cranium, torso, and left arm, they repositioned the right humerus beside the right femur. Residents remembered and revered the death and burial of this

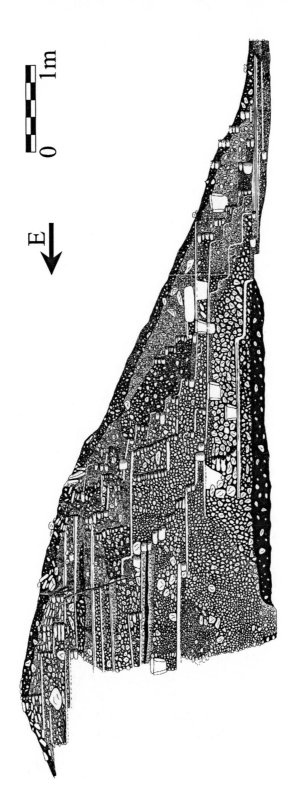

Figure 6.14. Profile of central east structure of E-Group (Structure 5-center). (Illustration by Nasario Puc.)

individual for generations, and in fact centuries, initiating a practice of remembering and revisiting ancestral burials across time at Chan.

Beginning in the Late Preclassic period and continuing into the Terminal Classic period, Chan's E-Group became the community's primary location for ancestral burials (Novotny 2012). In its earliest Late Preclassic form, the E-Group consisted of an 80-centimeter-high eastern structure (Structure 5) and a 50-centimeter-high western structure (Structure 7). Through time, residents reconstructed these structures, ultimately raising them to 5.6 and 4.9 meters in height, respectively (figure 6.14 and figure 5.3 lower). They expanded the eastern structure from a single to a tripartite building. The traces of incense burners visible and chemically identifiable in the floors of the eastern structure, the caching of an incense burner, and the deposition of incense-burning and food-bearing vessels across a room floor are the lines of evidence that build a picture of the ritual use of the E-Group: burning of incense and the serving of food accompanied ritual events at the E-Group. The sight and smell of the incense rising from the ceremonial event would have been an integral part of the experience of those events.

Like other E-Groups, Chan's E-Group served as a shrine for a select group of ancestors from the community. Adults (both men and women) and children were among the twenty individuals buried in fourteen graves that the project excavated from the E-Group (Novotny 2012). Many of the ancestors buried in the E-Group were young individuals. Chan's residents identified youth, a feature highly regarded in Classic Maya royal society, as a selection factor for ancestral burial.

Religion and Everyday Life

Previously, I provide a broad overview of ceremonial life at Chan; in this section, I describe how everyday life and religious life were implicated in, rather than separate from, one another (Kosakowsky et al. 2012; Kosakowsky and Robin 2010). The material objects that residents and ritual practitioners typically chose to use in ritual were objects that they also used in daily life, not a specialized set of objects produced solely for ritual use. The ceramic vessels that ritual practitioners placed in ritual deposits—the most numerous items they placed in these deposits—were used items. They were people's possessions and containers for food and other items (Kosakowsky et al. 2012; Kosakowsky and Robin 2010). Even the luxury items that ritual practitioners incorporated into ritual deposits show evidence of use. They included shell detritus from marine shell bead production in ritual deposits in the Preclassic period (Keller 2012). Jade objects, beads, celts, and other polished pieces were used, broken, or formerly strung (Keller 2008; Robin 2002a). There were a few items that appear to have been specially produced for ritual use, such as a unique thirty-eight-centimeter-long honey-brown-colored chert blade from northern Belize and eccentric chert objects (crescents, serpents, and celestial forms) that do not show signs of use and are not found in domestic nonritual inventories (Hearth, personal communication, 2009). But most of the objects that ritual practitioners interred in ritual deposits were items people had used in daily life.

Because the objects that ritual practitioners incorporated into ritual deposits were objects that residents used in daily life and could typically be found in domestic inventories, ritual and everyday life were linked at Chan. Residents' concerns for the sacred and supernatural were tied to, not separate from, the experiences of everyday life, through the incorporation of ordinary objects in ritual. As community members gathered on special occasions to observe even the largest of community-wide ritual events at Chan's community center, they not only experienced a sacrosanct periodic event but also recognized, through the manipulation of daily objects in these events, the way in which the sacred and the meaning of special events was deeply tied to the conditions of their daily lives.

Many of the objects that residents deposited in the earliest Middle and Late Preclassic burials and caches in the Central Plaza were partial objects: pieces of a larger serpentine or jade object, shell-working detritus, a fragment of a figurine, or individual shell beads that may have been part of a larger piece of jewelry. In one case, ritual practitioners successively interred four fragments of the same jade object in three different caches and as a grave offering to Burial 1 (Keller 2008). Pieces of objects were interred in ritual deposits, and other pieces of those same objects either would have remained in circulation in daily life at Chan or would have been sequestered by ritual practitioners until the next ritual event. Regardless, ritual practitioners placed pieces of objects in ritual deposits, and other pieces of those same objects remained and were curated in the living community, perhaps being used in later rituals and in some cases being interred in a subsequent ritual deposit. The part of the object that remained in circulation in the community referenced the buried part of that object and the earlier ritual event. By burying and curating partial objects, people linked themselves and their lives to their history and community (Robin, Meierhoff, Kestle, et al. 2012).

Ritual was not restricted to Chan's community center; it was pervasive across daily life at Chan (e.g., Blackmore 2011, 2012; Kosakowsky et al. 2012; Kosakowsky and Robin 2010; Robin 2002a). Ritual was an integral part of domestic life at households across the community. All of Chan's households, from its humblest farmer to its community leader, housed incense burners for the production of smoke and scent in rituals, and all residents interred material offerings in their homes (Blackmore 2011, 2012; Robin 2002a; Robin, Meierhoff, and Kosakowsky 2012; Wyatt 2012). The tiny fragments of hardwood and pine, less than 0.01 grams in weight and less than 1 millimeter in length, that Wyatt identified across agricultural terrace excavations were part of a process through which farmers amended soil through the application of household waste. But because pine gives off a particularly odiferous scent, produces a great deal of smoke, and is associated with ritual offerings elsewhere at the community, the incorporation of tiny pine fragments into agricultural fields may also attest to agricultural rituals (Wyatt 2008b, 2012).

The complexity and pervasiveness of domestic ritual at Chan illustrates that people developed the same range of depth of ritual knowledge within their homes as they performed in community center rituals. In the Middle Preclassic period, members of Chan's leading families buried a single blue-green teardrop-shaped jade *adorno* at the center of their residence (Structure 2), located on the north end of the Central Group, which was at that time a 25-centimeter-high stone platform that supported a perishable structure (Keller 2008). While the north residence grew in size through time, ultimately rising to a height of 1.5 meters, the position of the jade adorno remained the center point of the structure across its subsequent two-thousand-year history. This domestic ritual practice, using jade to consecrate the center of a home, parallels the community-wide ritual practices of using green objects to consecrate the center of the community, as discussed above.

In the late Late Classic period, the humble farming family living at household CN5 at Chan Nòohol consecrated their house as the center of the Maya cosmogram through the caching of ordinary river cobbles, detailed in chapter 4. Residents placed river cobbles with yellow (south), red (east), black (west), and white (north) markings in a quincunx pattern oriented to the cardinal directions around a worn serpentine fragment (see figure 4.3). The color-directional symbolism of the river cobble cache establishes a Maya cosmogram centering the house. In community center rituals in the Terminal Preclassic, ritual practitioners placed a cache of two lip-to-lip Pucte Brown or Balanza Black basal flange bowls in the plaza area in front of the west structure of the E-Group (Structure 7). This cache contained numerous small jade, shell, slate, and chert items, at the base of which were five small figures placed in a quincunx pattern (Keller 2012). The central figure is slate. Around this are a yellowish and reddish *Spondylus* figure, a green jade figure, and a white shell profile face. The colors associated with this quincunx, as well, serve to sanctify the center of the Chan community as the center of the Maya cosmogram. The placement of the black figure in the center, rather than the green figure, perhaps signifies the western location of this cache in the plaza, as west is associated with black.[4] Again, domestic and community-level ritual practices at Chan drew upon comparable understandings of religious beliefs.

Across domestic and community-wide ritual, Chan's residents drew upon a wealth of ritual knowledge about the sacred order and organization of the Maya world. While the association of green with the center is a common element of Maya ideology from the Preclassic period onward (e.g., McAnany 2004), the association of the colors white, yellow, red, and black with a quincunx and the directions north, south, east, and west is most standardized during the period of contemporary ethnographies (e.g., Hanks 1990; Vogt 1976). Postclassic sources do note color-directional symbolism, but there is variation as to what colors go in what directions. Quincunx patterns themselves have a deep history going back to the Preclassic period. In comparing domestic and community-wide ritual at Chan, residents, from the humblest of farmers to community leaders, were among the actors who through their specific ritual practices took part in creating what would become the highly conventionalized structures of ritual practices of much later times. As Chan's deep history attests, its residents were not emulators of Classic Maya royal ritual practices, as traditional archaeological thinking would suggest; instead, they were agents who developed understandings of the sacred world that were as deep as those of the natural world around them.

The two-thousand-year history of domestic and community-wide ritual at Chan attests to the ways in which ritual and daily life interpenetrated each other, through ritual practices that incorporated objects of daily use, through the performance of ritual across the spaces and places of daily life, and through the process of remembering past rituals. In terms of the broader history of religious practices in the Maya area—long seen through grand royal ritual acts—Chan's history illustrates that complex religious knowledge was initially developed in farmers' community centers and homes and then later adopted by society's nobility. At Chan, venerating a select group of ancestors and reentering their graves to involve them in contemporary rituals and possibly decision making has a deep history going back to the Middle Preclassic period. The ritual activities at the center of the Central Plaza all materially represent ideas about the meaning and importance of the center and its color, divinity, and cosmological associations. Chan's architects planned and organized the Central Group around the cardinal directions to make visible statements about power and ideology. Noble Maya art, iconography, and hieroglyphs make clear that all of these practices were key aspects of later Classic period state religion and city planning. But here at Chan, ordinary people were formulating complex sets of ritual knowledge through material objects dating back to the Middle Preclassic period. Chan's historical depth illustrates that many of the ideas that later in time became part of a Maya noble and royal ideology and political strategy were in fact initially conceived by farmers in farming communities. Chan's residents, and many others like them across the Maya area, constructed a popular religion that only later in time was adopted by nobility into state-level religious practices.

Community Governance at Chan

Having just explored the relationship between religion and everyday life, I now want to turn to the equally entwined nature of politics and everyday life at Chan. I begin this section by examining what project investigators were able to identify about the nature of community governance, and I then discuss politics and everyday life.

At Chan, and across Maya society, politics and religion were not isolated spheres. Chan's leaders governed the community through the orchestration of community-wide festivals, through the sponsoring of large-scale feasts, and by presiding over the administrative and adjudicative functions of the community (Keller 2012; Robin, Meierhoff, and Kosakowsky 2012).

As noted, Chan's leading families were not the only ones who hosted feasts at Chan: head families across neighborhoods at Chan, such

Figure 6.15. Central rooms of Chan's *audiencia*. Two of five quincunx holes in the west section of Room 2 are visible in the photograph. (Photograph by James Meierhoff.)

as the head families in the Northeast Group neighborhood and the family living adjacent to the aguada at Chan Nòohol, also hosted smaller neighborhood-wide feasts (Blackmore 2011, 2012; Robin 2002a). Modern Maya communities often hold community-wide ceremonies in a ceremonial round, in which small-scale ceremonies are first held by head families of subgroups within the community and then all members of the community come together for a single community-wide event (Vogt 1976). The evidence of feasting at neighborhoods across Chan may indicate a similar sequence of feasting and ceremony prehistorically that would have successively brought together larger and more inclusive groups across the community while simultaneously foregrounding the distinction of those that held feasts. Alternatively, the prehistoric neighborhood-level and community-wide feasts at Chan could have been distinct events.

While feasting represents a type of sociopolitical activity that is associated with head families across Chan, other types of political activity took place only at the Central Group. The unusually well preserved architecture and unusual array of terminal deposits in the rooms of the southern *audiencia*-style range structure, Structure 6, at the Central Group provide a rare glimpse into the nature of day-to-day community administration and adjudication (Robin, Meierhoff, and Kosakowsky 2012).

Structure 6 is a unique building at Chan, as it is the only vaulted masonry building in the community. In its final late Late Classic form, Structure 6-east, the larger and easternmost of Structure 6's two buildings,[5] had twelve vaulted rooms (figure 6.15). Ten rooms formed part of a tandem-layout range structure with north, south, and interior doorways. The south doorways opened to a rear patio bounded by two rooms to the east and west. The project excavated ten of the twelve rooms. Each room contained a substantial bench, which took up at least half of the room and was elevated to a height of sixty centimeters.

The administrative building not only was architecturally unique at Chan but also was used differently from other residential and ritual buildings: the activities conducted across room floors, bench sizes, ritual deposits, and plant use differed from other buildings (Lentz et al. 2012; Robin, Meierhoff, and Kosakowsky 2012). The types of organic waste-producing activities ongoing in domestic and ritual contexts were not ongoing in the administrative building (Hetrick 2007).

The central front room (Room 1), which opens onto the Central Plaza, is comparable to an *audiencia*—a place where Chan's leaders could have held meetings and settled disputes. In terms of its form, Room 1 is similar to the other smaller rooms in Structure 6, which may likewise have served as meeting places for smaller groups of people.

Comparable in size to Room 1, Room 2 (the central rear room) is distinct among the rooms of Structure 6, in that it is the only room to have internal divisions. Three narrow interior masonry walls, or screens, divide the space of Room 2 into three areas. The levels of the floors and benches in each of the three subdivisions differed in height. Multiple interior dividing walls and differing floor and bench elevations made movement in Room 2 more physically complex. In addition, at the end of its use in the Terminal Classic period, residents covered Room 2 with a lens of fine *sascab* to preserve a series of deposits they placed in this room. Carefully covering room floors with sascab was not something people did anywhere else at Chan. This gave excavators the first insight that there was a reason why people took special care to "bury" this room before they abandoned it. The unique architecture and deposits in Room 2 at Structure 6 are strikingly comparable to those of the divination building (Structure 12) at the farming community of Cerén in El Salvador that was buried by volcanic ash (Simmons and Sheets 2002). This illustrates the way in which divination and governance were entwined in farming communities situated on two ends of the Maya world.

The west division of Room 2 at Chan's Structure 6 has the highest floor and bench elevations and consists almost entirely of a raised bench area. Its builders cut five holes forming a quincunx pattern into this bench. They also carved a *patolli* board into the bench floor and inscribed horizontal and vertical lines into the south wall of Room 2 in this area. Patolli boards are part of a game that could be used in divination (Connell 2000). The five quincunx holes, as discussed above, represent the division of the Maya world into the four cardinal directions plus the center.

The central division of Room 2 has the lowest floor elevation and a bench. As residents ended their use of this room in the Terminal Classic period, they placed a terminal deposit on the bench that consisted of a pile of 548 jutes covering a spindle whorl. Adjacent to these they placed a pedestal base from a Roaring Creek Red vessel reworked as a cord holder (Kosakowsky et al. 2012). Cerén's diviners used beans and minerals in their divination; the jute pile at Chan may have served a similar divination purpose. Jutes not only were a source of food but also held ritual meaning for Chan's residents (Keller 2012). Modern shamans collect seashells as *cuentecitos*, objects used to access supernatural power, and this may have been the case for jutes at Chan (Linda Brown personal communication, in Simmons and Sheets 2002).

The east division of Room 2 has floors with two different elevations and no bench. During the final reconstruction of Room 2, builders placed a cache containing six deer antler fragments and two chert bifaces, one broken and one whole, within the north floor in the east division of Room 2. Deer antler was part of a diviner's toolkit, as the deer has important ritual association in Maya beliefs and divination and deer headdresses were worn by ritual practitioners (Simmons and Sheets 2002).

The diviner working in Structure 6, Room 2, could have communicated with the leaders who were meeting in Structure 6, Room 1, through the doorway that connected the two rooms. Divination was directly tied to resolving issues of community interest and settling disputes. This joining of administrative and judiciary functions in the governance of the community is perhaps unsurprising, because in preindustrial societies administrative and judiciary functions tend not to be differentiated (Durkheim [1893] 1997; Evans-Pritchard 1940; Inomata and Houston 2001).

The political strategies that Chan's leaders developed across its two-thousand-year history were always a blend of what Blanton and colleagues (1996) refer to as individual-centered (exclusionary) and group-oriented (corporate) strategies, but by the Classic period, political strategy at Chan had become dominated by group-focused strategies (Robin, Meierhoff, and Kosakowsky 2012). Individual-centered political strategies involve principles of hierarchy and political actors' monopoly control of sources of power. Classic Maya royal politics, with its emphasis on the cult of the divine king, is the key example of individual-centered politics in Blanton and colleagues' model. Group-oriented strategies involve principles of heterarchy and sharing of sources of power among groups. Group-oriented political strategies do not result in egalitarian societies, as hierarchy does still exist, but hierarchy and monopolies of control are restricted. Individual-centered and group-oriented political strategies always coexist within any political system, but typically one strategy or the other is dominant.

At Chan, individual-centered political strategy can be seen in the veneration of individual ancestors and the revisitation of their graves across the Preclassic and Classic periods, although ancestor veneration was also a group endeavor, as the living relatives of the deceased were responsible for the burial of ancestors, and larger groups of people—even at times the whole community—came together to revere their burial. Additionally, the feasting taking place as part of community-wide festivals across the Preclassic and Classic periods would have underscored group-oriented political dynamics in all periods.

The focus on the individual ancestor as a part of ritual and political process was most marked at Chan in the Preclassic period. Ritual practitioners interred Preclassic ancestors with more grave offerings than their Classic period counterparts received (Novotny 2012). Residents buried curated Middle Preclassic figurines with unique facial characteristics that may represent actual portraiture with Late Preclassic ancestors, possibly to link the deceased with founding members of Chan (Kosakowsky et al. 2012). In terms of shell ornamentation, only two burials at Chan, Late Preclassic Burial 10 and Terminal Preclassic Burial 2, were accompanied by shell ornaments that marked individual identity (Keller 2012).

While the political strategy of Chan's leaders always combined both individual-centered and group-focused strategies, by the Classic period their political strategy had become dominated by group-focused strategies. Ritual activity in Chan's community center shifted from a focus on individual ancestors to a focus on the community as a whole (Robin, Meierhoff, Kestle, et al. 2012). This is seen in a shift away from burying ceramics and other material objects with individual ancestors and placing these items in caches and terminal deposits, foregrounding the community, rather than the specific ancestor, as the focus of ritual activity (Kosakowsky et al. 2012) and an increase in the number of multiple- over single-interment ancestor burials (Novotny 2012). The dominant mode of political life at Chan in the Classic period, with its focus on the community, was strikingly different from that seen at Maya royal centers, where politico-ritual focused on the cult of the divine king.

Politics and Everyday Life

Having discussed the nature of politics and governance at Chan, I now turn to a discussion of how everyday life necessarily feeds into political life at Chan and how assumptions about the nature of political life in Classic Maya society have led to misconceptions about the history of politics in the region. The group- and community-oriented political strategies that were important at Chan in the Classic period, and certainly earlier, were not divorced from everyday practice. Had they simply been a political rhetoric of community and group orientation with no foundation in people's daily experience, they might not have engendered such a long-enduring sway over political life at Chan. The focus on the community rather than the individual in political and ritual practice and the hosting of feasts was paralleled in daily life by the absence of extreme social stratification within the community and the comparability in the quality of luxury items possessed and housing resided in by residents. These were aspects of everyday life, visible across the community, that provided a daily and experiential basis for the group-oriented political strategies that Chan's leaders espoused.

The group-focused political strategies seen at Chan are distinct from the political strategies of Classic period kingship practiced at royal centers across the Maya area, which epitomize the individual-centered strategy in Blanton and colleagues' model. Group-oriented political strategies are documented, at the end of the Classic period, as having been associated with political fragmentation of systems of kingship (Fash et al. 1992; Fash 1993; Tate 1992) and in the Postclassic period (G. Braswell 2001; Ringle and Bey 2001). Such political strategies are generally seen as a breakdown in the Classic Maya system of kingship. But the Classic period development of group-oriented political strategies at Chan indicates that there was a greater variety of forms of governance in the Classic period than systems of kingship (Keller 2012). Group-focused political strategies of the Postclassic and colonial period may have owed as much to the development of such strategies on the part of Classic period farming communities as they did to the breakdown of the system of kingship. Even during the Classic period there were tensions between the more centralized and extractive forces of kingship and the long duration of kinship structures that disperse authority more broadly (McAnany 1995).

Decline and Abandonment

For sixteen hundred years Chan grew and expanded, but by the Terminal Classic period, more people were leaving or dying at Chan than were continuing to live there. Because there was no expansion of mortuary contexts in the Terminal Classic period, population decline in this period seems to have been the result of people moving elsewhere. The people who remained at Chan, which was still a sizable community with between

379 and 637 inhabitants, continued to live across the entirety of the community, and Chan's community center retained its full range of religious, administrative, and judiciary functions. In terms of architectural construction in domestic, agricultural, and ceremonial contexts, residents largely made additions to existing constructions, such as adding a step, expanding a platform, or raising a floor level, rather than constructing new buildings or agricultural terraces.

Chan's newest late Late Classic farming families were among those who left Chan in the Terminal Classic period. Across the Belize Valley in the Terminal Classic people were leaving; when residents moved in this period, they voted with their feet to move to more distant areas beyond the Belize Valley. Chan's more long-standing residents, farmers and community leaders alike, were among those who stayed, perhaps because of their long ties to the place and people of the community. The local craft producers, including stone quarriers and chert biface producers, who were among Chan's newest late Late Classic residents, were also among those who stayed, perhaps because they had become so enmeshed in community-level exchange networks.

There may have been some premonitions about Terminal Classic residents' decisions to stay or leave the community in the day-to-day choices made by preceding generations. Across the Belize Valley, residents used a range of red, black, polychrome, and unslipped ceramic vessels in their daily lives. In the Late Classic, distinct ceramic style zones developed for the first time in the Belize Valley: one focused on the upper Belize Valley around Xunantunich, where Mt. Maloney Black vessels make up over 30 percent of ceramic assemblages; and one focused on the central Belize Valley, where black vessels make up only a small portion of ceramic assemblages and red vessels predominate (LeCount 1996, 2001, 2010). Because a range of red and black vessels were available to residents of the Belize Valley, the differential use of Mt. Maloney Black vessels represents a conscious signaling of people's sociopolitical affiliations (LeCount 1996, 2001, 2010). In addition to their daily use, at Xunantunich, Mt. Maloney Black vessels constitute a common vessel found in civic ritual deposits (LeCount 2010; Jamison 2010: table 6.1). In established and craft-producing households at Chan, Mt. Maloney Black vessels are found in proportions comparable to those identified at Xunantunich (table 6.4). In households established in the late Late Classic period, in contrast, they are found in greater proportions. Residents' choices in using Mt. Maloney vessels thus signaled their participation in an upper Belize Valley socio-political sphere that included Xunantunich.

There are also some key differences between Chan's and Xunantunich's residents' use of red and black pottery (Kosakowsky 2012). At Xunantunich, people were not only using higher frequencies of Mt. Maloney Black vessels, but also using quite low frequencies of all of the primary Late Classic red vessels (Dolphin Head Red, Belize Red, Roaring Creek Red, and Vaca Falls Red). Overall, people used over twice as many black as red vessels at Xunantunich. The black coloration of ceramic assemblages at Xunantunich seen on a day-to-day basis would have been a quite visible statement of sociopolitical affiliation (LeCount 2001, 2010). In contrast, Chan's established and craft-producing residents used roughly equal numbers of red and black vessels, each making up about 30 percent of ceramic assemblages (table 6.4). Considering only slipped calcite wares,

Table 6.4. Major Late Classic ceramic wares and groups at Chan and Xunantunich

Major wares and groups	Uaxactun Unslipped Ware	Mt. Maloney Group	Dolphin Head Red Group	Belize Red Group	Chunhuitz Group	Other	Rim count
	%	%	%	%	%	%	N
Chan established residents (all contexts)	28.6	31.1	24.1	9.2	1.9	5.1	12,156
Chan established residents (occupation)	28.5	36.4	14.0	15.0	0	6.1	214
Chan new residents (occupation)	25.6	53.4	8.6	2.9	3.5	6.0	313
Xunantunich (occupation)	22.6	38.3	4.5	11.5	12.3	10.8	1,175

Note: Frequencies are based on rim sherd counts. Given Chan's long temporal span, single-phase occupation deposits as identified at Xunantunich are not common at Chan. To facilitate comparison with the Xunantunich sample (which comes solely from occupation contexts), data from Chan's single-phase occupation contexts are presented here. Note the comparability between frequencies from all contexts and single-phase occupation contexts at Chan.

the basic daily cooking and serving wares, there are 8.5 times as many black vessels as red vessels at Xunantunich and only 2.6 times as many at Chan's established and craft-producing households. In terms of ritual practices, Chan's ritual practitioners only infrequently incorporated Mt. Maloney vessels in community center ritual deposits at Chan, while they did use Dolphin Head Red, Belize Red, and Roaring Creek Red, as well as unslipped wares (Kosakowsky et al. 2012: table 15.1). Established and craft-producing residents' greater incorporation of red vessels into their domestic assemblages may have signaled their maintenance of ties to a broader range of regional centers across the Belize Valley. By using red rather than black vessels in ritual and ceremonial contexts, Chan's leading families may have been saying something about where their alliances lay or about the different ways they chose to deploy their affiliations in different contexts.

Chan's newly established late Late Classic period farming families used red and black vessels in more comparable proportions or used higher proportions of black vessels than seen at Xunantunich. This perhaps indicates some of the tensions that may have existed in Chan at this time, between its newest residents, who perhaps felt a greater allegiance to Xunantunich, and its long-term residents, who were more ambivalent about the promises of new sociopolitical relationships. Alternatively, Laura Kosakowsky (personal communication, 2011) pointed out to me that it may have been Xunantunich's leaders who were trying to link themselves to a broadly established upper Belize Valley household pattern of the use of black vessels, while Chan's long-established families highlighted the breadth of their connections across the broader upper and central Belize Valleys in their ceramic choices. Certainly, there are many other examples of elites emulating ways of life from Chan. Regardless, residents' choices about which ceramics to use for daily and ritual needs in the late Late Classic period, and the sociopolitical affiliations implied by these choices, do seem to resonate with the choices their descendants made in the Terminal Classic period about whether to stay or leave Chan.

The last construction that residents built at Chan was a small, low, square shrine (Structure 1) measuring 2.6 meters by 2.0 meters with an elevation of 20 centimeters (see figure 4.4). Residents built the shrine at the cusp of the Terminal Classic/Early Postclassic periods at the center of the community in the plaza of the Central Group, directly over the area of original Preclassic caches that consecrated the center of the community.

They oriented the shrine to the intercardinal rather than cardinal directions, paralleling the orientation of Middle Preclassic Burial 1.

The shrine was associated with a 2-meter-high stela (Stela 1). A second late stela (Stela 2) marked the West Plaza's broad southern staircase that served as an entryway into the community center (Cap 2012). Although much of Chan's ritual and political practices previously discussed in this chapter were not cases of farmers emulating the ideas of Maya nobility, the presence of these late stelae at Chan seems evidence of Chan's leaders emulating and appropriating the symbols of the most divine of Classic Maya kings. Stelae are the quintessential marker of the ritual and political power of the Maya kings and are widely found across Maya centers as early as the Late Preclassic period (Hammond 1982). Stelae entered into Chan's ritual and political assemblage only late in its history and well after noble actors across Maya society had established their salient meaning. The dates and inscriptions on carved stelae at larger Maya centers suggest that in the Early Classic period, the distribution of carved stelae was restricted to the largest centers, and these stelae were erected only by the highest levels of royalty. As the power and authority of the Classic Maya kings waned at the end of the Classic period, carved stelae became more widely distributed at smaller royal seats of power, such as at Xunantunich, and were erected by more inclusive groups of lesser royalty and nobility (e.g., Martin and Grube 2000). Chan's two late uncarved stelae seem to represent the furthest extension of this process of appropriation and emulation as even smaller nonroyal centers were able to usurp the original symbols of the divine kings for their own purposes.

By the Early Postclassic period, scant populations of farmers were living in scattered farmsteads across the Belize Valley, as a few were living in the vicinity of what used to be the Chan community. Only one community, Tipu, along the Macal River, is known to have had substantial Postclassic occupation in the upper Belize Valley at this time (see figure 5.1). Chan is unlikely to have been a full-scale community in the Postclassic. Although Xunantunich had been a mighty power during the Late Classic, when the Belize Valley's remaining Postclassic farmers chose a location to revere their ancestors they chose Chan, not the Late Classic hilltop center of Xunantunich (Robin, Meierhoff, Kestle, et al. 2012). Belize Valley residents deposited two Early Postclassic caches that continued to consecrate the center of the Chan community through their material form on each of the two mosaic altars associated with the Structure 1 shrine (Kosakowsky et al. 2012). The caches were well equipped and contained incense burners, figurines, jade beads and chunks, and an entire necklace of eleven *Spondylus* shell beads. People were also using the West Plaza at this time (Cap 2012).

Comparably, the only location where Postclassic farmers went to perform rituals around Xunantunich was Group E, an important Preclassic ritual center east and downhill from the Late Classic hilltop polity capital (Brown 2010). Considering the location of Postclassic ritual around Xunantunich, Brown suggests that the choice of Group E as the focus of Early Postclassic ritual rather than the hilltop polity capital may have been a conscious rejection of the ideologies that Late Classic Xunantunich represented. It seems too that Postclassic ritual at Chan venerated what was enduring about human societies, not what was grand. In a distant realm, after the fall of the Zapotec capital of Monte Alban in Oaxaca, Mexico, commoners reused elite monuments in their house construction and even, in one case, ground corn on a stela fragment that depicted the face of a Late Classic king, suggesting that they too were rejecting earlier ideas of Zapotec kingship (Joyce and Weller 2007). These cases illustrate how some of the ordinary people living across Mesoamerica responded to the collapse of institutions of kingship.

By the Early Postclassic period, farming communities and civic-centers alike in the upper Belize Valley had largely been abandoned. The promise that the Belize Valley had held for centuries, of expanding farming populations and rising and declining civic-centers, was no longer what it used to be. For two thousand years, farming communities such as Chan and civic-centers such as Actuncan, Buenavista, Cahal Pech, Guacamayo, Las Ruinas, and Xunantunich had been enmeshed in complex and overlapping relationships of influence and authority and in something larger than their own history: the constitution of an upper Belize Valley society. The reason people left the upper Belize Valley does not appear to be environmental; certainly at Chan the mature forest still thrived (Lentz et al. 2012). Changes were afoot in Maya society that were bigger than communities, large and small, in the upper Belize Valley, indeed, bigger than the upper Belize Valley itself. Traditional seats of power in the Maya lowlands had collapsed, and new seats of power were being established in other parts of the Maya world. Residents of the Belize Valley once again voted with their feet, this time largely leaving the upper Belize Valley region and moving elsewhere.

Conclusion: Daily Practices of Social and Environmental Sustainability

For two millennia Chan was home to a diverse array of ancient Maya people from farmers to craft producers, diviners, and community leaders. Exploring residents' everyday lives reveals a socially, politically, intellectually, and technologically vibrant community that researchers might not have initially envisioned, given the scale of architecture and settlement at Chan. Chan's residents innovated conservation-wise agricultural technologies and forest management strategies. A mature, closed-canopy, tropical forest maintenance strategy, terracing to avoid erosion and maximize water infiltration, knowledge of sustainable agriculture established over centuries and passed down generation after generation, and the use of local resources are some of the environmentally effective strategies developed by Chan's farmers and local craft producers that enabled the community to endure. The type of sustainable forest management practiced at Chan is distinct from the more extractive practices of Tikal's elites, who culled the last mature *Manilkara zapota* from the forest around AD 741 (Lentz and Hockaday 2009).

Across Chan, from the homes of the humblest residents to those of community leaders and within the community center, residents developed community-focused ritual practices and heterarchical social and political strategies. Residents developed a popular religion that included many elements that elites later incorporated into state-level religious practices, such as the veneration of ancestors and the revisitation of their graves, an understanding of the order and organization of the Maya cosmos involving interrelated concepts of cardinal directionality and coloration that had both divine and worldly political implications, and the sanctification of homes and communities as central places in the Maya world and cosmology through the incorporation of green objects. But other aspects of social, political, and religious practices that people developed at Chan were not broadly adopted by the upper echelons of Maya society: the Classic period group-oriented political strategies practiced at Chan were distinct from the more hierarchical rule of the Classic Maya divine kings, and only later in time did they become a more prevalent political strategy across Maya society. Avoidance of extremes of wealth and power, maintenance of good health, avoidance of exclusionary ritual and political practices, feasting, community-wide ceremonies, and reasonably equitable distributions of exotic items are some of the socially effective strategies that enabled Chan's farmers to establish a long-lived community.

Major centers in the Belize River valley, such as the polity capital of Xunantunich, may have been impressive in their time but had rising and falling political histories. In contrast to the forest maintenance practices at Chan and the consistent health of community residents across its two-thousand-year history, at Tikal in Guatemala—one of the largest and most opulent Maya civic-centers, with hierarchical political institutions and the most inequitable distribution of wealth—poor health and deforestation mark the end of the Classic period.

From a traditional archaeological perspective, Chan would be considered a minor center, unremarkable in terms of size and architectural elaboration. Its residents would be classified as occupying a lower stratum of Maya society, people who certainly had less privilege and possessions than did society's power brokers. There is absolutely nothing inaccurate about this characterization of Chan and its residents. But missing from such a characterization of Chan is any exploration of the everyday lives of its residents. In the absence of studies of everyday life at Chan, it would be possible to assume that its residents were simply an underclass oppressed by the state and that the community had little role to play in the broader developments of Maya society. But actively exploring the everyday lives of Chan's residents across its two-thousand-year history and comparing the community's longevity and its social and environmental strategies with those of the much more opulent centers, with their monumental temple-pyramids and palaces and waxing and waning political histories, reveals how erroneous such a perspective can be. There is a richness of life that can be found within everyday life in even a smaller, "poorer" community, and the innovations developed there can greatly affect society. In the end, some of the most important lessons about human societies and the importance of social and economic sustainability may be learned by exploring everyday life in a seemingly unremarkable place such as Chan.

7 ❋ Why Everyday Life at Chan Matters

In chapter 6 I lay out what everyday life was like at Chan for its myriad residents. Understanding the technical and religious innovations, social and environmental sustainability, and political strategies developed by Chan's residents across their daily lives illustrates the kinds of significant insights into human society that would be missed without a lens focused on studying everyday life. In this chapter I explore how everyday life at Chan relates back to broader questions in archaeology, anthropology, and indeed across the social sciences. Understanding the intricacies of everyday life and addressing broader theoretical concerns about human societies are not mutually exclusive exercises; in fact, as I argue in this chapter, failure to take everyday life into account in the development of theoretical models of human societies leads to a silencing of the very people whose lives researchers are attempting to theorize, particularly a silencing of the lives of ordinary people in the past. Developing a critical understanding of farmers' everyday lives at Chan challenges researchers to rethink and to reformulate a wide range of anthropological theories about the constitution of human societies and the nature of human agency and to consider a greater role for ordinary people in the past. The explorations of everyday life at Chan undertaken in chapter 6 prompt the revision of prominent anthropological concepts, such as the role of population pressure and state control in the emergence of intensive agriculture; the relationship between ideology, false consciousness, and power; the nature of political economies; and the relationship between cities and rural producers. By comparing and contrasting the Chan study to archaeological models of farmers in complex societies that do not consider everyday life, I illustrate how archaeologists' models of the past may be flawed when researchers fail to take everyday life into account.

Population Pressure and State Control in the Emergence of Intensive Agriculture

Although the subjects of wide-ranging critique, the pioneering ideas of Ester Boserup and Karl Wittfogel remain as much discussed today as they were half a century ago (Fedick 1995; Marcus and Stanish 2006). The work of economist Ester Boserup (1965) in *The Conditions of Agricultural Growth: The Economics of Agrarian Change under Population Pressure* furthers the idea that farmers will undertake labor-intensive agricultural techniques only under the duress of expanding populations. The work of historian Karl Wittfogel (1957) in *Oriental Despotism: A Comparative Study of Total Power* concludes that centralized bureaucratic control and technological knowledge are required for the construction of large-scale irrigation works for intensive agricultural systems. In Boserup's and Wittfogel's model, traditional farmers' daily agricultural production is unchanging, based on rudimentary techniques and extensive production. Intensive agriculture involving more complex technologies and greater labor investment emerges only because of forces external to farmers' everyday lives, such as population pressure or state control.

Boserup's critical intervention into the study of agriculture growth is to interrogate a simple and undeniable equation: when there are more people, they will need more food. This remains the lasting contribution of Boserup's work and a raison d'être for the enduring nature of her research: there is a relationship between population growth and food production. At issue with Boserup's work is that she sees a single, unilinear, causal relationship between population growth and agricultural intensification, not the potential for multiple, historically and contextually situated relationships between the two.

Prior to Boserup's work, prevailing scholarship on the development of agricultural intensification followed the work of Thomas Malthus (1798), who posited the converse relationship between population growth and agricultural intensification: as people innovated new technologies and increased production, population growth became possible. For Boserup, the opposite is the case: as populations rise, there are new pressures placed on the natural environment. In order to maintain an adequate food supply, people must respond by intensifying their agricultural production; thus, "necessity is the mother of invention." When populations are low, agricultural production will be extensive and involve low labor inputs, such as in slash-and-burn agriculture, in which farmers rotate fields after each crop cycle and allow fallowing to restore fertility. Following an evolutionary progression, only when population pressure demands, will agricultural intensification happen.

For Malthus, war, disease, natural disasters, and so on were what would keep population expansion in check, leading to a very pessimistic view of the future of humanity and the implications of the human innovations that lead to population expansion. Boserup's inversion provided an alternative and optimistic outlook: new innovations in agricultural intensification could provide solutions for increasing world populations (Wilk 1996: 602; Wyatt 2008a: 16).

For Wittfogel, the prime mover driving agricultural intensification was state control rather than population pressure. Drawing on the work of Karl Marx, he believed that there were two modes of production: an Asiatic mode of production developed around large-scale irrigation works, which required centralized management and forced labor and resulted in the highly centralized and despotic Oriental states; and the contrasting Western mode of production in which authority was traditionally decentralized, leading to the development of industrial capitalism. The Asiatic mode of production was not characteristic of all Oriental societies, nor was it exclusive to Oriental societies: Wittfogel listed ancient Egypt, Mesopotamia, India, China, the Aztec Empire, and the Inca Empire among hydraulic civilizations. He theorized that ancient civilizations developed through the use of managerial control and forced labor in large-scale irrigation projects, which required an organizational hierarchy and governmental control. Wittfogel was also aware that despotic societies could develop in the absence of large-scale irrigation projects because he considered Russia to be an example of a despotic society, and Russian agriculture is not hydraulic. To resolve this issue, he created different types of despotic societies. Marginal-type hydraulic societies develop in the geographical periphery of a hydraulic zone through the diffusion of despotic strategies. Wittfogel considered the ancient Maya a marginal-type hydraulic society because their agricultural systems did not include large-scale irrigation works but they were located in the geographical periphery of a later hydraulic society: the Aztecs. Wittfogel's work lacked archaeological investigation into the ancient civilizations he discussed that could demonstrate a correlation between the development of large-scale irrigation projects and despotism. Among the early criticisms of *Oriental Despotism* (1957), Robert McCormick Adams (1966) in *The Evolution of Urban Society: Early Mesopotamia and Prehispanic Mexico* used archaeological data from ancient civilizations to illustrate that large-scale irrigation was not a primary cause of political coercion.

As Andrew Wyatt's research on Chan's agricultural terraces (discussed in chapter 6) illustrates, the correlates of Boserup's and Wittfogel's models do not apply in the case of agricultural intensification at Chan. The Preclassic development of terrace agriculture at Chan preceded periods of population expansion and the development of a regional state at Xunantunich. Terrace agriculture at Chan was a local development by farmers to manage production in hilly terrain, avoid soil erosion, and maximize water infiltration. This knowledge of sustainable agriculture established over the centuries and passed down generation after generation is one of the means through which Chan's residents sustained their community for two thousand years. The Chan case illustrates what is absent from Boserup's and Wittfogel's theories on the development of intensive agriculture: the everyday lives of farmers and a consideration of local ingenuity.

Chan's farmers certainly do not represent all farmers (even within the Belize Valley itself, as also discussed in chapter 6). History and prehistory show a range of ways in which farmers, intensification, population increases, and the state may interact (Marcus and Stanish 2006). Neither are Chan's farmers unique in terms of their local development of intensive agriculture and ability to effect communities and society through farmwork (e.g., Bradley 2005; Erickson 1993, 2006; Fedick 1994; A. Joyce 2010; Robb 2007; Rodríguez 2006; Sheets 2002; Walker 2011). What farmers or others do across their everyday lives has an effect on the formation of their societies, for people are not simply the outcome of expanding populations or state demands.

Still, agricultural developments at Chan were not isolated from increasing populations and the rise of states, illustrating the enduring aspects of Boserup's and Wittfogel's ideas just noted: there are relationships among population, states, and agriculture, just not single, unilinear, and causal relationships. At Chan's population peak in the Late Classic, terrace agriculture concomitantly reached its maximum level of expansion

(Wyatt 2008a, 2008b, 2012), and there was the greatest amount of forest clearance in terms of local hardwood trees at that time (Lentz et al. 2012). As population increased and land clearance for agricultural and construction projects increased, Chan's farmers faced new dilemmas about how to balance forest management and expanding agricultural projects and construction demands. While I do not know precisely what forest management strategies Chan's farmers chose, I do know that those strategies allowed the mature, tropical forest to continue to thrive; thus, these forest management strategies were apparently not shared by residents living in larger Maya cities such as Tikal. Chan's period of greatest population and agricultural expansion was also concurrent with the rise of the polity capital of Xunantunich. Xunantunich certainly would have attempted to extract tribute in the form of agriculture from Chan, and I will leave the broader discussion of tribute relationships between Chan and Xunantunich for the end of this chapter. Were Chan's farmers exploited by Xunantunich, agricultural production would have been their weakness, but it is also possible that their long-term agricultural production provided a constraint with which the emerging polity capital had to reckon, and it is the latter situation that best fits the Chan case. As populations expand and states emerge, there are greater needs for food, and these certainly affect agricultural production and the political and economic positions of farmers in society. But these relationships are neither singular, causal, nor unilinear. In any rethinking of theories of the development of intensive agriculture, the Chan data demand the inclusion of an important third variable: local ingenuity alongside population pressure and state demands. Incorporating a concern for understanding local ingenuity puts everyday life, people, and agency back into anthropological models of the development of intensive agriculture and avoids unilinear and causal explanations.

Ideology, False Consciousness, and Power

Concepts of ideology and false consciousness articulated by Karl Marx and Friedrich Engels ([1932] 1970) in *The German Ideology* and later developed by Louis Althusser (1971) and Antonio Gramsci (1971) posit that ideological knowledge is created by dominant groups to support their position in society. Because ordinary people are mystified and lack the knowledge to critically assess the dominant ideology, it is imposed on their consciousness and they become a complicit, unquestioning mass. This set of ideas, commonly referred to as the dominant ideology thesis, attempts to free power from necessarily involving coercive force (e.g., Abercrombie et al. 1980; Blackmore 2011; Lohse 2007; Scott 1985).

Marx and Engels ([1932] 1970) define the dominant ideology as elites' conscious management of worldviews to enforce their own self-interests. Through the concept of false consciousness, a society's dominant ideology hides the self-interests of dominators from duped subordinates. Gramsci (1971) incorporates the idea of a false consciousness produced by great men into his concept of hegemony. Hegemony is the inalienable ability of the dominant group to control other groups. Through the existence of false consciousness, the dominant group does not need coercive force to exert control. Within hegemony, the dominant ideology is impenetrable by subordinate groups, who are therefore condemned to support and reproduce it. While hegemony is a social construct, only knowledgeable elites have the capacity to create or modify it.

As I discuss in chapter 2, James Scott (1985: 314–50) uses everyday life research to directly confront Gramsci's notions of hegemony, which Scott feels is quite dangerous for studies of class relations. To assume that dominant classes can and do impose their visions of the social order on the consciousness of others who are mystified and passively comply with the means of their domination denies the existence of enforcement, coercion, and sanctions in legitimating class relations. Are subordinate people really dupes and dopes who do not understand the conditions of their domination? Scott's work on the everyday lives of Malaysian peasants indicates that peasants (not surprisingly) could comprehend what was going on in the world around them and recognized the inequalities in their society. Coercion of some kind is indeed needed to enforce inequality.

Certainly the research on Chan's farmers reveals a comparable situation: ancient farmers were neither dupes nor dopes. The Chan data illustrates that complex ideational knowledge was initially developed in the homes and communities of farmers, dating back to the Middle Preclassic period (also see Lucero 2010, McAnany 2004, and Walker and Lucero 2000 for comparable evidence across the Maya area for ordinary people's production of complex ideational knowledge and Bradley 2005 for a comparable example from prehistoric Europe). This "popular religion" was only later adopted by society's ruling class and elevated to a "state religion." The dominant ideology, then, was not impenetrable to the ordinary

Maya person, who had the knowledge to critically assess it. The everyday lives of ordinary people can be a fertile ground for the development of complex ideational knowledge that may later in time be incorporated into dominant ideologies.

In a comparable vein, Elizabeth Brumfiel (1996) explores whether residents of Xaltocan in central Mexico who were conquered by the Aztecs passively accepted the dominant ideology of the Aztec state. Looking at figurines used at Xaltocan before and after the Aztec conquest, she sees no appropriation of Aztec ideology. Here again people are not dopes or dupes but have the means to assess dominant ideologies (also see Joyce and Weller 2007 for a Zapotec example).

A critical shortcoming of the dominant ideology thesis, as seen at Chan and other ancient cases, is its assumption that ordinary people do not have the will or intellectual capacity to assess dominant ideologies, a position that Scott (1985) and Abercrombie and colleagues (1980) also take to task with contemporary data. Such a position arises because of a misunderstanding of the role of everyday life in the formation of higher knowledge. Assuming that such knowledge arises beyond the domain of everyday life and is the purview of only certain people or institutions in society leads to the assumption that ordinary people across their everyday lives cannot comprehend higher knowledge. Recognizing that higher knowledge is developed within everyday life allows for the possibility that the masses can understand, see through, and potentially contest dominant ideologies. The most dangerous aspect of the dominant ideology thesis is that it denies the existence of enforcement, coercion, and sanctions in legitimating class relations. Power is precisely what is missing from the dominant ideology thesis. If researchers seek to understand why inequalities exist in society, they must understand the power relationships through which certain groups assert and maintain their claims to superiority and the channels that may be open to challenge these claims: avoiding power does not help researchers get any closer to understanding the operation of inequality in society.

Political, Domestic, and Moral Economies

Humans are continually involved in the busy nature of everyday economic activities. In its broadest definition, a political economic approach seeks to understand the relationship between politics and economics in human societies. The anthropological concept of political economy can be traced back to the writings of Karl Marx, who drew on the work of Adam Smith (*An Inquiry into the Nature and Causes of the Wealth of Nations*, 1776). Marx and Smith were interested in understanding the economic means through which wealth was controlled and inequalities emerged in state-level societies. Archaeologists and anthropologists have modified the term to embrace the intersection of political and economic practices across all societies (e.g., Brumfiel and Earle 1987; Johnson and Earle 1987; Roseberry 1989). Some researchers envision the political economy operating at the suprahousehold level in economic exchanges between households and contrast this with a domestic economy, what households do for themselves (e.g., D'Altroy and Hastorf 2001; Earle 2002; Johnson and Earle 1987), although others disagree with this distinction (e.g., Hirth 1996; Michael Smith 2004). The latter position resonates with an understanding of political and economic relationships derived from the Chan study, where what households produced and consumed for themselves operated in political ways as much as did the exchanges between households. This also meshes with the feminist, household, and consumption literature discussed in chapters 2 and 3, which expose the political nature of mundane acts such as eating, consuming, and provisioning oneself. Domestic economies are political.

The political economy can also refer to a process of extraction, exchange, or mobilization of surplus from households used to finance societal institutions (Johnson and Earle 1987). In this way the political economy is associated with processes of wealth accumulation that promote inequality that lead to the evolution of ranking, complexity, and states. Types of political economies that operate by extracting surplus from households to promote inequality include patron-client systems, staple finance systems, wealth finance systems, tribute systems, and so on. Hirth (1996) criticizes archaeological approaches to political economy that subsume discussion within a broader project of understanding the evolution of complex societies rather than focusing on defining the nature and components of prehistoric political economies. Political economic approaches that focus on the process of extracting surplus also draw attention to the agency of elites as those people who extract surplus and shape society over the agency of ordinary people (Erickson 2006).

Less discussed in the archaeological literature is the moral economy (but see González-Ruibal 2011). Moral economies involve economic transactions that are mutually beneficial across groups and promote collective well-being over individual wealth because they rely on a moral character rather than individual self-interest. Political economies generate inequality and moral economies promote equality. The term *moral economy* can be traced to the works of Marxist historian E. P. Thompson (1971) and political scientist James Scott (1976). Although the term *moral economy* has not seen great resonance in archaeology, Blanton and colleagues' (1996) distinction between individual-centered and group-oriented political strategies (discussed in chapter 6) and Crumley's (1995) concepts of hierarchy and heterarchy encapsulate parallel concerns.

Like the political economy, the moral economy was initially defined in reference to Western capitalism and its transformation of feudalist economic systems, particularly in relation to working-class or peasant groups who resisted unequal treatment in initial or later stages of capitalist systems. But as with the political economy, it is more broadly applicable across societies. E. P. Thompson used the term in relation to understanding eighteenth-century food riots in England as society transitioned from feudalism to capitalism. The communal moral systems of just prices for bread under feudalism eroded with the development of capitalism, and peasants rioted at what they saw as an injustice. Moral economic studies of later capitalist societies, for which the concept has also been deployed, have been critiqued for focusing too heavily on the role of nonmarket "moral" principles in modern societies in which markets and market economic principles are inescapably a part of people's daily lives.

While some scholars define the political economy and the moral economy as two opposing types of economies, other scholars who draw on the broad definition of political economy as the relationship between economics and politics in society see moral economies as another form of political economy or a form of political and economic relationships that advance morality over self-interest (e.g., Best and Paterson 2010; Munro 1998), and even other scholars have adopted the term *politico-moral economy* to indicate that both political and moral reasoning can take place in economic transactions (e.g., Bredel 2007).

Chan's economy, particularly during the Classic period—with its lesser degree of social stratification, more equitable distribution of wealth objects, and maintenance of forest and human health—does seem closer to a moral economy than a political economy (defining these terms in an oppositional way). But at the same time, political economic strategies were in operation at Chan as leaders accumulated relatively more wealth than others, and Chan's economy certainly operated within a broader Maya economy that highlighted principles of extenuating inequality. While political and moral economies are typically considered to be opposing types of economies, an appropriate way to rethink these concepts is to see them as contrasting strategies that can be in operation (and in tension) in any society rather than differing types of economies into which societies need to be categorized. Exploring the implications of political economic interactions that promote equality, as well as those that create inequality, and understanding the politics of domestic economies will be important in future archaeological research.

Cities and Rural Producers

Archaeologists and anthropologists have long recognized that farmers and the relationships between rural producers and cities are critical to studies of complex societies (e.g., Adams 1966; Kroeber 1948; Redfield 1941; Redman 1978; Trigger 1972; Wolf 1955). Rural producers are critical to the development of complex societies because they produce the agricultural surpluses that allow for the development and promotion of the quintessential human achievement—states and their constituent cities and elites.

Despite, or perhaps because of, this recognized importance, early researchers focused on the humdrum nature of everyday life in farming communities and the susceptibility of farmers' agricultural production to elite extraction and exploitation, which led to rural farmers being viewed as a timeless and unchanging mass who played little role in the innovations and changes in their societies. The innovations in technology, religion, and politics within the Chan community stand in sharp contrast to a position that posits that society's greatest advancements come from its cities and elites.

In Redfield's pioneering discussions of the rural-urban continuum, the "little community" of peasant studies was a homogeneous community of self-sufficient agricultural producers (Redfield 1960). With farmers dependent on the necessities of agricultural production, the unchanging nature of everyday life in the peasant farming community is what promotes its ability to be a type of community that exists through time and around the world. Because of the homogeneity of everyday life in a "little community," a researcher can study a small part of it to ascertain the whole: "A compact community of four thousand people in Indian Latin-America can be studied by making direct personal acquaintance with one section of it" (Redfield 1960: 4). This methodology is theoretically self-fulfilling, for if researchers explore only one portion of a community and assume that portion to be representative of the whole community, then homogeneity is a given. Redfield's American structural-functionalist methodological approach is comparable to Lévi-Strauss's French structuralist methodological approach to research, which could involve "'just a quarter of an hour alone' with a man from a distinct or extinct culture" (Lefebvre [1958] 2008: 7), a poignant subject of critique in Lefebvre's *Critique of Everyday Life* (as discussed in chapter 2). In archaeology, the question of how to study a representative sample of a community was a key question of processual archaeology in its development of sampling strategies (e.g., Flannery 1976), as well as an aspect of postprocessual and feminist approaches that focus on understanding diversity (e.g., Brumfiel 1992; Conkey and Gero 1997; Johnson 2010a; Meskell and Preucel 2004). The sampling strategy I employed in excavating Chan (chapter 6) engages these concerns for attaining representative samples of the diversity within communities.

At the same time that archaeologists began questioning how to understand diversity in small communities, these questions were also being raised across social science and humanities disciplines. After growing up in a Welsh border village, when Marxist literary critic Raymond Williams began his academic career at Cambridge University he was struck by the images of rural life that filled the pages of academic literature. In *The Country and the City* (1973: 1) he demonstrates the deeply embedded assumptions about countries and cities that have developed across the history of Western thought, which he sums up as follows: "On the country has gathered the idea of a natural way of life: of peace, innocence, and a simple virtue. On the city has gathered the idea of an achieved center: of learning, communication, light. Powerful hostile associations have also developed: on the city as a place of noise, worldliness and ambition; on the country as a place of backwardness, ignorance, limitation. A contrast between country and city, as fundamental ways of life, reaches back into classical times."

Karl Marx's ([1869] 1963: 123–24) now-overcited commentary on nine-teenth-century French peasants, which does not fully capture Marx's per-spective on peasants, epitomizes the traditional peasant model:

> The small holding peasants form a vast mass, the members of which live in similar conditions but without entering into manifold rela-tions with one another. Their mode of production isolates them from one another instead of bringing them into mutual intercourse. . . . Their field of production, the small holding, admits of no division of labor in its cultivation, no application of science and, therefore, no diversity of development, no variety of talent, no wealth of social re-lationships. Each individual peasant family is almost self-sufficient; it itself directly produces the major part of its consumption and thus acquires its means of life more through exchange with nature than in intercourse with society. . . . In this way, the great mass of the French nation is formed by simple addition of homologous magni-tudes, much as potatoes in a sack form a sack of potatoes.

Because peasants produce their subsistence through their own labor as they work off of the land, they are characterized as simple folk, who live within nature and outside of the culture and changes ongoing in society.

To challenge the traditional peasant model, anthropologist Robert Netting in *Smallholders, Householders: Farm Families and the Ecology of Intensive, Sustainable Agriculture* (1993) reexamined contemporary agrar-ian communities practicing intensive agriculture across Africa, Asia, Eu-rope, and the Americas. These intensive agriculturalists are active and dynamic, existing and changing through their flexible and adaptive inno-vation of intensification strategies in relation to the different and changing political-economic systems within which they live (Netting 1993: 15, 330). Netting refers to these active and heterogeneous intensive agricultural-ists as smallholding farmers, to differentiate them from the traditionally defined passive and homogeneous peasants. Smallholding farmers are able to be active participants in their society because (1) they develop socioeconomically heterogeneous relations within and beyond their com-munity, (2) they utilize intensification to produce higher yields on small and/or marginal land plots, and (3) they also produce nonagricultural items for household, community, and/or extracommunity economies (Netting 1993: 12). Archaeologists who embrace the application of Netting's model to ancient agriculturalists, particularly those practicing intensive agriculture, are equally critical of the seemingly endless flexibility and adaptability of Netting's smallholding farmers, which appears to paint them into the opposite extreme of traditionally defined peasants (e.g., Erickson 2006: 253; Pyburn 1997, 1998). Researchers need to assess, not assume, how, when, and to what extent farmers had active and changing roles in their society. This implies methodological procedures that allow investigation of the range and variability in farming life in a community or society, procedures that are the opposite of those invoked by Redfield in his "little community" studies.

Anne Pyburn (1997, 1998) argues that Netting's work is particularly applicable for the ancient Maya who practiced intensive agriculture, as the archaeological data indicate for Chan. Chan's farmers do seem to fit the smallholder type better than they fit the peasant type, although as Chan's Early Postclassic disillusionment indicates, farmers' flexibility and adaptability was not endless. Changing economic strategies—developments in terms of religion and politics as well as agriculture and forest maintenance—defy a homogeneous and unchanging lifestyle at Chan and attest to the innovations and broader societal connections that were always part of life across the community.

Interpreting Maya Society and Ancient Societies in the Absence of Farmers' Everyday Lives

A substantial set of cross-temporal and cross-cultural archaeological case studies have now emerged documenting that ancient farming communities are socioeconomically heterogeneous, with innovative abilities for specialized production in agricultural and nonagricultural products, deeply engaged in the production of ideational knowledge, and active and integrated within their societies (e.g., Bradley 2005; Erickson 1993, 2006; Falconer 1995; Gonlin and Lohse 2007; A. Joyce 2010; A. Joyce et al. 2001; A. Joyce and Weller 2007; R. Joyce 1991; Kuijt 2000; Lohse and Valdez 2004; Marcus and Stanish 2006; McAnany 2004; Pyburn 1998; Robb 2007; Scarborough and Valdez 2009; Scarborough et al. 2003; Schwartz and Falconer 1994; Sheets 2002; Michael Smith 1994; Stein 1999, 2002; Walker 2011; Wattenmaker 1998). Given this preponderance of research, it should be that the traditional peasant model is little more than part of the intellectual history of the field, as most would argue. But the host of

assumptions about cities and countrysides that Raymond Williams identifies as being so deeply ingrained in Western literature and art leads to
a persistence of traditional peasant models even as researchers attempt
to eschew these ideas through empirical studies. Persistent assumptions
about farmers still haunt archaeological research in the form of assumptions about innate elite control and commoner subordination that are
implicit in models of agricultural intensification, ideology and power,
and rational political economies. And herein lies the Trojan horse, even
though anthropologists and archaeologists no longer embrace a traditional peasant model: assumptions about farmers' everyday lives originally formulated in the traditional peasant model underlie models that researchers continue to draw upon. This problem resonates with questions
of evidential reasoning and evidential constraint discussed by Wylie and
explored in chapter 4. I develop this point further in this section.

While single, unilinear, and causal equations between population pressure, state control, and intensive agriculture have rarely been documented
in empirical archaeological research in the ancient world (e.g., Adams
1966; Erickson 1993; Fedick 1994, 1996; Morrison 1996; Pyburn 1998;
Renfrew and Bahn 2005: 165; Scarborough 1998), theoretical models of
ancient state societies continue to posit elite interests and/or population
pressure as driving forces in the development of intensive agriculture and
the development of states (e.g., Blanton et al. 1996; Conrad and Demarest 1984; Johnson and Earle 1987; Kolata 1993, 1996, 2002; Redman 1999;
Stanish 2006; see Erickson 2006 for a more comprehensive discussion).
Whether archaeologists acknowledge the intellectual legacies of Boserup
and Wittfogel in their work or they do not, this has also been the case in
Maya archaeology (e.g., Abrams 1995; Adams and Culbert 1977; LeCount
and Yaeger 2010; Leventhal and Ashmore 2004; Neff 2010; Schortman
2010; Turner 1978, 1983; see Wyatt 2012 for a more comprehensive discussion). Morrison (1996) refers to the unexamined aspects of Boseru-
pian theory that pervade archaeological discussions as an archaeological
dogma. Indeed, Wittfogelian ideas are implicated in political economic
perspectives that posit elite forces as the prime movers in the development of state societies (Erickson 2006). Boserup's and Wittfogel's theories
are not simply about the development of intensive agriculture; they have
implications for the development of state societies and for the specific,
hierarchical, and unequal power relationships between elites and commoners that allow elites to engineer state societies and exploit farmers.

Working within this intellectual tradition in Maya archaeology, Abrams (1995) and Neff (2010) apply ideas from Wittfogel and Boserup to understand the relationship between agricultural intensification, the development of states, and elite-commoner power struggles in the Copan and Xunantunich areas. Neff's work explores settlement survey data from the Xunantunich region that includes the communities of Chan, Dos Chombitos, Succotz, and Callar Creek (see figure 5.1 for community locations). He generates labor value estimates and population estimates from the settlement survey data and uses these to examine how population growth and labor value affect the relationship between rulers and farmers. He concludes that by the late Late Classic period, particularly in areas of high population, there was a drop in agricultural labor value in the Xunantunich area, leading to a situation in which rulers were able to exploit agricultural workers. LeCount and Yaeger (2010: 345) draw upon Neff's work to illustrate that in the late Late Classic Xunantunich area "the labor value of hinterland farmers was decreasing, leaving them in a weaker position to negotiate their places in the local and regional relationships of the polity's political economy." Schortman (2010: 371–74) further explores the implications of Neff's model by using it to suggest that Xunantunich's royals may have been able to fund their rise to power through a program of staple finance (a system in which rulers extract food and other items from subjects and use these as rewards [D'Altroy and Earle 1985]). Xunantunich's royals accomplished this by developing terrace agricultural systems, establishing exclusive claims to those lands, and encouraging a compliant immigrant population of tribute payers to settle and work the terraced fields. "Terracing slopes that, presumably, had been marginal to earlier subsistence systems was an effective way to create new lands devoted to funding novel, overarching political institutions. . . . Such vulnerability to state demands would have only been exacerbated by the increasingly unfavorable labor imbalances outlined by Neff" (Schortman 2010: 371–72).

A model of decreasing labor values works only if the population estimates and labor value estimates entered into the model are correct. If populations were lower or ancient labor values were higher than the model estimates, the model would generate the opposite conclusion: that there was an increase in agricultural labor value in the late Late Classic, leading to a situation in which farmers had greater leverage with rulers.[1]

While arguments could be made endlessly about the parameters of a model, the value of a model is in its application to archaeological data. As LeCount and Yaeger (2010: 354) note, one of the implications of a model of decreasing labor values is that "state polities may have been more coerce [sic] in areas of highest density and, conversely, more cajoling in parts of the valley that exhibited less explosive growth." Chan is the ideal place to test this hypothesis because it is located in the area where the highest mound densities have been identified in the Xunantunich region (Yaeger 2010: table 11.1). If the model is correct, Chan's farmers would have been the most coerced and exploited of farmers in the Xunantunich vicinity. The data on everyday life at Chan presented in this book do not fit the model: Chan's small-scale farmers were comparably well-off in the region in terms of both well-being (as measured though human health, forest health, and lesser degrees of intracommunity social stratification) and material possessions (as measured through access to exotic items relative to higher-status members of their own community and comparable-status members of neighboring communities).

A central part of the decreasing labor value model is not just state exploitation of farmers but the means of that exploitation: as they accept gifts in the form of luxury items from Xunantunich's rulers, leaders of farming communities in turn collect tribute in the form of foodstuffs for Xunantunich's rulers from the farmers in their communities (Neff 2010: 266). Given a paucity of prestige items identified at Xunantunich relative to powerful civic-centers in the Maya area (Jamison 2010; LeCount 2010), Schortman (2010: 373) suggests that "the role of wealth finance, therefore, in encouraging resettlement and directing agricultural labor among all population segments remains unclear." Only thirteen pieces of jade or jadeite were identified in forty-three caches and burials excavated at Xunantunich's civic-center, and most of these predated Xunantunich's peak in power in the late Late Classic period or were undated (Jamison 2010: 138–39, table 6.1, 6.2). Three additional pieces of jade were identified at the nonroyal elite residential group (Group D) connected by a causeway to the Xunantunich civic-center (J. Braswell 1998). Only three palace-school vases were identified at Xunantunich, suggesting that that community's rulers had a "tenuous place on the political landscape of the eastern Petén" (LeCount 2010). Obsidian sourcing at Chan (as discussed in chapter 6) additionally suggests that gifts from Xunantunich's royals were not the source of exotic Pachuca obsidian at Chan, which comes from a source 1,070 kilometers distant from the community (Meierhoff et al.

2012). Pachuca obsidian has not been identified at Xunantunich, while it has been identified at other Belize Valley civic-centers such as Buenavista and Cahal Pech as well as smaller communities such as San Lorenzo and Chaa Creek. Chan's leaders seem to have acquired their Pachuca obsidian through long-standing ties with other neighboring centers or even centers beyond the Belize Valley, rather than through Xunantunich.

At Chan, when only Late to Terminal Classic deposits are considered (because these are the time periods most comparable to those of the rise and fall of the hilltop capital of Xunantunich), 3 pieces of jade or jade-ite were found in twenty-nine ritual deposits and burials in the Central Group, 7 were associated with head families in the Northeast group, and 3 were associated with small farming households. No palace-school vases were identified at Chan (Kosakowsky 2012). While jade is scarcer at Chan's Central Group than at the hilltop center of Xunantunich in these periods, with 0.1 jade pieces per offering or burial at Chan compared to 0.3 at Xunantunich, these differences are not as pronounced as might be expected between a polity capital and a farming community. Late Classic burial 196 at the capital of Tikal, one of the most elaborate Maya burials identified, contained 40 ceramic vessels, 11 jade items (including an entire jade bead necklace, wristlet, and jade and shell belt), and 4 pyrite plaques, among other shell, bone, wood, alabaster, pearl, hematite, and cinnabar items. This perhaps indicates the difficulty that all residents of the peripheral Belize Valley area, from royals to farmers, had in acquiring jade in the politically turbulent Late Classic period.

The paucity of prestige items at Xunantunich leads Schortman (2010: 374) to question "how commoner compliance with elite demands was rewarded." He asks a series of questions: "Might the rewards for service have been more direct? Were the supposed immigrants former residents of neighboring areas who were landless and desperately in need of sustenance? Could these movements have been instigated by those seeking protection in unsettled times, Xunantunich's magnates offering shelter from the political storms sweeping the Maya lowlands during the seventh and eighth centuries?" (Schortman 2010: 373). Given a lack of fit between the model and the archaeological evidence, Schortman suggests that future research should consider looking for new lines of evidence that could support the model. But at what point have researchers collected enough archaeological evidence to consider revising or rejecting a model rather than looking for further evidence to support a model? This is precisely what is at stake for Wylie in evidential reasoning and evidential constraint (see chapter 4). Researchers must maintain a constant interplay between theory and evidence and triangulate back and forth between multiple lines of evidence and prior models. If theory does not stand alone as an abstraction, as the everyday life thinkers argue, and it is deeply implicated in what data researchers bring to it, then researchers must be able to determine when their evidence is sufficient to use to re-enter into a dialogue with prior models and reformulate them based on new evidence.

Eric Wolf's (1955) distinction between open and closed communities suggests that if farming community leaders were being drawn into a highly stratified system of kingship in which rulers coerced local leaders who coerced farmers, then researchers would expect to see high degrees of social stratification at Chan and a growing distinction between leaders and the led. Wolf further posits that the organization of a farming community thus exploited (open communities) would come to mirror that of the state and diverge from preexisting community orders. But the late Late Classic Chan community was not marked by high degrees of social stratification. A deep history of ancestor veneration was maintained, and heterarchy—not hierarchy—best exemplifies the sociopolitical organization of the community. Although Chan does appear to have heightened its internal economic production in the Late and Terminal Classic periods, which would have allowed the community to buffer itself from outside demands, it does not fit Wolf's classic definition of a closed community, because the Late and Terminal Classic were also periods of heightened external relations (as seen through the importation of non-Guatemalan obsidian and finished marine shell ornaments) and at all points in Chan's history the community engaged the broader political economy of Maya society. The lack of fit between Late and Terminal Classic developments at Chan and that of an open community further highlights the problems in applying the exploited farmer model to the Chan case.

Unlike the major centers of Tikal or Copan, Xunantunich itself did not attract a large settlement in the Late Classic (Yaeger 2010: table 11.1). This is an intriguing settlement pattern, because neighboring communities such as Chan did attract larger populations at this time. Perhaps this settlement data along with the paucity of prestige goods found at Xunantunich and its short political history indicate that Xunantunich's rulers failed to collect sizable tribute from surrounding populations and thus were unable to amass great wealth, attract a large populace to their city, or assert their authority for a sustained period of time. Perhaps Chan's leaders and the farmers they represented had amassed a type of wealth that cannot be measured in terms of the quantity of luxury items and the size and elaboration of houses but should instead be measured through long-term personal ties to people and places: something that people today often capture with the expression "quality of life." This local "wealth" may have provided a formidable constraint on the policies of Xunantunich's rulers.

At the heart of this discussion is a question about how to model tribute. Could Xunantunich's rulers have demanded tribute from places like Chan, or were material goods and labor offered more voluntarily? While Spanish colonial documents about the Postclassic period do not represent Classic period systems, in the *Relaciones Histórico-geográficas de la Gobernación de Yucatán* (de la Garza et al. 1983), Late Postclassic tribute arrangements vary considerably. "Historiographical concerns aside, sometimes tribute was small and almost voluntary, at tribute payers' volition and only what they wanted or managed to give" (Jeff Buechler, personal communication 2010; also see Foias 2002: 226–27).[2] Chan's local "wealth" may have enabled the community to set its own standards for tribute payment as other Maya communities were able to do later in time.

The archaeological data from Chan turn the model of exploited farmers on its head: the exploited farmers seem to have had quite a bit of wealth and power. Chan's residents developed a range of local production, manipulated local resources, and perhaps even played off competing Belize Valley powers. Because of this, Xunantunich was unable to dominate resources and production and thereby predetermine a network of dependency (also see Schortman and Urban 1992, 1994 for a comparable example of interactions between the less complex non-Maya peoples in the Naco Valley of Honduras and their more complex Maya neighbors). As this discussion illustrates, "peopling the past is a radical alternative to viewing farmers as faceless masses, the passive recipients of what the elite impose on them through direct coercion or state ideology" (Erickson 2006: 253).

From the perspective of Chan looking out onto Maya society, the powerful polity capital of Xunantunich appears to have been caught in a double bind of constraint. At the regional level, Xunantunich rose to power at the end of the Late Classic period, a period during which the system of divine kingship that its leaders had adopted was weakening and the powerful

Petén polities of its patrons such as Naranjo were experiencing politically tumultuous times and declining. At the local level, Xunantunich was situated in a provincial part of the Maya world, one with a long history of interacting centers. None of the upper Belize Valley's major centers other than Xunantunich had forty-three-meter-high temples or its own emblem glyph or reached a level of regional power equal to that achieved by Xunantunich, but they had their own sources of local power. Even smaller communities such as Chan had developed resources and production and complex webs of sociopolitical and economic relations that constrained the development of a network of exploitation by Xunantunich.

Interpretations derived from analyses that do not consider archaeological evidence for farmers' everyday lives would come to conclusions about Chan and its residents that are quite different from those I have presented in this book. Profoundly different and inaccurate interpretations of the operation of society can be reached when researchers do not take everyday life into account.

Conclusion

Understanding everyday life at Chan is not only significant for understanding Chan, it is significant for building method and theory in archaeology. Everyday life at Chan has revealed a remarkable range of innovation and ingenuity in agricultural, religious, political, social, and economic domains of life that belies traditional conceptions of everyday life as simply mundane. This prompts reconsideration of traditional anthropological theories about the emergence of intensive agriculture; the relationship between ideology, false consciousness, and power; the nature of political economies; and the relationship between cities and rural producers. Revising these models in light of the Chan study to reinsert everyday life and its potential for local ingenuity can develop models of human societies open to the agency and potential of all groups of people who made up a society.

The Chan study illustrates that in order to understand the development of intensive agriculture, researchers must pay as much attention to farmers' practices and local ingenuity as they do to population pressure and managerial control. Theoretical notions of hegemony and false consciousness must be viewed with a careful eye because ordinary people are neither dopes nor dupes of elite ideologies. Given the importance of economic transactions in society, political economic decision making that reduces inequality must always be considered alongside decision making that promotes inequality.

When farmers' everyday lives are not considered in building models about human societies, outdated models of farmers as passive victims of state demands and population pressure reemerge. As Eric Wolf (1982) has long noted, there is a profound impact of Western and capitalist penetration in the world today. If scholars seek to understand the diversity of human social organization, then the importance of discussions drawing upon prehistoric data grows for all scholars. Situating research within a critical everyday life approach is a way to immerse analyses in data from the past and open up the possibility of understanding a past that was different from the present as well as from preconceived models.

8 ✳ Conclusion
Everyday Life Matters

Standing on top of El Castillo, the central temple at Xunantunich, and looking four kilometers to the southeast, all one sees is a vast expanse of trees where the contemporary Belizean forest has reclaimed Chan (figure 8.1 upper). From this distant perspective the vibrant rain forest that covers Chan appears to be a homogeneous mass to the onlooker, and the long-abandoned community is rendered invisible. Just as the trees that hide Chan appear homogeneous from this distant perspective, so too are the diversity and complexity of everyday life at Chan obscured from an anthropological perspective that stands at a distance from people's everyday lives.

When we switch the view to look from Chan to Xunantunich, the perspective is quite different (figure 8.1 lower). From most locations at Chan, if viewers look to the northwest, they can see a distant vista of El Castillo: royal pomp and circumstance reduced to a small, two-dimensional image in the background of the colors and dynamism of everyday life at Chan. At least in the Late Classic period when El Castillo was constructed, this small and distant image of monumental construction, which was unlike anything at Chan, would have been a constant reminder to the people of Chan of the broader world in which they lived. It may also have reminded residents of the limits of their social world and the social differences that existed in their society. As Xunantunich's power waned in the Terminal Classic and the center was abandoned, this distant image may have symbolized something different: the failures of highly centralized and stratified states.

If we switch the focus again, to within Chan, our view becomes even more dynamic. For its ancient residents, Chan was a place filled with the

Figure 8.1. *Top*: View from the top of El Castillo at Xunantunich looking southeast. White arrow points to the location of Chan. *Bottom*: Cynthia Robin and Santiago Juarez surveying at Chan. To the northwest (upper left-hand corner of image), El Castillo is visible in the distance.

motions and hustle and bustle of everyday life, a warm bowl of corn gruel shared with family under the midday sun, the outstretched branches of a mahogany tree swaying above as farmers till the earth with bifacial hoes, good days and bad days, happiness and remorse. There was time to understand the promise of the land and time to understand the mysteries of the cosmos.

The swaying branch of the mahogany tree was part of the monotony of everyday life at Chan. Preserving this tree, as was done by generation after generation at Chan, was part of the repetitiveness of daily life, the maintenance of a tradition, a type of agriculture, in which the forest and field could coexist. The same daily act that preserved a mahogany tree and others like it and countless other mature closed-canopy tropical forest trees around Chan also produced what was dynamic and changing at Chan: a community that thrived and grew for two thousand years. Healthy forests and healthy people have the time and disposition to innovate and to organize a farm, a community, a society, and in the process to develop counterhegemonic political practices as well. Everyday life is central in the production and reproduction of society, and also for its transformation. Across the rhythms of daily life at Chan, people reproduced established norms and produced counternormative acts, often through the same actions.

At first glance, the Chan community is unremarkable: in this rolling landscape, pole-and-thatch houses encircled by their terraced agricultural fields surround a central plaza with six buildings dedicated to community-level ceremony, administration, and adjudication. In many ways, Chan was this unremarkable place. With its 5.6-meter-high eastern E-Group temple it was among the smaller end of minor centers in the Maya area. Compared to Maya elites who inhabited vaulted stone houses, Chan's residents living in pole-and-thatch houses occupied a lower stratum in society. Chan's residents certainly had less privilege and fewer possessions than society's power brokers did.

While there is nothing inaccurate about such a characterization of Chan and its inhabitants, the same characteristics that make Chan seem so unremarkable are actually what make it quite remarkable. Across a 3.2-square-kilometer area and 274 farmsteads, every resident from community leader to humble farmer lived in a perishable house with a thatch roof. The broad commonalities in housing types at Chan would have been as visible to neighbor and visitor at Chan in the past as they are to archaeologists today. The lesser degree of stratification in housing types at Chan is remarkable in comparison to both the opulence of housing at Maya regal centers and the visible hierarchy of housing types at nearby Belize Valley communities such as Chaa Creek and San Lorenzo. At Chan, in terms of housing and possessions, there was a more equitable distribution of wealth than is the norm in the highly stratified society of the Maya Classic period. While Chan's leaders may have had less than expected for community leaders, Chan's humble farmers had more than would be expected, and this appears to be part of a political strategy that is heterarchical and group centered and highlights the importance of community over the importance of the individual.

Taking everyday life seriously reveals the complex and vibrant nature of daily life at Chan. For two thousand years, Chan was a home for a diverse array of ancient Maya people, from farmers to craft producers, diviners, and community leaders. Exploring residents' everyday lives reveals a socially, politically, intellectually, and technologically vibrant community that researchers might not have initially envisioned given the scale of architecture and settlement at Chan. Chan's residents innovated conservation-wise agricultural technologies and forest management strategies. A mature, closed-canopy, tropical forest maintenance strategy, terracing to avoid erosion and maximize water infiltration, knowledge of sustainable agriculture established over centuries and passed down generation after generation, and the use of local resources are some of the environmentally effective strategies developed by Chan's farmers and local craft producers that enabled the community to endure. The type of sustainable forest management practiced at Chan is distinct from the more extractive practices of Tikal's royals, who culled the last mature *Manilkara zapota* from the forest around AD 741 (Lentz and Hockaday 2009).

Across Chan, from the homes of the humblest residents to those of community leaders and within the community center, residents developed community-focused ritual practices and heterarchical social and political strategies. Residents developed a popular religion, which included many elements that elites later incorporated into state-level religious practices. But other aspects of social, political, and religious practices that people developed at Chan were not broadly adopted by the upper echelons of Maya society: the Classic period group-oriented political strategies practiced at Chan were distinct from the more hierarchical rule of the Classic Maya divine kings, and only later in time did they become a more prevalent political strategy across Maya society. Avoidance of extremes of wealth and power, maintenance of good health, avoidance of exclusionary ritual and political practices, feasting, community-wide ceremonies, and reasonably equitable distributions of exotic items are some of the socially effective strategies that enabled Chan's farmers to establish a long-lived community.

In the absence of studies of everyday life at Chan, it would be possible to assume that Chan's residents were simply an underclass oppressed by the state, living in small houses, and that the community had little role to play in the broader developments of Maya society. But by actively exploring the everyday lives of Chan's residents across its two-thousand-year history and comparing the community's longevity and its social and environmental strategies with much more opulent centers, with their monumental temple-pyramids and palaces, and waxing and waning political histories, we can increasingly see how erroneous such a perspective can be. Major centers in the Belize River valley, like the polity capital of Xunantunich, may have been impressive in their time, but they had rising and falling political histories. There is a richness that can be found within everyday life in even a smaller, "poorer" community and in the innovations developed there that can greatly affect society. In the end, some of the most important lessons about human societies and the importance of social and economic sustainability may be learned by exploring everyday life in a seemingly unremarkable place such as Chan.

If people create and are constrained by the material and spatial practices of day-to-day life, then an academic understanding of people cannot be found at the abstract level but must be located in the practice of studying people's everyday lives. The Chan research maintained a constant interplay between theoretical interests and evidential constraints (sensu stricto Wylie 1992, 2002). I continually triangulated back and forth between theoretical issues raised by everyday life thinkers, intensive archaeological methods and scientific microanalytical techniques that revealed ever more details about ancient everyday life, and systematic insights from Belizean staff that did not fit neatly into either scientific or humanistic academic traditions. By taking everyday life seriously, I was able to ask questions about how the seemingly ordinary things people do across their everyday lives might affect their societies. In terms of examining the relationship between farmers and farming communities and states, this allowed me to develop additional sets of questions beyond the traditional ones that have framed these inquires. Thus, rather than simply ask a set of questions about how commoner compliance with elite demands was rewarded, I was able to ask a broader range of questions that also included whether or not farmers were compliant, and if they were, to what extent they were compliant.

Taking seriously the idea that Chan was a resilient community, a socially and environmentally sustainable community, rather than an oppressed community, requires researchers to rethink and to reformulate a wide range of anthropological theories about the constitution of human societies and the nature of human agency. Everyday life at Chan revealed a remarkable range of innovation and ingenuity in agricultural, religious, political, social, and economic domains of life that belies traditional conceptions of everyday life as simply mundane. This prompts reconsideration of traditional anthropological theories about the emergence of intensive agriculture; the relationship between ideology, false consciousness, and power; the nature of the political economy; and the relationship between cities and rural producers. By revising these models in light of the Chan study to reinsert everyday life and its potential for local ingenuity, we can develop models of human societies that are open to the agency and potential of all the groups of people who made up a society.

The Chan study illustrates that in order to understand the development of intensive agriculture researchers must pay as much attention to farmers' practices and local ingenuity as they do to population pressure and managerial control. Theoretical notions of hegemony and false consciousness must be viewed with a careful eye because ordinary people are neither dopes nor dupes of elite ideologies. Given the importance of economic transactions in society, political-economic decision making that enhances equality must always be considered alongside decision making that creates inequality.

When farmers' everyday lives are not considered in building models about human societies, outdated models of farmers as passive victims of state demands and population pressure reemerge. As Eric Wolf (1982) has long noted, Western and capitalist perspectives have had a profound impact on the world today. If scholars seek to understand the diversity of human social organization, then the importance of discussions drawing upon prehistoric data grows for all scholars. Situating research within a critical everyday life approach is a way to immerse analyses in data from the past and open up the possibility of understanding a past that was different from the present or preconceived models.

Everyday life is the matter of much of the archaeological record, and when archaeologists bring a host of social theoretical, scientific, and nontraditional forms of knowledge to bear on studying everyday life in the past, the richness of the everyday imprints that constitute much of the archaeological record can open up a critical commentary on human societies. Understanding ancient everyday life matters because what people do on a daily basis is central in the construction of their societies, and as researchers gain better insights into everyday life in the past they may discern that some of what is truly remarkable about human societies is situated in deep understandings of the ways of daily lives. Studying everyday life also matters for archaeologists' interpretations of human societies, because without careful attention to the operation of everyday life, models of the operation of human societies may be flawed.

Notes

Chapter 2. Social Theory and Everyday Life

1. The group of scholars that I bring together in this chapter represent my attempt at formulating a critical everyday life perspective. Although the book-length reviews of everyday life thinkers are more in depth than this chapter, they are equally selective in their review. Gardiner's (2000) *Critiques of Everyday Life*, for example, brings together the work of the Dadaists, Surrealists, Bakhtin, Lefebvre, the Situationist International, Heller, de Certeau, and Smith. Highmore's (2002a) *Everyday Life and Cultural Theory: An Introduction* highlights Simmel, Surrealism, Benjamin, Mass-Observation, Lefebvre, and de Certeau. Sheringham's (2006) *Everyday Life: Theories and Practices from Surrealism to the Present* follows the French tradition, with a focus on the work of Lefebvre, Barthes, de Certeau, and Perec. Highmore's (2002b) *Everyday Life Reader* provides the most comprehensive set of readings in everyday life, including excerpts from thirty-six authors.

Chapter 5. Situating Chan

1. Given that 562 mounds were identified across the 3.2 km^2 Chan survey area, I estimate that there were 552 mounds within a 1 km radius of the Central Group. Detailed excavations at a 10 percent sample of Chan's mound groups allowed me to gauge what percentage of these mounds were residential. Twelve type 1 single mounds were investigated. Of these, full-scale horizontal excavations were undertaken at eight type 1 mounds. The remaining type 1 mounds were investigated only through extramural post-hole testing. Of the eight intensively excavated type 1 mounds, seven were residential (Kestle 2012; Robin 1999, 2002a, 2002b; Wyatt 2008a, 2008b, 2012) and one was nonresidential (Cap 2012). Thus, for the purpose of calculating populations, I estimate that seven-eighths of type 1 mounds were residential.

Chan's single type 7 mound group, the Central Group, was mapped with nine mounds, only one of which was residential (Robin, Meierhoff, and Kosakowsky 2012); thus, for this group I include only one residential mound in the population estimates. For type 4 to 6 mound groups, which represent the households of head or higher-status families across Chan (Blackmore 2008, 2011, 2012; Robin, Meierhoff, and Kosakowsky 2012), two-thirds of mounds were residential and one-third were ancillary structures based on excavation data. For type 2 mound groups where all mounds in a group were excavated, in two cases all mounds were residential (Robin 1999, 2002a) and in one case one mound was residential and one was an ancillary structure (Hearth 2012). For the type 3 mound groups investigated, investigations did not explore all mounds in a group (Blackmore 2008, 2011, 2012; Kestle 2012). For type 2 to 3 mound groups, I estimate that five-sixths of mounds were residential.

The extensive program of posthole testing that extended from the architectural cores of mound groups for 30 to 50 meters beyond the architectural core and in two cases extended across whole neighborhoods allowed exploration of the existence of nonmound architecture (Blackmore 2008, 2011, 2012; Hearth 2012; Robin 1999, 2002a; Robin, Meierhoff, and Kosakowsky 2012). Indeed, a number of nonmound structures were identified through posthole testing, but all of these were ancillary structures; they include the lithic workshop within mound group C-199 (Hearth 2012) and the ancillary structures in the humble farming mound groups located south of the Central Group (Robin 1999, 2002a). I do not believe that substantial numbers of residences were missed by the survey.

Using the figures discussed above, I estimate that there were 436 residential mounds within a 1-kilometer radius of the Central Group. This number is generated from the number of mounds present in a group at the end of its occupation history; thus, it may overrepresent the number of mounds in a group from earlier periods of Chan's occupation. Given that deeply buried earlier architecture is likely to be underrepresented in the surface collection samples, I feel it is appropriate to use mound counts based on the number of mounds present in a group at the end of its history as a proxy for all time periods.

Not all residences in a community will be inhabited contemporaneously, particularly where there are extended family compounds and perishable houses, as at Chan. The residence of an older couple in a compound, upon their death, may go out of use for a time. Likewise, the residence of a young family may go out of use for a time when they move elsewhere in the community or to another community and start their own house compound. Given these issues of the developmental cycling of households and families (Goody 1971), an estimate of contemporaneity must be factored into population estimates. Recently, Mesoamericanists have used estimates ranging from 75 percent (Beekman 1998) to 90 percent (Tourtellot 1990) to account for the numbers of residences that may be unoccupied in a community at any one time. Initially, scholars used much lower figures; for example, Ricketson and Ricketson (1937) considered that only 25 percent of mounds were occupied contemporaneously at Uaxactun. But these lowest-end figures assume that swidden farming was practiced, which was certainly not the case at Chan. I used 75 percent and 90 percent to calculate minimum and maximum population estimates.

Mayanists typically estimate that between 4 and 5.6 persons lived in an ancient house based on a range of ethnographic and environmental analogies (Beekman 1998; Rice and Rice 1990; Tourtellot et al. 1990; Webster and Freter 1990). I employed both figures to generate minimum and maximum population estimates.

I advocate a model of continuous occupation (Tourtellot 1990); thus, I did not standardize residence counts based on length of occupation phase. Temporal standardization has the effect of making population estimates unrealistically low for the long temporal spans of the Preclassic period. But as a result, estimates for Chan's population at its peak in the late Late Classic period may overestimate population. To calculate a minimum population estimate I used the following equation: 436 residential mounds × percentage dated to phase × 75 percent contemporaneity × 4 persons per residence. For a maximum estimate I used 436 residential mounds × percentage dated to phase × 90 percent contemporaneity × 5.6 persons per residence.

Chapter 6. Everyday Life at Chan

1. Expedient chert tools are quickly made tools typically produced from single flakes that may be used as is or retouched. Expedient flake tools can be used for a wide range of cutting and scrapping needs. They require less technological knowledge in their production than do the formal bifaces produced by specialized tool producers at Chan that are discussed later in this chapter.

2. Yaeger used a different mound group typology than that used at Chan, but the mound groups at San Lorenzo range from single mounds less than 1 meter in height (type 1 in the Chan typology) to formal platform groups with at least one mound between 2 and 5 meters in height (type 6 in the Chan typology).

3. Connell used the same mound group typology as used at Chan in the Chaa Creek work.

4. The precise cardinal directional orientation of the four figures surrounding the central slate figure is unknown because the lip-to-lip cache vessels containing this cache were quite fragmentary. To preserve the vessels and materials they contained, excavators removed the vessels from the field still encased in soil matrix. They were then carefully excavated in the controlled laboratory environment. It was during this excavation that the interior cache was identified.

5. Structure 6 consists of two buildings, Structure 6-east and Structure 6-west. These were connected by a vaulted passageway and interior stair. The smaller of the two buildings, Structure 6-west, was heavily looted; thus, only salvage excavations were conducted there. The form of Structure 6-west is comparable to but smaller in scale than that of Structure 6-east.

Chapter 7. Why Everyday Life at Chan Matters

1. Neff (2010: 264) states that his model "assumes the presence of an intensive hydraulic agricultural system, or a system equivalent to it." Using total-productivity model simulation data, given a population growth index of 8, a total product of 63 ("total product is the yield of agricultural product per unit of land"), an average product of 7.87 ("average product is total product divided by the number of laborers per unit of land"), and a marginal product of -1 ("marginal product represents the change in agricultural production achieved by adding additional workers to a given unit of land"), during the late Late Classic period at Chan and in neighboring communities, a point of diminishing returns was reached, in which the labor that farmers put into terrace agriculture could no longer produce higher outputs, diminishing the value of their labor and making them vulnerable to Xunantunich's demands (Neff 2010: 260–63, table 11.4).

As Neff notes, and is discussed in chapter 5, Mayanists use various methods to derive population estimates from settlement survey data. The number of people who live in a structure, the percentage of structures that are residential, the percentage of structures that are inhabited contemporaneously, and the time span of a given phase of occupation all have to be estimated. Neff estimates that 5 people lived in a structure. He estimates that all identified structures were residential and that all structures were inhabited contemporaneously. Using these estimating procedures, he calculates that there were 524 people per square kilometer living in the Chan area. This falls into the upper end of the population estimates I generated for the late Late Classic Chan community (between 317 and 532 people per square kilometer) using the more compressive set of variables as discussed in chapter 5 note 1. Were the lower end Chan population estimates a more accurate estimation of absolute ancient populations than the higher end population estimates, labor value may not have decreased in the late Late Classic period.

Estimating ancient labor values is even more challenging than estimating ancient populations. Neff derived his labor values from the work of Abrams (1995), who in turn derived his labor values from the work of Boserup (1965). Boserup's labor value data are hypothetical and not based on any actual studies of the time, labor, and value involved in agricultural work, as Abrams points out. Abrams (1995: 201) indicates that he "would have preferred to use empirically based marginal-productivity data, but . . . [has] found it very difficult to obtain such data for contemporary agricultural systems in Latin America, despite their clear importance in decision making." Robert McC. Netting (1993: 105) in *Smallholders, Householders: Farm Families and the Ecology of Intensive Agriculture* addresses this issue as well, noting the same problem with Boserup's work on the value of intensive agriculture versus extensive swidden agriculture, which are hypothetical and not based on actual data from these types of agricultural systems. Netting (1993: 102–22) shows through detailed cross-cultural ethnographic studies that there is a complex relationship between the inputs and the outputs in intensive agricultural systems that relates to a wide range of variables, including but not limited to the nature of the intensification, family size, farm size, soil quality, climatic conditions, types of crops grown, divisions of labor, types of markets for crops, and so forth. All of these variables need to be considered in estimating labor value in agriculture. Netting does concur with Boserup that there are conditions under which populations become too high for farmers to be able to continue to add value to their land and labor through intensification. One such documented situation is among the Owerre-Ebeire of Nigeria, where there is a population density of 1,200 people per square kilometer. All other differences between the contemporary Owerre-Ebeire and the ancient Belize Valley farmers aside, Owerre-Ebeire populations are anywhere from two to four times higher than population estimates for Chan. Netting also points out that farm families do not just farm, and they can enhance the value of their labor through the production of nonagricultural goods for both household use and extrahousehold markets. Because the famers at Chan were involved in nonagricultural production at the household and community level, this adds another dimension to the value of their labor. Were labor values higher at Chan for any of these reasons than Neff estimated, a situation of diminishing returns may not have been reached in the late Late Classic period.

2. Three different cases of relatively voluntary tribute are recounted in the *Relaciones Histórico-geográficas de la Gobernación de Yucatán* (de la Garza et al. 1983):

"[Tutul Xiu] . . . tuvo a todos de los señores de la tierra debajo de su dominio más por maña que por fuerza de armas, y dicen de él que fue muy sabio, que enseño las letras y la cuenta de los meses y años a los naturales. . . . Los tributos que llevaban sus vasallos eran de maíz, gallinas, miel y alguna ropilla de algodón, todo muy limitado y casi voluntario, que no era más que un reconocimiento de su señorío, salvo que eran los vasallos obligados a servir en la guerra con sus personas" (Relación de Dzan, Panabchen, y Muna, 252–53; Relación de Mama y Kantemo, 110; Relación de Tabi y Chunhuhub, 164).

" . . . el mayor señor de la dicha provincia, a quien todos eran sujetos . . . al cual cada año le tributaban sus vasallos de su voluntad, sin ser forzados a ello, lo que su posible alcanzaba y el propio tributario le quería dar, lo cual le daban de maíz . . . la cantidad que el súbdito quería" (Relación de Muxuppipp, 376–77).

"En tiempo de su gentilidad no tenían más señor que al cacique y éste los gobernaba y aun los tiranizaba; y no le tributaban más que maíz, frijoles ya ají, y unos patiejos o mantillas de poco más que una vara" (Relación de Cacalchen, Yaxa, y Sihunchen, 342).

References

Abercrombie, Nicholas, Stephen Hill, and Bryan S. Turner. 1980. *The Dominant Ideology Thesis*. London: G. Allen and Unwin.

Abrams, Elliot M. 1995. "A Model of Fluctuating Labor Value and the Establishment of State Power: An Application to the Prehispanic Maya." *Latin American Antiquity* 6 (3): 196–213.

Abu-Lughod, Lila. 1993. *Writing Women's Worlds: Bedouin Stories*. Berkeley: University of California Press.

Adams, Richard E. W., and T. Patrick Culbert. 1977. "The Origins of Civilization in the Maya Lowlands." In *The Origins of Maya Civilization*, edited by R.E.W. Adams, 3–24. Albuquerque: University of New Mexico Press.

Adams, Robert McC. 1966. *The Evolution of Urban Society: Early Mesopotamia and Prehispanic Mexico*. Chicago: Aldine.

Aimers, James J., and Prudence M. Rice. 2006. "Astronomy, Ritual and the Interpretation of Maya 'E-Group' Architectural Assemblages." *Ancient Mesoamerica* 17 (1): 79–96.

Allison, Penelope Mary. 1999. *The Archaeology of Household Activities: Dwelling in the Past*. New York: Routledge.

Althusser, Louis. 1971. *Lenin and Philosophy and Other Essays*. New York: Monthly Review Press.

Aragon. 1926. *Le paysan de Paris*. Paris: Gallimard.

Ashmore, Wendy. 1991. "Site-Planning Principles and Concepts of Directionality among the Ancient Maya." *Latin American Antiquity* 2 (3): 199–226.

———. 2000. "Leaving Home Abruptly." *Mayab* 13: 108–12.

———. 2002. "Decisions and Dispositions: Socializing Spatial Archaeology." *American Anthropologist* 104 (4): 1172–83.

———. 2004. "Classic Maya Landscapes and Settlements." In *Mesoamerican Archaeology*, edited by J. A. Hendon and A. A. Joyce, 169–91. Oxford, U.K.: Blackwell.

———. 2010. "Antecedents, Allies, Antagonists: Xunantunich and Its Neighbors." In *Classic Maya Provincial Politics: Xunantunich and Its Hinterlands*, edited by L. J. LeCount and J. Yaeger, 46–66. Tucson: University of Arizona Press.

Ashmore, Wendy, Samuel V. Connell, Jennifer J. Ehret, Chad H. Gifford, and L. Theodore Neff. 1994. The Xunantunich Settlement Survey. In *Xunantunich Archaeological Project: 1994 Field Season*, edited by R. Leventhal, 248–80. Report submitted to the Belize Institute of Archaeology, Belmopan.

Ashmore, Wendy, and Arthur Bernard Knapp. 1999. *Archaeologies of Landscape: Contemporary Perspectives.* Oxford, U.K.: Blackwell.

Ashmore, Wendy, and Jeremy A. Sabloff. 2002. "Spatial Orders in Maya Civic Plans." *Latin American Antiquity* 13 (2): 201–15.

Ashmore, Wendy, and Richard R. Wilk. 1988. "Household and Community in the Mesoamerican Past." In *Household and Community in the Mesoamerican Past,* edited by R. R. Wilk and W. Ashmore, 1–27. Albuquerque: University of New Mexico Press.

Ashmore, Wendy, and Gordon R. Willey. 1981. "A Historical Introduction to the Study of Lowland Maya Settlement Patterns." In *Lowland Maya Settlement Patterns,* edited by W. Ashmore, 3–17. Albuquerque: University of New Mexico Press.

Ashmore, Wendy, Jason Yaeger, and Cynthia Robin. 2004. "Commoner Sense: Late and Terminal Classic Social Strategies in the Xunantunich Area." In *The Terminal Classic in the Maya Lowlands: Collapse, Transition, and Transformation,* edited by D. S. Rice, P. M. Rice, and A. A. Demarest, 302–23. Boulder, Colo.: Westview Press.

Atran, Scott. 1993. "Itza Maya Tropical Agro-Forestry." *Current Anthropology* 34 (5): 633–700.

Awe, Jaime Jose. 1992. "Dawn in the Land Between the Rivers: Formative Occupation at Cahal Pech, Belize and Its Implications for Preclassic Development in the Maya Lowlands." PhD diss., University of London.

Bailey, Douglass W. 1990. "The Living House: Signifying Continuity." In *The Social Archaeology of Houses,* edited by R. Samson, 19–48. Edinburgh: University of Edinburgh Press.

Bakhtin, M. M. (1930) 1981. *The Dialogic Imagination: Four Essays.* Edited by Michael Holquist. Austin: University of Texas Press.

———. (1941) 1984. *Rabelais and His World.* Translated by Hélène Iswolsky. Bloomington: Indiana University Press.

———. 1993. *Toward a Philosophy of the Act.* Edited by Vadim Liapunov and Michael Holquist. Austin: University of Texas Press.

Ball, Joseph W. 1993. "Pottery, Potters, Palaces, and Polities: Some Socioeconomic and Political Implications of Late Classic Maya Ceramic Industries." In *Lowland Maya Civilization in the Eighth Century AD,* edited by J. A. Sabloff and J. S. Henderson, 243–72. Washington, D.C.: Dumbarton Oaks.

Ball, Joseph W., and Jennifer T. Taschek. 1991. "Late Classic Lowland Maya Political Organization and Central-Place Analysis: New Insights from the Upper Belize Valley." *Ancient Mesoamerica* 2 (2): 149–65.

———. 2001. "The Buenavista–Cahal Pech Royal Court: Multi-Palace Court Mobility and Usage in a Petty Lowland Maya Kingdom." In *Royal Courts of the Ancient Maya,* vol. 2, *Data and Case Studies,* edited by T. Inomata and S. D. Houston, 165–200. Boulder, Colo.: Westview Press.

———. 2004. "Buenavista del Cayo: A Short Outline of Occupational and Cultural History at an Upper Belize Valley Regal-Ritual Center." In *The Ancient Maya of the Belize Valley: Half a Century of Archaeological Research,* edited by J. F. Garber, 149–67. Gainesville: University Press of Florida.

Barba, Luis, and Agustín Ortiz. 1992. "Análisis químico de pisos de ocupación: Un caso etnográfico en Tlaxcala, México." *Latin American Antiquity* 3 (1): 63–82.

Battle-Baptiste, Whitney. 2011. *Black Feminist Archaeology*. Walnut Creek, Calif.: Left Coast Press.

Beauvoir, Simone de. 1953. *The Second Sex*. New York: Knopf.

Beekman, Christopher S. 1998. "A Comparison of Different Methods to Estimate Population among Sites in the La Venta Corridor, Highland Jalisco." Paper presented at Midwest Mesoamericanist Meeting, East Lansing, Mich.

Bell, Ellen E. 2002. "Engendering a Dynasty: A Royal Woman in the Margarita Tomb, Copan." In *Ancient Maya Women*, edited by T. Ardren, 89–104. Walnut Creek, Calif.: Altamira Press.

Bender, Barbara. 1993. *Landscape: Politics and Perspectives, Explorations in Anthropology*. Providence, R.I.: Berg.

———. 1998. *Stonehenge: Making Space, Materializing Culture*. Oxford, U.K.: Berg.

Best, Jacqueline, and Matthew Paterson. 2010. *Cultural Political Economy*. London: Routledge.

Binford, Lewis Roberts. 1977. *For Theory Building in Archaeology: Essays on Faunal Remains, Aquatic Resources, Spatial Analysis, and Systemic Modeling*. New York: Academic Press.

———. 1978. *Nunamiut Ethnoarchaeology*. New York: Academic Press.

———. 1982. "The Archaeology of Place." *Journal of Anthropological Archaeology* 1 (1): 5–31.

———. 1989. *Debating Archaeology*. San Diego: Academic Press.

Blackmore, Chelsea. 2003. "Operation 1, C-001." In *The Chan Project: 2003 Season*, edited by C. Robin, 36–51. Report submitted to the Belize Institute of Archaeology, Belmopan.

———. 2007. "Commoner Ritual and Socio-Political Life in a Late Classic Neighborhood: Archaeological Investigations at the Northeast Group, Chan, Belize." In *Research Reports in Belizean Archaeology* 4: 24–46.

———. 2008. "Challenging 'Commoner': An Examination of Status and Identity at the Ancient Maya Village of Chan, Belize." PhD diss., University of California–Riverside.

———. 2011. "Ritual among the Masses: Deconstructing Identity and Class in an Ancient Maya Neighborhood." *Latin American Antiquity* 22 (2): 159–77.

———. 2012. "Recognizing Difference in Small-Scale Settings: An Examination of Social Identity Formation at the Northeast Group, Chan." In *Chan: An Ancient Maya Farming Community*, edited by C. Robin, 173–91. Gainesville: University Press of Florida.

Blanton, Richard E., Gary M. Feinman, Stephen A. Kowalewski, and Peter N. Peregrine. 1996. "A Dual-Processual Theory for the Evolution of Mesoamerican Civilization." *Current Anthropology* 37 (1): 1–14.

Boserup, Ester. 1965. *The Conditions of Agricultural Growth: The Economics of Agrarian Change under Population Pressure*. Chicago: Aldine Publishing Co.

Bourdieu, Pierre. 1977. *Outline of a Theory of Practice*. Cambridge: Cambridge University Press.

———. 1998. *Practical Reason: On the Theory of Action*. Stanford: Stanford University Press.

Bradley, Richard. 2005. *Ritual and Domestic Life in Prehistoric Europe*. London: Routledge.

Braswell, Geoffrey E. 2001. "Post-Classic Maya Courts of the Guatemalan Highlands: Archaeological and Ethnohistorical Approaches." In *Royal Courts of the Ancient Maya*, edited by T. Inomata and S. D. Houston, 308–34. Boulder, Colo.: Westview Press.

Braswell, Jennifer Briggs. 1998. "Archaeological Investigations at Group D, Xunantunich, Belize." PhD diss., Tulane University, New Orleans.

Braudel, Fernand. 1972. *The Mediterranean and the Mediterranean World in the Age of Philip II*. New York: Harper and Row.

Bredel, Ralf. 2007. *The Ethical Economy of Conflict Prevention and Development: Towards a Model for International Organizations*. Leiden: M. Nijhoff.

Breton, André. 1924. *Manifeste du surréalisme: Poisson soluble*. Paris: Éditions du Sagittaire.

———. 1928. *Nadja*. Paris: Gallimard.

Brier, Bob, and A. Hoyt Hobbs. 2008. *Daily Life of the Ancient Egyptians*. Westport, Conn.: Greenwood Press.

Brown, M. Kathryn. 2010. "From Sunrise to Sunset: Preliminary Investigations of Preclassic and Postclassic Ritual Activity at Xunantunich, Belize." *Research Reports in Belizean Archaeology* 7: 37–44.

Brown, M. Kathryn, Jaime J. Awe, and James Garber. 2009. "The Preclassic in the Mopan River Valley: Preliminary Investigations at Nohoch Ek and Xunantunich." *Research Reports in Belizean Archaeology* 6: 63–72.

Bruhns, Karen Olsen, and Karen E. Stothert. 1999. *Women in Ancient America*. Norman: University of Oklahoma Press.

Brumfiel, Elizabeth M. 1991. "Weaving and Cooking: Women's Production in Aztec Mexico." In *Engendering Archaeology: Women and Prehistory*, edited by J. M. Gero and M. W. Conkey, 224–54. Oxford, U.K.: Blackwell.

———. 1992. "Breaking and Entering the Ecosystem: Gender, Class, and Faction Steal the Show." *American Anthropologist* 94 (3): 551–67.

———. 1996. "Figurines and the Aztec State: Testing the Effectiveness of Ideological Domination." In *Gender in Archaeology: Essays in Research and Practice*, edited by R. P. Wright, 143–66. Philadelphia: University of Pennsylvania Press.

———. n.d. "A Role for Archaeology in Feminist and Gender Studies." Manuscript in the possession of the author.

Brumfiel, Elizabeth M., and Timothy K. Earle. 1987. *Specialization, Exchange, and Complex Societies*. Cambridge: Cambridge University Press.

Bullard, William R., Jr. 1960. "Maya Settlement Pattern in Northwestern Petén, Guatemala." *American Antiquity* 25 (3): 355–72.

Búriková, Zuzana, and Daniel Miller. 2010. *Au Pair*. Cambridge, U.K.: Polity Press.

Cantwell, Anne-Marie E., and Diana diZerega Wall. 2001. *Unearthing Gotham: The Archaeology of New York City*. New Haven, Conn.: Yale University Press.

Cap, Bernadette. 2012. "'Empty' Spaces and Public Places: A Microscopic View of Chan's West Plaza." In *Chan: An Ancient Maya Farming Community*, edited by C. Robin, 150–72. Gainesville: University Press of Florida.

Casey, E. 1996. "How to Get from Space to Place in a Fairly Short Stretch of Time." In *Senses of Place*, edited by S. Feld and K. Basso, 13–52. Albuquerque, N.Mex.: School of American Research Press.

Clark, John E. 1990. "Fifteen Fallacies in Lithic Workshop Interpretation: An Experimental and Ethnoarchaeological Perspective." In *Ethnoarqueologi: Primer Coloquio Bosch Gimpera*, edited by Y. Y. Sugiura and P.M.C. Serra, 497–512. Mexico City: Universidad Autónoma de México.

Clarke, David L. 1968. *Analytical Archaeology*. London: Methuen.

———. 1977. *Spatial Archaeology*. New York: Academic Press.

Conkey, Margaret W., and Joan M. Gero. 1997. "Programme to Practice: Gender and Feminism in Archaeology." *Annual Review of Anthropology* 26: 411–37.

Conlon, James M., and Terry G. Powis. 2004. "Major Center Identifiers at a Plazuela Group near the Ancient Maya Site of Baking Pot." In *The Ancient Maya of the Belize Valley: Half a Century of Archaeological Research*, edited by J. F. Garber, 70–85. Gainesville: University Press of Florida.

Connell, Samuel V. 2000. "Were They Well Connected? An Exploration of Ancient Maya Regional Integration from the Middle-Level Perspective of Chaa Creek, Belize." PhD diss., University of California, Los Angeles.

———. 2003. "Making Sense of Variability among Minor Centers: The Ancient Maya of Chaa Creek, Belize." In *Perspectives on Ancient Maya Rural Complexity*, edited by S. V. Connell and G. Iannone, 27–41. Los Angeles: Cotsen Institute of Archaeology.

———. 2010. "A Community to Be Counted: Chaa Creek and the Emerging Xunantunich Polity." In *Classic Maya Provincial Politics: Xunantunich and Its Hinterlands*, edited by L. J. LeCount and J. Yaeger, 295–314. Tucson: University of Arizona Press.

Conrad, Geoffrey W., and Arthur Andrew Demarest. 1984. *Religion and Empire: The Dynamics of Aztec and Inca Expansionism*. New Studies in Archaeology. Cambridge: Cambridge University Press.

Crumley, Carole L. 1995. "Heterarchy and the Analysis of Complex Societies." In *Heterarchy and the Analysis of Complex Societies*, edited by R. M. Ehrenreich, C. L. Crumley, and J. E. Levy, 1–5. Archaeological Papers of the American Anthropological Association, 6. Oxford, U.K.: Wiley-Blackwell.

Culbert, T. Patrick, and Don S. Rice. 1990. *Precolumbian Population History in the Maya Lowlands*. Albuquerque: University of New Mexico Press.

D'Altroy, T. N., and T. K. Earle. 1985. "Staple Finance, Wealth Finance, and Storage in the Inca Political-Economy." *Current Anthropology* 26 (2): 187–206.

D'Altroy, Terence N., and Christine Ann Hastorf. 2001. *Empire and Domestic Economy: Interdisciplinary Contributions to Archaeology*. New York: Kluwer Academic.

Dark, K. R. 2004. *Secular Buildings and the Archaeology of Everyday Life in the Byzantine Empire*. Oxford, U.K.: Oxbow Books.

David, Bruno, and Julian Thomas. 2008a. "Landscape Archaeology: Introduction." In *Handbook of Landscape Archaeology*, edited by B. David and J. Thomas, 27–43. Walnut Creek, Calif.: Left Coast Press.

David, Bruno, and Julian Thomas. 2008b. "Living Landscapes: The Body and the Experience of Place." In *Handbook of Landscape Archaeology*, edited by B. David and J. Thomas, 245. Walnut Creek, Calif.: Left Coast Press.

de Certeau, Michel. 1984. *The Practice of Everyday Life*. Berkeley: University of California Press.

de Certeau, Michel, Luce Giard, and Pierre Mayol. 1998. *The Practice of Everyday Life*. Vol. 2, *Living and Cooking*. Minneapolis: University of Minnesota Press.

Deetz, James. 1977. *In Small Things Forgotten: The Archaeology of Early American Life*. Garden City, N.Y.: Anchor Press/Doubleday.

de la Garza, Mercedes, Ma. del Carmen León Cázares, Ana Luisa Izquierdo, Tolita Figueroa, and Carlos Ontiveros. 1983. *Relaciones Histórico-Geográficas de la Gobernación de Yucatán*. Merida: Universidad Nacional Autónoma de México.

Docster, Elise. 2008. "GIS and Settlement Pattern Analysis at Chan, Belize." BA thesis, Northwestern University.

Driver, W. David, and James F. Garber. 2004. "The Emergence of Minor Centers in the Zones between Seats of Power." In *The Ancient Maya of the Belize Valley: Half a Century of Archaeological Research*, edited by J. F. Garber, 287–304. Gainesville: University Press of Florida.

Durkheim, Émile. (1893) 1997. *The Division of Labor in Society*. New York: Free Press.

Earle, Timothy K. 2002. *Bronze Age Economics: The Beginnings of Political Economies*. Boulder, Colo.: Westview Press.

Ehret, Jennifer. 1995. "The Xunantunich Settlement Survey Test-Pitting Program." In *Xunantunich Archaeological Project: 1995 Field Season*, edited by R. M. Leventhal, 164–92. Report submitted to the Belize Institute of Archaeology, Belmopan.

Eley, Geoff. 1995. Foreword to *The History of Everyday Life: Reconstructing Historical Experiences and Ways of Life*, edited by A. Lüdtke, vii–xiii. Princeton: Princeton University Press.

Erickson, Clark L. 1993. "The Social Organization of Prehispanic Raised Field Agriculture in the Lake Titicaca Basin." In *Economic Aspects of Water Management in the Prehispanic New World*, edited by V. L. Scarborough and B. L. Isaac, 369–426. Greenwich, Conn.: JAI Press.

———. 2006. "Intensification, Political Economy, and the Farming Community: In Defense of a Bottom-Up Perspective of the Past." In *Agricultural Strategies*, edited by J. Marcus and C. Stanish, 233–65. Los Angeles: Cotsen Institute of Archaeology.

Evans-Pritchard, Edward W. 1940. *The Nuer: A Description of the Modes of Livelihood and Political Institutions of a Nilotic People*. Oxford: Oxford University Press.

Falconer, Steven E. 1995. "Rural Responses to Early Urbanism: Bronze Age Household and Village Economy at Tell el-Hayyat, Jordan." *Journal of Field Archaeology* 22 (4): 399–419.

Farriss, Nancy. 1984. *Maya Society under Colonial Rule: The Collective Enterprise of Survival*. Princeton: Princeton University Press.

Fash, Barbara, William L. Fash, Sheree Lane, Rudy Larios, Linda Schele, Jeffrey Stomper, and David Stuart. 1992. "Investigations of a Classic Maya Council House at Copán, Honduras." *Journal of Field Archaeology* 19 (4): 419–42.

Fash, William L. 1993. *Scribes, Warriors, and Kings: The City of Copán and the Ancient Maya*. London: Thames and Hudson.

Fedick, Scott L. 1994. "Ancient Maya Agricultural Terracing in the Upper Belize River Area: Computer-Aided Modeling and the Results of Initial Field Investigations." *Ancient Mesoamerica* 5 (1): 107–27.

———. 1995. "Indigenous Agriculture in the Americas." *Journal of Archaeological Research* 3 (4): 257–303.

———. 1996. *The Managed Mosaic: Ancient Maya Agriculture and Resource Use*. Salt Lake City: University of Utah Press.

Fladmark, K. R. 1982. "Microdebitage Analysis: Initial Considerations." *Journal of Archaeological Science* 9 (2): 205–20.

Flannery, Kent V. 1976. *The Early Mesoamerican Village: Studies in Archeology*. New York: Academic Press.

Flannery, K. V., and J. Marcus. 1976. "Formative Oaxaca and Zapotec Cosmos." *American Scientist* 64 (4): 374–83.

Foias, Antonia E. 2002. "At the Crossroads: The Economic Basis of Political Power in the Petexbatun Region." In *Ancient Maya Political Economies*, edited by M. A. Masson and D. A. Freidel, 223–48. Walnut Creek, Calif.: Altamira Press.

Ford, Anabel, and Scott Fedick. 1992. "Prehistoric Maya Settlement Patterns in the Upper Belize River Area: Initial Results of the Belize River Archaeological Settlement Survey." *Journal of Field Archaeology* 19 (1): 35–49.

Freud, Sigmund. 1914. *Psychopathology of Everyday Life*. English edition with introduction by A. A. Brill. London: T. Fisher Unwin.

Friedan, Betty. 1963. *The Feminine Mystique*. New York: Norton.

Garber, James F., ed. 2004. *The Ancient Maya of the Belize Valley: Half a Century of Archaeological Research*. Gainesville: University Press of Florida.

Garber, James F., M. Kathryn Brown, Jaime J. Awe, and Christopher J. Hartman. 2004. "Middle Formative Prehistory of the Central Belize Valley: An Examination of Architecture, Material Culture, and Sociopolitical Change at Blackman Eddy." In *The Ancient Maya of the Belize Valley: Half a Century of Archaeological Research*, edited by J. F. Garber, 25–47. Gainesville: University Press of Florida.

Gardiner, Michael E. 2000. *Critiques of Everyday Life*. London: Routledge.

Geertz, Clifford. 1973. *The Interpretation of Cultures*. New York: Basic Books.

Geller, Pamela L., and Miranda K. Stockett. 2006. *Feminist Anthropology: Past, Present, and Future*. Philadelphia: University of Pennsylvania Press.

Gero, Joan, and M. Cristina Scattolin. 2002. "Beyond Complementarity and Hierarchy: New Definitions for Archaeological Gender Relations." In *Pursuit of Gender: Worldwide Archaeological Approaches*, edited by S. M. Nelson and M. Rosen-Ayalon, 155–71. Walnut Creek, Calif.: Altamira.

Gilchrist, Roberta. 1999. *Gender and Archaeology: Contesting the Past*. London: Routledge.

Goffman, Erving. 1959. *The Presentation of Self in Everyday Life*. Garden City, N.Y.: Doubleday.

Gonlin, Nancy, and Jon C. Lohse. 2007. *Commoner Ritual and Ideology in Ancient Mesoamerica*. Boulder: University Press of Colorado.

González-Ruibal, Alfredo. 2011. "The Politics of Identity: Ethnicity and the Economy of Power in Iron Age Northwest Iberia." In *Landscape, Ethnicity, Identity in the Archaic Mediterranean Area*, edited by S. Stoddart and G. Cifani, 245–66. Oxford, U.K.: Oxbow Books.

Goody, Jack. 1971. *The Developmental Cycle in Domestic Groups*. London: Cambridge University Press.

Graham, Elizabeth A. 2011. *Maya Christians and Their Churches in Sixteenth-Century Belize*. Gainesville: University Press of Florida.

Gramsci, Antonio. 1971. *Selections from the Prison Notebooks of Antonio Gramsci*. Edited and translated by Quintin Hoare and Geoffrey Nowell Smith. New York: International Publishers.

Guyer, Jane I. 1988. "The Multiplication of Labor: Historical Methods in the Study of Gender and Agricultural Change in Modern Africa." *Current Anthropology* 29: 247–72.

Hall, Martin, and Stephen W. Silliman. 2006. *Historical Archaeology*. Oxford, U.K.: Blackwell.

Hammond, Norman. 1975. "Maya Settlement Hierarchy in Northern Belize." In *Contributions of the University of California Archaeological Research Facility 27*, edited by J. A. Graham, 40–55. Berkeley: University of California Archaeological Research Facility.

———. 1978. "The Myth of the Milpa: Agricultural Expansion in the Maya Lowlands." In *Prehispanic Maya Agriculture*, edited by P. D. Harrison and B. L. Turner II, 23–43. Albuquerque: University of New Mexico Press.

———. 1982. "A Late Formative Period Stela in the Maya Lowlands." *American Antiquity* 47 (2): 396–403.

———. 1994. *Ancient Maya Civilization*. New Brunswick, N.J.: Rutgers University Press.

Hanks, William F. 1990. *Referential Practice: Language and Lived Space among the Maya*. Chicago: University of Chicago Press.

Hart, Siobhan M., Maxine Oland, and Liam Frink. 2012. "Finding Transitions: Global Pathways to Decolonializing Indigenous Histories in Archaeology." In *Decolonizing Indigenous Histories: Exploring Prehistoric/Colonial Transitions in Archaeology*, edited by M. Oland, S. M. Hart, and L. Frink, 1–18. Tucson: University of Arizona Press.

Hastorf, Christine A. 1991. "Gender, Space, and Food in Prehistory." In *Engendering Archaeology: Women and Prehistory*, edited by J. M. Gero and M. W. Conkey, 132–62. Oxford, U.K.: Blackwell.

———. 1999. "Recent Research in Paleoethnobotany." *Journal of Archaeological Research* 7 (1): 55–103.

Hauser, Mark W. 2008. *An Archaeology of Black Markets: Local Ceramics and Economies in Eighteenth-Century Jamaica*. Gainesville: University Press of Florida.

Haviland, William A. 1967. "Stature at Tikal, Guatemala: Implications for Ancient Maya Demography and Social Organization." *American Antiquity* 32 (3): 316–25.

Head, Lesley, Jennifer Atchinson, and Richard Fullagar. 2002. "Country and Garden: Ethnobotany, Archaeobotany and Aboriginal Landscapes near the Keep River, Northwestern Australia." *Journal of Social Archaeology* 2: 173–96.

Healy, Paul. 2004. "Preclassic Maya of the Belize Valley: Key Issues and Questions." *Research Reports in Belizean Archaeology* 3: 13–30.

Healy, Paul F., David Cheetham, Terry G. Powis, and Jaime J. Awe. 2004. "Cahal Pech: The Middle Formative Period." In *The Ancient Maya of the Belize Valley: Half a Century of Archaeological Research*, edited by J. F. Garber, 103–24. Gainesville: University Press of Florida.

Hearth, Nicholas F. 2008. "Analysis of Lithic Artifacts from Various Contexts at Chan, Belize." In *The Chan Project: 2008 Season*, edited by C. Robin, 57–83. Report submitted to the Belize Institute of Archaeology, Belmopan.

———. 2012. "Organization of Chert Tool Economy during the Late and Terminal Classic Periods at Chan: Preliminary Thoughts Based upon Debitage Analysis." In *Chan: An Ancient Maya Farming Community*, edited by C. Robin, 192–206. Gainesville: University Press of Florida.

Heller, Agnes. (1970) 1984. *Everyday Life*. London: Routledge and Kegan Paul.

Helliwell, Christine. 1992. "Good Walls Make Bad Neighbours: The Dayak Longhouse as a Community of Voices." *Oceania* 62 (3): 179–93.

Helmke, Christophe, Jaime J. Awe, and Nikolai Grube. 2010. "The Carved Monuments and Inscriptions of Xunantunich: Implications for Terminal Classic Sociopolitical Relationships in the Belize Valley." In *Classic Maya Provincial Politics: Xunantunich and Its Hinterlands*, edited by L. J. LeCount and J. Yaeger, 97–144. Tucson: University of Arizona Press.

Hendon, Julia A. 1996. "Archaeological Approaches to the Organization of Domestic Labor: Household Practice and Domestic Relations." *Annual Review of Anthropology* 25: 45–61.

———. 2004. "Living and Working at Home: The Social Archaeology of Household Production and Social Relations." In *A Companion to Social Archaeology*, edited by L. Meskell and R. W. Preucel, 272–86. Oxford, U.K.: Blackwell.

———. 2010. *Houses in a Landscape: Memory and Everyday Life in Mesoamerica*. Durham, N.C.: Duke University Press.

Hetrick, Christopher. 2007. "No Tortillas in the Temple: Ritual and Domestic Space in an Ancient Maya Village." BA thesis, Northwestern University, Evanston, Ill.

Hicks, Dan, and Mary Carolyn Beaudry. 2006. *The Cambridge Companion to Historical Archaeology*. Cambridge: Cambridge University Press.

Highmore, Ben. 2002a. *Everyday Life and Cultural Theory: An Introduction*. London: Routledge.

———. 2002b. *The Everyday Life Reader*. London: Routledge.

Hirth, K. G. 1996. "Political Economy and Archaeology: Perspectives on Exchange and Production." *Journal of Archaeological Research* 4: 203–40.

Hodder, Ian. 1982. *Symbolic and Structural Archaeology*. Cambridge: Cambridge University Press.

———. 1987. *The Archaeology of Contextual Meanings*. Cambridge: Cambridge University Press.

———. 1990. *The Domestication of Europe: Structure and Contingency in Neolithic Societies*. Oxford, U.K.: Blackwell.

———. 1992. *Theory and Practice in Archaeology*. London: Routledge.

———. 1999. *The Archaeological Process: An Introduction*. Oxford, U.K.: Blackwell.

———. 2006. *The Leopard's Tale: Revealing the Mysteries of Çatalhöyük*. New York: Thames and Hudson.

Hodder, Ian, and Craig Cessford. 2004. "Daily Practice and Social Memory at Catalhoyuk." *American Antiquity* 69 (1): 17–40.

Hodder, Ian, and Clive Orton. 1976. *Spatial Analysis in Archaeology*. Cambridge: Cambridge University Press.

Hollimon, Sandra E. 1997. "The Third Gender in Native California: Two Spirit Undertakers among the Chumash and Their Neighbors." In *Women in Prehistory*, edited by C. Claassen and R. A. Joyce, 173–88. Philadelphia: University of Pennsylvania Press.

Houston, Stephen D., David Stuart, and Karl A. Taube. 1992. "Image and Text on the Jauncy Vase." In *The Maya Vase Book*, edited by J. Kerr, 499–512. New York: Kerr Associates.

Hutson, Scott. 2010. *Dwelling, Identity, and the Maya: Relational Archaeology at Chunchucmil*. Lanham, Md.: AltaMira Press.

Iannone, Gyles, and Sam V. Connell. 2003. *Perspectives on Ancient Maya Rural Complexity*. Los Angeles: Cotsen Institute of Technology.

Ingold, Tim. 2000. *The Perception of the Environment: Essays on Livelihood, Dwelling and Skill*. London: Routledge.

———. 2011. *Being Alive: Essays on Movement, Knowledge and Description*. London: Routledge.

Inomata, Takeshi. 2006. "Plazas, Performers, and Spectators: Political Theater of the Classic Maya." *Current Anthropology* 47 (5): 805–42.

Inomata, Takeshi, and Stephen D. Houston. 2001. "Opening the Maya Royal Court." In *Royal Courts of the Ancient Maya*, vol. 1, *Theory, Comparison, Synthesis*, edited by T. Inomata and S. D. Houston, 3–26. Boulder, Colo.: Westview Press.

Jamison, Thomas R. 2010. "Monumental Building Programs and Changing Political Strategies at Xunantunich." In *Classic Maya Provincial Politics: Xunantunich and Its Hinterland*, edited by L. J. LeCount and J. Yaeger, 122–44. Tucson: University of Arizona Press.

Johnson, Allen W., and Timothy K. Earle. 1987. *The Evolution of Human Societies: From Foraging Group to Agrarian State*. Stanford: Stanford University Press.

Johnson, Matthew. 1996. *An Archaeology of Capitalism: Social Archaeology*. Oxford, U.K.: Blackwell.

———. 2007. *Ideas of Landscape*. Oxford, U.K.: Blackwell.

———. 2010a. *Archaeological Theory: An Introduction*. 2nd ed. Oxford, U.K.: Blackwell.

———. 2010b. *English Houses, 1300–1800: Vernacular Architecture, Social Life*. Harlow, U.K.: Pearson Longman.

Jones, Andrew. 2002. *Archaeological Theory and Scientific Practice*. Cambridge: Cambridge University Press.

Jones, Grant D. 1998. *The Conquest of the Last Maya Kingdom.* Stanford: Stanford University Press.

Joyce, Arthur A. 2004. "Sacred Space and Social Relations in the Valley of Oaxaca." In *Mesoamerican Archaeology,* edited by J. A. Hendon and R. A. Joyce, 192–216. Oxford, U.K.: Blackwell.

———. 2010. *Mixtecs, Zapotecs, and Chatinos: The Ancient Peoples of Southern Mexico.* Oxford, U.K.: Blackwell.

Joyce, Arthur A., Laura Arnaud Bustamante, and Marc N. Levine. 2001. "Commoner Power: A Case Study from the Classic Period Collapse on the Oaxaca Coast." *Journal of Archaeological Method and Theory* 8 (4): 343–85.

Joyce, Arthur A., and Errin T. Weller. 2007. "Commoner Rituals, Resistance, and the Classic-to-Postclassic Transition in Ancient Mesoamerica." In *Commoner Ritual and Ideology in Ancient Mesoamerica,* edited by N. Gonlin and J. C. Lohse, 143–84. Boulder: University of Colorado Press.

Joyce, Rosemary A. 1991. *Cerro Palenque: Power and Identity on the Maya Periphery.* Austin: University of Texas Press.

———. 2000. *Gender and Power in Prehispanic Mesoamerica.* Austin: University of Texas Press.

———. 2004. "Mesoamerica: A Working Model for Archaeology." In *Mesoamerican Archaeology,* edited by J. A. Hendon and R. A. Joyce, 1–42. Oxford, U.K.: Blackwell.

Joyce, Rosemary A., and Jeanne Lopiparo. 2005. "PostScript: Doing Agency in Archaeology." *Journal of Archaeological Method and Theory* 12 (4): 365–74.

Juarez, Santiago. 2003. "The Terraces of Chan: Ancient Maya Villagers and Agriculture." BA thesis, Northwestern University, Evanston, Ill.

Kaplan, A., and K. Ross. 1987. "Introduction." *Yale French Studies* 73: 1–4.

Keller, Angela. 2008. "Jade and Other Stone Artifacts from the Chan Site." Access database in the possession of the author.

———. 2012. "Creating Community with Shell." In *Chan: An Ancient Maya Farming Community,* edited by C. Robin, 253–70. Gainesville: University Press of Florida.

Kestle, Caleb. 2012. "Limestone Quarrying and Household Organization at Chan." In *Chan: An Ancient Maya Farming Community,* edited by C. Robin, 207–30. Gainesville: University Press of Florida.

Kidder, Alfred Vincent. 1924. *An Introduction to the Study of Southwestern Archaeology with a Preliminary Account of the Excavations at Pecos.* New Haven, Conn.: Yale University Press.

———. 1961. "Archaeological Investigations at Kaminaljuyu, Guatemala." *American Philosophical Society Proceedings* 105 (6): 559–70.

Kindon, Andrew, and Samuel Connell. 1999. "Wealth Items and the Prestige-Goods Model: Obsidian at Xunantunich." Paper presented at the Society for American Archaeology Meetings, Chicago.

King, Julia A. 2006. "Household Archaeology, Identities, and Biographies." In *The Cambridge Companion to Historical Archaeology,* edited by D. Hicks and M. C. Beaudry, 293–313. Cambridge: Cambridge University Press.

King, R. B., I. C. Baillie, T.M.B. Abell, J. R. Dunsmore, D. A. Gray, J. H. Pratt, H. R. Versey, A.C.S. Wright, and S. A. Zisman. 1992. *Land Resource Assessment of Northern Belize*. London: Natural Resources Bulletin.

Kolata, Alan L. 1993. *The Tiwanaku: Portrait of an Andean Civilization*. Oxford, U.K.: Blackwell.

———. 1996. *Tiwanaku and Its Hinterland: Archaeology and Paleoecology of an Andean Civilization*. Vol. 1. Smithsonian Series in Archaeological Inquiry. Washington, D.C.: Smithsonian Institution Press.

———. 2002. *Tiwanaku and Its Hinterland: Archaeology and Paleoecology of an Andean Civilization*. Vol. 2. Smithsonian Series in Archaeological Inquiry. Washington, D.C.: Smithsonian Institution Press.

Kosakowsky, Laura J. 2007. "Preliminary Report on the Analysis of the Ceramics from the Chan Project: 2007 Laboratory Season." In *The Chan Project Report: 2007 Season*, edited by C. Robin, 3–24. Report submitted to the Belize Institute of Archaeology, Belmopan.

———. 2009. "Preliminary Report on the Analysis of the Ceramics from the Chan Project: 2009 Laboratory Season." In *The Chan Project Report: 2009 Season*, edited by C. Robin, 3–36. Report submitted to the Belize Institute of Archaeology, Belmopan.

———. 2012. "Ceramics and Chronology at Chan." In *Chan: An Ancient Maya Farming Community*, edited by C. Robin, 42–70. Gainesville: University Press of Florida.

Kosakowsky, Laura J., Anna C. Novotny, Angela H. Keller, Nicholas F. Hearth, and Carmen Ting. 2012. "Contextualizing Ritual Behavior: Caches, Burials, and Problematical Deposits from Chan's Community Center." In *Chan: An Ancient Maya Farming Community*, edited by C. Robin, 289–310. Gainesville: University Press of Florida.

Kosakowsky, Laura J., and Cynthia Robin. 2010. "Contextualizing Ritual Behavior at the Chan Site: Pottery Vessels and Ceramic Artifacts from Burials, Caches, and Problematical Deposits." In *Research Reports in Belizean Archaeology* 7: 45–54.

Kroeber, Alfred L. 1948. *Anthropology: Race, Language, Culture, Psychology, Prehistory*. New York: Harcourt Brace.

Kuijt, Ian. 2000. *Life in Neolithic Farming Communities: Social Organization, Identity, and Differentiation*. New York: Springer.

Lane, Paul J. 2008. "The Use of Ethnography in Landscape Archaeology." In *Handbook of Landscape Archaeology*, edited by D. Bruno and J. Thomas, 237–44. Walnut Creek, Calif.: Left Coast Press.

Langford, R. 1983. "Our Heritage—Your Playground." *Australian Archaeology* 16: 1–6.

Latsch, Michael. 2003. "Operation 2, C-001." In *The Chan Project: 2003 Season*, edited by C. Robin, 52–62. Report submitted to the Belize Institute of Archaeology, Belmopan.

LeCount, Lisa J. 1996. "Pottery and Power: Feasting, Gifting, and Displaying Wealth among the Late and Terminal Classic Lowland Maya." PhD diss., University of California, Los Angeles.

———. 2001. "Like Water for Chocolate: Feasting and Political Ritual among the Late Classic Maya at Xunantunich, Belize." *American Anthropologist* 103 (4): 935–53.

———. 2004. "Looking for a Needle in a Haystack: The Early Classic Period at Actuncan, Cayo District." *Research Reports in Belizean Archaeology* 1: 27–36.

———. 2010. "Mount Maloney People? Domestic Pots, Everyday Practice, and the Social Formation of the Xunantunich Polity." In *Classic Maya Provincial Politics: Xunantunich and Its Hinterlands*, edited by L. J. LeCount and J. Yaeger, 209–32. Tucson: University of Arizona Press.

LeCount, Lisa J., and Jason Yaeger. 2010. "Conclusion: Placing Xunantunich and Its Hinterland Settlements in Perspective." In *Classic Maya Provincial Politics: Xunantunich and Its Hinterlands*, edited by L. J. LeCount and J. Yaeger, 337–69. Tucson: University of Arizona Press.

LeCount, Lisa J., Jason Yaeger, Richard M. Leventhal, and Wendy Ashmore. 2002. "Dating the Rise and Fall of Xunantunich, Belize." *Ancient Mesoamerica* 13 (1): 41–63.

Lefebvre, Henri. 2004. *Rhythmanalysis: Space, Time, and Everyday Life*. London: Continuum.

———. 2008. *Critique of Everyday Life*. 3 vols. London: Verso. Vol. 1 reprinted 1958; vol. 2 reprinted 1961.

Lentz, David. 2000. *Imperfect Balance: Landscape Transformations in the Precolumbian Americas*. New York: Columbia University Press.

Lentz, David L., and Bryan Hockaday. 2009. "Tikal Timbers and Temples: Ancient Maya Agroforestry and the End of Time." *Journal of Archaeological Science* 36 (7): 1342–53.

Lentz, David, Sally Woods, Angela Hood, and Marcus Murph. 2012. "Agroforestry and Agricultural Production of the Ancient Maya at Chan." In *Chan: An Ancient Maya Farming Community*, edited by C. Robin, 89–112. Gainesville: University Press of Florida.

Leone, Mark P. 1984. "Interpreting Ideology in Historical Archaeology: Using the Rules of Perspective in the William Paca Garden in Annapolis, Maryland." In *Ideology, Power and Prehistory*, edited by D. Miller and C. Tilley, 25–35. Cambridge: Cambridge University Press.

Leventhal, Richard M., and Wendy Ashmore. 2004. "Xunantunich in a Belize Valley Context." In *The Ancient Maya of the Belize Valley: Half a Century of Archaeological Research*, edited by J. F. Garber, 168–79. Gainesville: University Press of Florida.

Lightfoot, Kent G. 1995. "Culture Contact Studies: Redefining the Relationship between Prehistoric and Historical Archaeology." *American Antiquity* 60 (2): 199–217.

———. 2005. *Indians, Missionaries, and Merchants: The Legacy of Colonial Encounters on the California Frontiers*. Berkeley: University of California Press.

Lightfoot, K. G., A. Martinez, and A. M. Schiff. 1998. "Daily Practice and Material Culture in Pluralistic Social Settings: An Archaeological Study of Culture Change and Persistence from Fort Ross, California." *American Antiquity* 63 (2): 199–222.

Lohse, Jon C. 2007. "Commoner Ritual, Commoner Ideology: (Sub)-Alternate Views of Social Complexity in Prehispanic Mesoamerica." In *Commoner Ritual and Ideology in Ancient Mesoamerica*, edited by N. Gonlin and J. C. Lohse, 1–32. Boulder: University Press of Colorado.

Lohse, Jon C., and Fred Valdez, eds. 2004. *Ancient Maya Commoners*. Austin: University of Texas Press.

Lucero, L. J. 2010. "Materialized Cosmology among Ancient Maya Commoners." *Journal of Social Archaeology* 10 (1): 138–67.

Lüdtke, Alf. 1995. *The History of Everyday Life: Reconstructing Historical Experiences and Ways of Life*. Princeton: Princeton University Press.

Lyman, R. L., and M. J. O'Brien. 2001. "The Direct Historical Approach, Analogical Reasoning, and Theory in Americanist Archaeology." *Journal of Archaeological Method and Theory* 8 (4): 303–42.

Malthus, T. R. 1798. *An Essay on the Principle of Population*. London: J. Johnson.

Manzanilla, Linda, and Pingarron Luis Barba. 1990. "The Study of Activities in Classic Households: Two Case Studies from Coba and Teotihuacan." *Ancient Mesoamerica* 1 (1): 41–49.

Marcus, Joyce. 1993. "Ancient Maya Political Organization." In *Lowland Maya Civilization in the Eighth Century A.D.*, edited by J. A. Sabloff and J. S. Henderson, 111–83. Washington, D.C.: Dumbarton Oaks.

———. 1995. "Where Is Lowland Maya Archaeology Headed?" *Journal of Archaeological Research* 3 (1): 3–53.

———. 2001. "Breaking the Glass Ceiling: The Strategies of Royal Women in Ancient States." In *Gender in Pre-Hispanic Mesoamerica*, edited by C. Klein, 305–40. Washington, D.C.: Dumbarton Oaks.

Marcus, Joyce, and Charles Stanish. 2006. *Agricultural Strategies*. Los Angeles: Cotsen Institute of Archaeology.

Martin, Simon, and Nikolai Grube. 2000. *Chronicle of the Maya Kings and Queens: Deciphering the Dynasties of the Ancient Maya*. London: Thames and Hudson.

Marx, Karl. (1869) 1963. *The Eighteenth Brumaire of Louis Bonaparte, with Explanatory Notes*. New York: International Publishers.

Marx, Karl, and Friedrich Engels. (1932) 1970. *The German Ideology*. New York: International Publishers.

Matthews, W., C.A.I. French, T. Lawrence, D. F. Cutler, and M. K. Jones. 1997. "Microstratigraphic Traces of Site Formation Processes and Human Activities." *World Archaeology* 29 (2): 281–308.

McAnany, Patricia Ann. 1995. *Living with the Ancestors: Kinship and Kingship in Ancient Maya Society*. Austin: University of Texas Press.

———. 2004. *Kaxob: Ritual, Work, and Family in an Ancient Maya Village*. Los Angeles: Cotsen Institute of Archaeology.

McGuire, Randall H. 2008. *Archaeology as Political Action*. Berkeley: University of California Press.

McNiven, Ian J. 2008. "Sentient Seas: Seascapes as Spiritscapes." In *Handbook of Landscape Archaeology*, edited by B. David and J. Thomas, 149–58. Walnut Creek, Calif.: Left Coast Press.

Medick, Hans. 1995. "'Missionaries in the Rowboat'? Ethnological Ways of Knowing as a Challenge to Social History." In *The History of Everyday Life: Reconstructing Historical Experiences and Ways of Life*, edited by A. Lüdtke, 41–71. Princeton: Princeton University Press.

Meierhoff, James, Mark Golitko, and James D. Morris. 2012. "Obsidian Acquisition, Trade, and Regional Interaction at Chan." In *Chan: An Ancient Maya Farming Community*, edited by C. Robin, 271–88. Gainesville: University Press of Florida.

Merrifield, Andy. 2006. *Henri Lefebvre: A Critical Introduction*. New York: Routledge.

Meskell, Lynn. 1996. "The Somatisation of Archaeology: Institutions, Discourses, Corporeality." *Norwegian Archaeological Review* 29: 1–16.

———. 1999. *Archaeologies of Social Life: Age, Sex, Class et Cetera in Ancient Egypt*. Oxford, U.K.: Blackwell.

———. 2002. *Private Life in New Kingdom Egypt*. Princeton: Princeton University Press.

Meskell, Lynn, and Rosemary A. Joyce. 2003. *Embodied Lives: Figuring Ancient Maya and Egyptian Experience*. London: Routledge.

Meskell, Lynn, and Robert W. Preucel. 2004. *A Companion to Social Archaeology*. Oxford, U.K.: Blackwell.

Middleton, William D. 1998. "Craft Specialization at Ejutla, Oaxaca, Mexico: An Archaeometric Study of the Organization of Household Craft Production." PhD diss., University of Wisconsin, Madison.

———. 2004. "Identifying Chemical Activity Residues on Prehistoric House Floors: A Methodology and Rationale for Multi-elemental Characterization of Mild Acid Extract of Anthropogenic Sediments." *Archaeometry* 46: 47–65.

Middleton, William D., and T. Douglas Price. 1996. "Identification of Activity Areas by Multi-element Characterization of Sediments from Modern and Archeological House Floors Using Inductively Coupled Plasma-Atomic Emission Spectroscopy." *Journal of Archaeological Science* 23: 673–87.

Miller, Daniel. 1998. *A Theory of Shopping*. Ithaca, N.Y.: Cornell University Press.

———. 2008. *The Comfort of Things*. Cambridge, U.K.: Polity Press.

———. 2010. *Stuff*. Cambridge, U.K.: Polity Press.

———. 2012. *Consumption and Its Consequences*. Cambridge, U.K.: Polity Press.

Moore, Jerry D. 1996. *Architecture and Power in the Ancient Andes: The Archaeology of Public Buildings*. Cambridge, U.K.: Cambridge University Press.

Morgan, Lewis Henry. 1878. *Ancient Society; or, Researches in the Lines of Human Progress from Savagery through Barbarism to Civilization*. New York: H. Holt.

———. 1879. "A Study of the Houses of the American Aborigines with a Scheme of Exploration of the Ruins in New Mexico and Elsewhere." *Annual Report Archaeological Institute of America* 1880: 29–80.

———. 1881. *Houses and House-Life of the American Aborigines, Contributions to North American Ethnology*. Washington, D.C.: Government Printing Office.

Morrison, K. D. 1996. "Typological Schemes and Agricultural Change: Beyond Boserup in Precolonial South India." *Current Anthropology* 37 (4): 583–608.

Morson, Gary S., and Caryl Emerson. 1990. *Mikhail Bakhtin: Creation of a Prosaics*. Stanford: Stanford University Press.

Mould, Quita, Ian Carlisle, Esther A. Cameron, and York Archaeological Trust. 2003. *Craft, Industry and Everyday Life: Leather and Leatherworking in Anglo-Scandinavian and Medieval York*. York: Council for British Archaeology.

Munro, William A. 1998. *The Moral Economy of the State: Conservation, Community Development, and State Making in Zimbabwe*. Monographs in International Studies Africa Series. Athens: Ohio University Center for International Studies.

Neff, L. Theodore. 2010. "Population, Intensive Agriculture, Labor Value, and Elite-

Commoner Political Power Relations in the Xunantunich Hinterlands." In *Classic Maya Provincial Politics: Xunantunich and Its Hinterlands*, edited by L. J. LeCount and J. Yaeger, 250–71. Tucson: University of Arizona Press.

Neff, L. Theodore, Cynthia Robin, Kevin Schwartz, and Mary Morrison. 1995. "The Xunantunich Settlement Survey." In *Xunantunich Archaeological Project: 1995 Season*, edited by R. M. Leventhal, 164–92. Report submitted to the Belize Institute of Archaeology, Belmopan.

Nelson, Sarah M. 2003. *Ancient Queens: Archaeological Explorations*. Walnut Creek, Calif.: Altamira Press.

———. 2006. *Handbook of Gender in Archaeology*. Walnut Creek, Calif.: Altamira Press.

Netting, Robert M. 1993. *Smallholders, Householders: Farm Families and the Ecology of Intensive, Sustainable Agriculture*. Stanford: Stanford University Press.

Novotny, Anna C. 2012. "The Chan Community: A Bioarchaeological Perspective." In *Chan: An Ancient Maya Farming Community*, edited by C. Robin, 231–52. Gainesville: University Press of Florida.

Oland, Maxine. 2009. "Long-Term Indigenous History on a Colonial Frontier: Archaeology at a 15th–17th Century Maya Village, Progresso Lagoon, Belize." PhD diss., Northwestern University, Evanston, Ill.

———. 2012. "Lost among the Colonial Maya: Engaging Indigenous Maya Colonial History at Progresso Lagoon, Belize." In *Decolonizing Indigenous Histories: Exploring Prehistoric/Colonial Transitions in Archaeology*, edited by M. Oland, S. M. Hart, and L. Frink, 178–200. Tucson: University of Arizona Press.

Oland, Maxine, Siobhan M. Hart, and Liam Frink. 2012. *Decolonizing Indigenous Histories: Exploring Prehistoric/Colonial Transitions in Archaeology*. Tucson: University of Arizona Press.

Ortner, Sherry B. 1984. "Theory in Anthropology since the Sixties." *Comparative Studies in Society and History* 26: 126–66.

Özbal, Rana. 2006. "Households, Daily Practices and Cultural Appropriation at Sixth Millennium Tell Kurdu." PhD diss., Northwestern University.

Palerm, Angel. 1967. "Agricultural Systems and Food Patterns." In *Social Anthropology Handbook of Middle American Indians*, edited by N. Manning, 26–52. Austin: University of Texas Press.

Pauketat, Timothy R. 2001. "Practice and History in Archaeology." *Anthropological Theory* 1: 73–98.

Preucel, Robert W. 1991. *Processual and Postprocessual Archaeologies: Multiple Ways of Knowing the Past*. Carbondale: Center for Archaeological Investigations, Southern Illinois University at Carbondale.

Preucel, Robert W., and Lynn Meskell. 2004. "Knowledges." In *Companion to Social Archaeology*, edited by L. Meskell and R. W. Preucel, 3–22. Oxford, U.K.: Blackwell.

Preucel, Robert W., and Stephen A. Mrozowski. 2010. *Contemporary Archaeology in Theory: The New Pragmatism*. Oxford, U.K.: Wiley-Blackwell.

Pyburn, K. Anne. 1997. "The Archaeological Signature of Complexity in the Maya Lowlands." In *The Archaeology of City States: Cross-Cultural Approaches*, edited by D. Nichols and T. Charlton, 155–68. Washington, D.C.: Smithsonian Institution Press.

———. 1998. "Smallholders in the Maya Lowlands: Homage to a Garden Variety Ethnographer." *Human Ecology* 26 (2): 267–86.

———. 2004. *Ungendering Civilization*. London: Routledge.

Re Cruz, Alicia. 1996. *The Two Milpas of Chan Kom: Scenarios of a Maya Village Life*. Albany: State University of New York Press.

Redfield, Robert. 1941. *The Folk Culture of Yucatán*. Chicago: University of Chicago Press.

———. 1960. *The Little Community and Peasant Society and Culture*. Chicago: University of Chicago Press.

Redfield, Robert, and Alfonso Villa Rojas. 1934. *Chan Kom: A Maya Village*. Washington, D.C.: Carnegie Institution of Washington.

Redman, Charles L. 1978. *The Rise of Civilization: From Early Farmers to Urban Society in the Ancient Near East*. San Francisco: W. H. Freeman.

———. 1999. *Human Impact on Ancient Environments*. Tucson: University of Arizona Press.

Renfrew, Colin, and Paul G. Bahn. 1996. *Archaeology: Theories, Methods, and Practice*. London: Thames and Hudson.

———. 2005. *Archaeology: The Key Concepts*. London: Routledge.

Rice, Don S., and Prudence M. Rice. 1990. "Population Size and Population Change in the Central Petén Lakes Region, Guatemala." In *Precolumbian Population History in the Maya Lowlands*, edited by T. P. Culbert and D. S. Rice, 123–49. Albuquerque: University of New Mexico Press.

Rice, Prudence M. 2004. *Maya Political Science: Time, Astronomy, and the Cosmos*. Austin: University of Texas Press.

Ricketson, Oliver G., Jr., and Edith B. Ricketson. 1937. *Uaxactun, Guatemala: Group E: 1926–1931*. Publication 477. Washington, D.C.: Carnegie Institution of Washington.

Ringle, William M., and George J. Bey III. 2001. "Post-Classic and Terminal Classic Courts of the Northern Maya Lowlands." In *Royal Courts of the Ancient Maya*, edited by T. Inomata and S. D. Houston, 266–307. Boulder, Colo.: Westview Press.

Robb, John. 2007. *The Early Mediterranean Village: Agency, Material Culture, and Social Change in Neolithic Italy*. Cambridge: Cambridge University Press.

Robin, Cynthia. 1999. "Towards an Archaeology of Everyday Life: Maya Farmers of Chan Nòohol and Dos Chombitos Cik'in, Belize." PhD diss., University of Pennsylvania, Philadelphia.

———. 2001. "Peopling the Past: New Perspectives on the Ancient Maya." *Proceedings of the National Academy of Sciences* 98 (1): 18–21.

———. 2002a. "Outside of Houses: The Practices of Everyday Life at Chan Nòohol, Belize." *Journal of Social Archaeology* 2 (2): 245–68.

———. 2002b. "Gender and Farming: Chan Nòohol, Belize." In *Ancient Maya Women*, edited by T. Ardren, 12–30. Walnut Creek, Calif.: Altamira Press.

———. 2003. "New Directions in Classic Maya Household Archaeology." *Journal of Archaeological Research* 11 (4): 307–56.

———. 2004. "Social Diversity and Everyday Life within Classic Maya Settlements." In *Mesoamerican Archaeology*, edited by J. A. Hendon and R. A. Joyce, 148–68. Oxford, U.K.: Blackwell.

————. 2006. "Gender, Farming, and Long-Term Change: Maya Historical and Archaeological Perspectives." *Current Anthropology* 47 (3): 409–33.

————, ed. 2012a. *Chan: An Ancient Maya Farming Community*. Gainesville: University Press of Florida.

————. 2012b. "Introducing the Chan Site: Farmers in Complex Society." In *Chan: An Ancient Maya Farming Community*, edited by C. Robin, 1–18. Gainesville: University Press of Florida.

————. 2012c. "Learning from an Ancient Maya Farming Community." In *Chan: An Ancient Maya Farming Community*, edited by C. Robin, 311–42. Gainesville: University Press of Florida.

Robin, Cynthia, and Elizabeth M. Brumfiel. 2008. *Gender, Households, and Society: Unraveling the Threads of the Past and the Present*. Archaeological Papers of the American Anthropological Association 18. Oxford, U.K.: Blackwell.

Robin, Cynthia, James Meierhoff, Caleb Kestle, Chelsea Blackmore, Laura J. Kosakowsky, and Anna C. Novotny. 2012. "Ritual in a Farming Community." In *Chan: An Ancient Maya Farming Community*, edited by C. Robin, 113–32. Gainesville: University Press of Florida.

Robin, Cynthia, James Meierhoff, and Laura J. Kosakowsky. 2012. "Nonroyal Governance at Chan's Community Center." In *Chan: An Ancient Maya Farming Community*, edited by C. Robin, 133–49. Gainesville: University Press of Florida.

Robin, Cynthia, and Nan A. Rothschild. 2002. "Archaeological Ethnographies: Social Dynamics of Outdoor Space." *Journal of Social Archaeology* 2 (2): 159–72.

Robin, Cynthia, Andrew R. Wyatt, Laura J. Kosakowsky, Santiago Juarez, Ethan Kalosky, and Elise Enterkin. 2012. "A Changing Cultural Landscape: Settlement Survey and GIS at Chan." In *Chan: An Ancient Maya Farming Community*, edited by C. Robin, 19–41. Gainesville: University Press of Florida.

Robin, Cynthia, Jason Yaeger, and Wendy Ashmore. 2010. "Living in the Hinterlands of a Provincial Polity." In *Classic Maya Provincial Politics: Xunantunich and Its Hinterlands*, edited by L. J. LeCount and J. Yaeger, 315–36. Tucson: University of Arizona Press.

Rodriguez, V. P. 2006. "States and Households: The Social Organization of Terrace Agriculture in Postclassic Mixteca Alta, Oaxaca, Mexico." *Latin American Antiquity* 17 (1): 3–22.

Roseberry, William. 1989. *Anthropologies and Histories: Essays in Culture, History, and Political Economy*. New Brunswick, N.J.: Rutgers University Press.

Sabloff, Jeremy A. 2008. *Archaeology Matters: Action Archaeology in the Modern World*. Walnut Creek, Calif.: Left Coast Press.

Samson, Ross. 1990. Introduction to *The Social Archaeology of Houses*, edited by R. Samson, 1–18. Edinburgh: University of Edinburgh Press.

Scarborough, Vernon L. 1998. "Ecology and Ritual: Water Management and the Maya." *Latin American Antiquity* 9 (2): 135–59.

Scarborough, Vernon L., and F. Valdez. 2009. "An Alternative Order: The Dualistic Economies of the Ancient Maya." *Latin American Antiquity* 20 (1): 207–27.

Scarborough, Vernon L., Fred Valdez Jr., and Nicholas Dunning. 2003. *Heterarchy, Political Economy, and the Ancient Maya.* Tucson: University of Arizona Press.

Schele, Linda, and David A. Freidel. 1992. *A Forest of Kings: The Untold Story of the Ancient Maya.* New York: Quill/W. Morrow.

Scheper-Hughes, Nancy. 1992. *Death without Weeping: The Violence of Everyday Life in Brazil.* Berkeley: University of California Press.

Schortman, Edward M. 2010. "Provincial Politics at Xunantunich: Power, Differentiation, and Identity in a Classic-Period Maya Realm." In *Classic Maya Provincial Politics: Xunantunich and Its Hinterlands,* edited by L. J. LeCount and J. Yaeger, 370–84. Tucson: University of Arizona Press.

Schortman, Edward M., and Patricia A. Urban. 1992. *Resources, Power, and Interregional Interaction.* New York: Plenum Press.

———. 1994. "Living on the Edge: Core/Periphery Relations in Ancient Southeastern Mesoamerica." *Current Anthropology* 35 (4): 401–30.

Schwartz, Glenn M., and Steven E. Falconer. 1994. *Archaeological Views from the Countryside: Village Communities in Early Complex Societies.* Washington, D.C.: Smithsonian Institution Press.

Scott, James C. 1976. *The Moral Economy of the Peasant: Rebellion and Subsistence in Southeast Asia.* New Haven, Conn.: Yale University Press.

———. 1985. *Weapons of the Weak: Everyday Forms of Peasant Resistance.* New Haven, Conn.: Yale University Press.

———. 1990. *Domination and the Arts of Resistance: Hidden Transcripts.* New Haven, Conn.: Yale University Press.

Shanks, Michael, and Christopher Y. Tilley. 1988. *Social Theory and Archaeology.* Albuquerque: University of New Mexico Press.

———. 1992. *Re-constructing Archaeology: Theory and Practice.* London: Routledge.

Sheets, Payson D. 1992. *The Ceren Site: A Prehistoric Village Buried by Volcanic Ash in Central America.* Fort Worth, Tex.: Harcourt, Brace, Jovanovich.

———. 2000. "Provisioning the Ceren Household: The Vertical Economy, Village Economy, and Household Economy in the Southeastern Maya Periphery." *Ancient Mesoamerica* 11 (2): 217–30.

———, ed. 2002. *Before the Volcano Erupted: The Ancient Cerén Village in Central America.* Austin: University of Texas Press.

———. 2006. *The Ceren Site: An Ancient Village Buried by Volcanic Ash in Central America.* Belmont, Calif.: Thomson Higher Education.

Sheringham, Michael. 2006. *Everyday Life: Theories and Practices from Surrealism to the Present.* Oxford: Oxford University Press.

Silliman, Stephen W. 2004. *Lost Laborers in Colonial California: Native Americans and the Archaeology of Rancho Petaluma.* Tucson: University of Arizona Press.

Simmons, Scott E., and Payson Sheets. 2002. "Divination at Cerén: The Evidence from Structure 12." In *Before the Volcano Erupted: The Ancient Cerén Village in Central America,* edited by P. Sheets, 104–14. Austin: University of Texas Press.

Smith, Adam. 1776. *An Inquiry into the Nature and Causes of the Wealth of Nations.* 3 vols. Dublin: Whitestone.

Smith, Adam T. 2003. *The Political Landscape: Constellations of Authority in Early Complex Polities.* Berkeley: University of California Press.

Smith, Dorothy E. 1987. *The Everyday World as Problematic: A Feminist Sociology.* Boston: Northeastern University Press.

———. 1992. "Remaking a Life, Remaking Sociology: Reflections of a Feminist." In *Fragile Truths: Twenty-Five Years of Sociology and Anthropology in Canada,* edited by W. K. Carroll, L. Christiansen-Ruffman, R. F. Currie, and D. Harrison. Ottawa, Ont.: Carleton University Press.

———. 1994. "A Berkeley Education." In *Gender and the Academic Experience: Berkeley Women Sociologists,* edited by K. P. Meadow Orlans and R. A. Wallace, 45–56. Lincoln: University of Nebraska Press.

Smith, Michael E. 1994. "Social Complexity in the Aztec Countryside." In *Archaeological Views from the Countryside: Village Communities in Early Complex Societies,* edited by G. M. Schwartz and S. E. Falconer, 143–59. Washington, D.C.: Smithsonian Institution Press.

———. 2004. "The Archaeology of Ancient State Economies." *Annual Review of Anthropology* 33: 73–102.

Smith, Monica L. 1999. "The Role of Ordinary Goods in Premodern Exchange." *Journal of Archaeological Method and Theory* 6 (2): 109–35.

———. 2010. *A Prehistory of Ordinary People.* Tucson: University of Arizona Press.

Snead, James E. 2008. *Ancestral Landscapes of the Pueblo World.* Tucson: University of Arizona Press.

Sørensen, Marie Louise Stig. 2000. *Gender Archaeology.* Cambridge, Mass.: Blackwell.

Spencer-Wood, Suzanne M. 1991. "Towards a Historical Archaeology of Materialistic Domestic Reform." In *The Archaeology of Inequality,* edited by R. H. McGuire and R. Paynter, 231–86. Oxford, U.K.: Blackwell.

———. 1999. "Gendering Power." In *Manifesting Power: Gender and the Interpretation of Power in Archaeology,* edited by T. L. Sweely, 175–83. London: Routledge.

Stahl, Ann Brower. 2001. *Making History in Banda: Anthropological Visions of Africa's Past.* Cambridge: Cambridge University Press.

Stahl, Peter W., and James A. Zeidler. 1990. "Differential Bone-Refuse Accumulation in Food-Preparation and Traffic Areas on an Early Ecuadorian House Floor." *Latin American Antiquity* 1: 150–69.

Stanish, Charles. 2006. "Prehispanic Agricultural Strategies of Intensification in the Titicaca Basin of Peru and Bolivia." In *Agricultural Strategies,* edited by J. Marcus and C. Stanish, 364–400. Los Angeles: Cotsen Institute of Archaeology Press.

Steggerda, Morris. 1941. *Maya Indians of Yucatan.* Carnegie Institution of Washington Publication 531. Washington, D.C.: Carnegie Institution of Washington.

Stein, Gil. 1999. *Rethinking World-Systems: Diasporas, Colonies, and Interaction in Uruk Mesopotamia.* Tucson: University of Arizona Press.

———. 2002. "From Passive Periphery to Active Agents: Emerging Perspectives in the Archaeology of Interregional Interaction." *American Anthropologist* 104 (3): 903–16.

Strong, William Duncan. 1933. "The Plains Culture Area in the Light of Archaeology." *American Anthropologist* 35: 271–87.

Sweely, Tracy L. 1998. "Personal Interactions: The Implications of Spatial Arrangements for Power Relations at Cerén, El Salvador." *World Archaeology* 29 (3): 393–406.

Taschek, Jennifer J., and Joseph W. Ball. 1992. "Lord Smoke-Squirrel's Cacao Cup: The Archaeological Context and Socio-Historical Significance of the Buenavista-Jauncy Vase." In *The Maya Vase Book*, edited by J. Kerr, 490–97. New York: Kerr Associates.

Tate, Carolyn E. 1992. *Yaxchilan: The Design of a Maya Ceremonial City*. Austin: University of Texas Press.

Thomas, Julian. 1996. *Time, Culture, and Identity: An Interpretative Archaeology*. London: Routledge.

———. 2001. "Archaeologies of Place and Landscape." In *Archaeological Theory Today*, edited by I. Hodder, 165–86. Oxford, U.K.: Blackwell.

———. 2008. "Archaeology, Landscape, and Dwelling." In *Handbook of Landscape Archaeology*, edited by B. David and J. Thomas, 300–306. Walnut Creek, Calif.: Left Coast Press.

Thompson, Edward Herbert. 1892. "The Ancient Structures of Yucatan Not Communal Dwellings." *Proceedings of the American Antiquarian Society* 2: 262–69.

Thompson, Edward P. 1971. "The Moral Economy of the English Crowd in the Eighteenth Century." *Present and Past* 50: 76–136.

Tilley, Christopher Y. 1994. *A Phenomenology of Landscape: Places, Paths, and Monuments*. Oxford, U.K.: Berg.

———. 2010. *Interpreting Landscapes: Geologies, Topographies, Identities*. Walnut Creek, Calif.: Left Coast Press.

Tourtellot, Gair. 1990. "Population Estimates for Preclassic and Classic Seibal, Petén." In *Precolumbian Population History in the Maya Lowlands*, edited by T. P. Culbert and D. S. Rice, 83–102. Albuquerque: University of New Mexico Press.

Tourtellot, Gair, Jeremy A. Sabloff, and Michael P. Smyth. 1990. "Room Counts and Population Estimation for Terminal Classic Sayil in the Puuc Region, Yucatán, Mexico." In *Precolumbian Population History in the Maya Lowlands*, edited by T. P. Culbert and D. S. Rice, 245–62. Albuquerque: University of New Mexico Press.

Trebitsch, Michel. 2008. Preface to *Critique of Everyday Life*, edited by H. Lefebvre. London: Verso.

Trigger, Bruce. 1972. "Determinants of Urban Growth in Preindustrial Societies." In *Man, Settlement, and Urbanism*, edited by P. J. Ucko, R. Tringham, and G. W. Dimbleby, 575–99. London: Duckworth.

Tringham, Ruth E. 1991. "Households with Faces: The Challenge of Gender in Prehistoric Architectural Remains." In *Engendering Archaeology: Women and Prehistory*, edited by J. M. Gero and M. W. Conkey, 93–131. Oxford, U.K.: Blackwell.

Tsing, Anna Lowenhaupt. 1993. *In the Realm of the Diamond Queen: Marginality in an Out-of-the-Way Place*. Princeton: Princeton University Press.

Turner, B. L., II. 1978. "Ancient Agricultural Land Use in the Central Maya Lowlands." In *Pre-Hispanic Maya Agriculture*, edited by P. D. Harrison and B. L. Turner II, 163–83. Albuquerque: University of New Mexico Press.

———. 1983. *Once Beneath the Forest: Prehistoric Terracing in the Río Bec Region of the Maya Lowlands*. Dellplain Latin American Studies no. 13. Boulder, Colo.: Westview Press.

Vogt, Evon Z. 1976. *Tortillas for the Gods: A Symbolic Analysis of Zinacanteco Rituals.* Cambridge: Cambridge University Press.

Voss, Barbara L. 2008a. *The Archaeology of Ethnogenesis: Race and Sexuality in Colonial San Francisco.* Berkeley: University of California Press.

———. 2008b. "Sexuality Studies in Archaeology." *Annual Review of Anthropology* 7: 317–36.

Walker, John H. 2011. "Social Implications from Agricultural Taskscapes in the Southwestern Amazon." *Latin American Antiquity* 22 (3): 275–95.

Walker, William H., and Lisa J. Lucero. 2000. "The Depositional History of Ritual Power." In *Agency in Archaeology*, edited by M.-A. Dobres and J. Robb, 130–47. London: Routledge.

Wall, Diana diZerega. 1994. *The Archaeology of Gender: Separating the Spheres in Urban America.* New York: Plenum Press.

Wattenmaker, Patricia. 1998. *Household and State in Upper Mesopotamia: Specialized Economy and the Social Uses of Goods in an Early Complex Society.* Washington, D.C.: Smithsonian Institution Press.

Webster, David, and AnnCorrine Freter. 1990. "The Demography of Late Classic Copan." In *Precolumbian Population History in the Maya Lowlands*, edited by T. P. Culbert and D. S. Rice, 37–62. Albuquerque: University of New Mexico Press.

Wedel, Waldo Rudolph. 1938. *The Direct-Historical Approach in Pawnee Archeology.* Washington, D.C.: Smithsonian Institution.

Weiner, James F. 1991. *The Empty Place: Poetry, Space, and Being among the Foi of Papua New Guinea.* Bloomington: Indiana University Press.

Wells, E. C., and R. E. Terry. 2007. "Advances in Geoarchaeological Approaches to Anthrosol Chemistry. Part I: Agriculture—Introduction." Special issue, *Geoarchaeology: An International Journal* 22 (3): 285–90.

Wilk, Richard R. 1996. *Economies and Cultures: Foundations of Economic Anthropology.* Boulder, Colo.: Westview Press.

Wilk, Richard R., and Wendy Ashmore. 1988. *Household and Community in the Mesoamerican Past.* Albuquerque: University of New Mexico Press.

Wilk, Richard R., and William Rathje. 1982. "Household Archaeology." *American Behavioral Scientist* 25 (6): 617–39.

Wilkie, Laurie A. 2000. *Creating Freedom: Material Culture and African American Identity at Oakley Plantation, Louisiana, 1840–1950.* Baton Rouge: Louisiana State University Press.

———. 2003. *The Archaeology of Mothering: An African-American Midwife's Tale.* New York: Routledge.

Willey, Gordon R., William R. Bullard Jr., and J. B. Glass. 1955. "The Maya Community of Prehistoric Times." *Archaeology* 8 (1): 18–25.

Willey, Gordon R., William R. Bullard Jr., J. B. Glass, and James C. Gifford. 1965. *Prehistoric Maya Settlement in the Belize Valley.* Papers of the Peabody Museum of Archaeology and Ethnology 54. Cambridge, Mass.: Harvard University.

Willey, Gordon R., and Jeremy A. Sabloff. 1980. *A History of American Archaeology.* San Francisco: W. H. Freeman.

Williams, Raymond. 1973. *The Country and the City*. Oxford: Oxford University Press.

———. 1989. *Resources of Hope: Culture, Democracy, Socialism*. London: Verso.

Willis, Susan. 1991. *A Primer for Daily Life*. Studies in Culture and Communication. London: Routledge.

Wilson, Gregory D. 2008. *The Archaeology of Everyday Life at Early Moundville*. Tuscaloosa: University of Alabama Press.

Wittfogel, Karl August. 1957. *Oriental Despotism: A Comparative Study of Total Power*. New Haven, Conn.: Yale University Press.

Wobst, H. Martin. 1978. "The Archaeo-Ethnology of Hunter-Gatherers or the Tyranny of the Ethnographic Record in Archaeology." *American Antiquity* 43 (2): 303–9.

Wolf, Eric. 1955. "Types of Latin American Peasantry: A Preliminary Discussion." *American Anthropologist* 57: 452–71.

———. 1982. *Europe and the People without History*. Berkeley: University of California Press.

Wood, Margaret. 2002. "Women's Work and Class Conflict in a Working-Class Coal-Mining Community." In *The Dynamics of Power*, edited by M. O'Donovan, 66–87. Carbondale, Ill.: Center for Archaeological Investigations.

Wyatt, Andrew R. 2008a. "Gardens on Hills: The Archaeology of Ancient Maya Terrace Agriculture at Chan, Belize." PhD diss., University of Illinois at Chicago.

———. 2008b. "Pine as an Element of Household Refuse in the Fertilization of Ancient Maya Agricultural Fields." *Journal of Ethnobiology* 28 (2): 244–58.

———. 2012. "Agricultural Practices at Chan: Farming and Political Economy in an Ancient Maya Community." In *Chan: An Ancient Maya Farming Community*, edited by C. Robin, 71–88. Gainesville: University Press of Florida.

Wylie, Alison. 1985. "The Reaction against Analogy." *Advances in Archaeological Method and Theory* 8: 63–111.

———. 1991. "Gender Theory and the Archaeological Record: Why Is There No Archaeology of Gender?" In *Engendering Archaeology: Women and Prehistory*, edited by J. M. Gero and M. W. Conkey, 31–56. Oxford, U.K.: Blackwell.

———. 1992. "The Interplay of Evidential Constraints and Political Interests: Recent Archaeological Research on Gender." *American Antiquity* 57 (1): 15–35.

———. 2002. *Thinking from Things: Essays in the Philosophy of Archaeology*. Berkeley: University of California Press.

———. 2007. "Doing Archaeology as a Feminist: Introduction." *Journal of Archaeological Method and Theory* 14 (3): 209–16.

———. 2008. "Legacies of Collaboration: Transformative Criticism in Archaeology." Distinguished Lecture in Archaeology, Archaeology Division, American Anthropological Association, San Francisco, Calif.

Yaeger, Jason. 2000a. "Changing Patterns of Social Organization: The Late and Terminal Classic Communities at San Lorenzo, Cayo District, Belize." PhD diss., University of Pennsylvania, Philadelphia.

———. 2000b. "The Social Construction of Communities in the Classic Maya Countryside: Strategies of Affiliation in Western Belize." In *The Archaeology of Communities: A New World Perspective*, edited by M. Canuto and J. Yaeger, 123–42. London: Routledge.

———. 2003. "Untangling the Ties That Bind: The City, the Countryside, and the Nature of Maya Urbanism at Xunantunich, Belize." In *The Social Construction of Ancient Cities*, edited by M. L. Smith, 121–55. Washington, D.C.: Smithsonian Books.

———. 2008. "Charting the Collapse: Late Classic to Postclassic Population Dynamics in the Mopan Valley, Belize." *Research Reports in Belizean Archaeology* 5: 13–21.

———. 2010. "Landscapes of the Xunantunich Hinterlands." In *Classic Maya Provincial Politics: Xunantunich and Its Hinterlands*, edited by L. J. LeCount and J. Yaeger, 233–50. Tucson: University of Arizona Press.

Yaeger, Jason, and Marcello A. Canuto. 2000. "Introducing the Archaeology of Communities." In *Archaeology of Communities: A New World Perspective*, edited by M. A. Canuto and J. Yaeger, 1–15. London: Routledge.

Yaeger, Jason, Bernadette Cap, and Meaghan Peuramaki-Brown. 2009. "The 2007 Field Season of the Mopan Valley Archaeological Project: Buenavista del Cayo's East Plaza and Near-Periphery Settlement." *Research Reports in Belizean Archaeology* 6: 209–17.

Yaeger, Jason, and Samuel V. Connell. 1993. "Xunantunich Settlement Survey, 1993 Report." In *Xunantunich Archaeological Project: 1993 Field Season*, edited by R. M. Leventhal, 172–201. Report submitted to the Belize Institute of Archaeology.

Yaeger, Jason, and Cynthia Robin. 2004. "Heterogeneous Hinterlands: The Social and Political Organization of Commoner Settlements near Xunantunich, Belize." In *Ancient Maya Commoners*, edited by J. C. Lohse and F. Valdez, 147–74. Austin: University of Texas Press.

Index

Belize River valley, 10; ceramic use across, 168–69; Chan location and Maya area of, *92*; early occupation, 106; major centers of, 112, 174–75; society interpreted without everyday life, 188–95

Bench: masonry, 144; quincunx pattern in, 165

"Berkeley Education, A" (D. Smith), 38

Binford, Lewis, 47

Blackmore, Chelsea, 105, 133–36, *134*

Black vessels, 169, *170*

Boserup, Ester, 177–79, 189; hypothetical labor value data, 207n1

Bourdieu, Pierre, 5, 26–27; doxa concept, 29

Brechas, 98

Bringsvaerd, Tor Age, 69

Brumfiel, Elizabeth, 55, 58, 182

Budapest school, 39

Bullard, William, 112

Bureau of Surrealist Research, 21

Burials: ancestral, 156, *157*, 158, 166–67; figurines placed in, 167; objects placed with, 158–59, 166–67, 192; shift in focus from individual to group, 166–67; Xunantunich, 191

Búriková, Zuzana, 43

Camal, Bernabe, Sr., *74*, *75*, *101*

Camal, Bernabe, Jr., 76–77, *78*

Capitalism, 53–54, 184; consumer, 36

Cartesian and Platonic dualities, 19–20, 25

Center, cosmology of, 153

Central Group, 94, *95*; ceremonial spaces, 109, 153, 159–60; first ceremonial architecture, 109; hilltop location, 104; leading family residence in, *145*; orientation of, 155–56, 161–62; residential mounds of, 105, 205n1; structures at height of construction, 153

Ceramics: areas of large quantities of, 145; black vessels (Mt. Maloney), 169–70, *170*; Late Classic, 168–71, *170*; Mars Orange Ware, 108; Middle Preclassic, 108; Red vessels, 165, 169, *170*, 171; Terminal Preclassic, 109; Xunantunich and Chan, 169–71, *170*

Ceremonies/ceremonial space: Central Group, 109, 153, 158–60; community-level, 135, 155–58, *157*, 162, 164; festivals and feasts, 135, 162, 164; overview of

community center, 152–55; space requirements per person, 153–54. *See also* Ritual practices

Cerén, 85–86, 150, 165

Chaa Creek, 147, 149, 150, 207n3

Chan: Cerén and, 85–86; changing settlement patterns, *111*; Chan Nòohol (south), 76–77, *78*, 97; chronology and population, 105–12, *106*, 205n1; community identification, 100–102, *101*; construction peak at, 94, 153; cultural landscape, 102–5; decline and abandonment, 106, 168–71; economy of, 184–85; elites' emulation of commoners, 104; everyday life in, 116–75; governance of, 162, 164–68; homogeneous appearance of, 197–98; housing type comparison, 149–52, 207n2; last construction built at, 171–72; location of, 2, 91, *92*, 113; longevity of, 10–11, 95, 174–75; longue durée, 6, 21; material remains, 117, 119, *123*, *132*, 143; maximum population period, 179–80; as minor center, 11; Northeast Group, 105, 134, *134*, *136*; regional context for, 112–15; remarkable nature of, 199–200; residents, 9, 11, 92, 152; revised models in light of, 188–95, 202; site custodians, 71; site summary for, 91–96; social diversity of, 148–52; stelae found at, *79*, 79–81, 172; sustainability and, 10–11, 131–33, 148–52, 174–75, 180, 200; topography, *93*; traditional archaeology and, xvii, 61–62, 175; wealth accumulation in, 185; West Plaza, 153, 171–72; and why everyday life matters, 176–96; Xunantunich distance from, 114. *See also* Administrative building; Agricultural terraces; Agriculture; Central Group; Ceramics; Chan Nòohol (south); Community center; E-Group; Everyday life; Excavations; Exotic materials; Farming community, of Chan; Northeast Group; Settlement; *specific periods*

Chan, Derric, 71–72, 100

Chan, Ismael, Sr., 71, 100

Chan Nòohol (south), 76–77, *78*, 97; consecrated house in, 160–61; footpaths, 122

Chan project: Belizean archaeological workers on, 72–73; development and dates, 8; excavation and data set overview, 9; first phase, 73; funding, 8–9, 72;

research questions, 62, 97, 114–15. *See also* Excavations

Chert, ritual use of, 159

Chert biface craft workers, 137–43, *139*; expedient tools and, 122, 207n2

Chi, Everaldo, 79, *79*, 80

Chico zapote (Manilkara zapota*)*, 133, 174, 200

Chronology, Chan population and, 105–12, *106*, 205n1

Chultun, river cobble cache on, 76–77, *78*, 160–61

City-rural relations, 185–88, 202

Classic period: Chan economy during, 184–85; Early, 109–10; Late, 126–27, 168–72, *170*; Late late, 110, *111*; Terminal, 80, 95, 110–11, *111*, 114, 168–70. *See also* Postclassic period; Preclassic period

Class relations: dominant ideology thesis and, 180–82; Scott's focus on, 35–36

Collaboration: between farming families, 123–25; Wylie on, 71, 73–74

Collaborative archaeology, 70–81; Cerén example of, 85–86; importance highlighted by funding, 72; microanalysis enabled by, 84; river cobbles example, 76–77, *78*; stelae find and, *79*, 79–81

Colonial archaeology, 60, 62

Colonial period, 46

Color symbolism, 156, 160–61, 207n4

Comfort of Things, The (Miller), 43

Commoners, elites emulation of, 104, 171

Community: Chan identification of, 100–102; and community-level ceremonies, 135, 155–56, *157*, 158, 162–63; definition of, 101; and material production, 143; open and closed models of, 193

Community center, 10, 92, *95*; directional orientation of, 155–56; excavations, 117; functional similarity to large civic centers, 94; green color and, 156; individual-group focus shift in, 166–67; leading family residences and, *144*; Middle Preclassic existence of, 153; overview of ceremonial use, 152–55; ritual and politics, 152–73

Community leaders, 143–48, *144*, *145*, *151*

Conditions of Agricultural Growth, The (Boserup), 177–78, 179

Connell, Samuel V., 149, 207n3

Constraints: creativity and, 37–38;

evidential, 67–68, 192–93; on Xunantunich power, 147–48, 180, 195

Construction: last, 171; peak, 94, 153; pole-and-thatch, 124, 137. *See also* Reconstruction drawings

Consumer capitalism, 36

Consumption: De Certeau on production and, 32–33; household archaeology treatment of, 50; Miller's work on, 42–43

Continuous occupation model, 205n1

Cosmology: center symbolism in, 153; directional forces in, 155; river cobbles cosmogram, 160–61; site size and, 156

Country and the City, The (Williams), 186

Craft producers, 135–37; chert biface, 122, 137–43, *139*, 207n2; limestone, 82–83, 140–43, *141*; obsidian blade, 146; as remaining Late Classic residents, 168–69

Creativity: constraints and, 37–38; everyday life and, 30–37

Critique of Everyday Life (Lefebvre), 22, 24–25, 186

Cultural landscape, of Chan, 102–5

Data, theory and, 67–68

De Certeau, Michel, xviii, 5, 21, 30; break with structuralism, 37; on consumption and production, 32–33; on data-laden theory, 67; Lefebvre compared with, 31; Miller and, 43; place and space conceptual tools, 33–34; on spatial practices, 34

Decreasing labor value model, 190–92; hypothetical data in, 207n1

Deetz, James, 7

Deforestation, 1, 11, 175

De la Garza, Mercedes, 194, 209n2

Dialogic Imagination, The (Bakhtin), 39

Direct historical analogies, 74–75

Directions, cardinal, 155–56, 160–61, 207n4; quincunx pattern association with, 165

Docster, Elise, 98, 107

Domestic economies, as political, 183

Domestic spheres: Feminist and gender archaeology approach, 53–54; housework as subversive politics, 50–51

Dominant ideology thesis, 180–82

Doxa, 29

Dualities: Cartesian and Platonic, 19–20, 25; De Certeau's sets of oppositions, 32–33

Dwelling, 41, 57, 59–60

FDC. *See* Friends for Conservation and Development

Feminist and gender archaeology, 13, 52–55; politics of, 58–59; Public and private spheres in, 53–54; stages of, 54–55

Feminist scholarship: on everyday life, 30; feminist standpoint theory, 29–30; in the late twentieth century, 36–37; in the middle twentieth century onward, 27–30; in the 1970s and 1980s, 30; Smith, D., use of early works on, 29

Festivals and feasts, 135, 162, 164

Figurines, 167

Flake core production, 137

Flannery, Kent, 81–82

Forest management, 131–33, 174, 180, 200

Foucault, Michel, 38

Fragments: greenstone axe, 76–77; importance of, 77, 79; limestone, *79*, 79–81

French countryside analogy, 23

French peasants, 187

Freud, Sigmund, 21

Friends for Conservation and Development (FDC), 71

Funding, Chan project, 8–9, 72

Geographical Information Systems (GIS), 98

German Ideology, The (Engels and Marx), 180–81

GIS. *See* Geographical Information Systems

Goffman, Erving, 21

Governance, at Chan, 162, 164–67

Gramsci, Antonio, 35, 180–81

Grave revisitation, 156, 158–60, 161–62; periods of intensified, 167

Green (color), 156, 160–61

Greenstone axe fragment, 76–77

Group-centered political strategies, 166–67, 174–75, 184

Habitus, 27

Hard tabular limestone, 140–41, *141*

Hardwood trees, 131, *132*, 133

Hauser, Mark, 6

Health, 11, 151

Hearth, Nicholas F., 137, 138

Hearth deposit, 135, *136*

Hegemony, 181

Heidegger, Martin, 41, 57

Heller, Agnes, 39–40; Lefebvre's influence on, 39

Hendon, Julia, 5–6

Hernandez, Ciro, 79, *79*, 80

Hidden transcripts, 49

Historical archaeology: definition of, 46; politics of, 60–61; prehistoric and, 46–47

Hodder, Ian, 47

Horizontal excavation (open area), 81–84, 86; use of in Chan project, 127

Household archaeology, 13, 45, 48; consumption treated in, 50; emergence of, 51–52; European, 51; everyday life used interchangeably with, 63; excavation advocated by, 82; gender and, 52–53; hidden and public transcripts of, 49

Households: Chan excavations of, 116–17, 205n1; cycling of, 205n1; domestic and political economies of, 183; independence and interdependence of, 138, 142

Houses and housing types: Chan Nòohol's consecrated house, 160–61; and comparison of Chan with other minor centers, 149–52, 207n2; demarcation of lots, 145; interior of, 122; pole-and-thatch construction, 124, 137; reconstruction drawing of farmer, *121*; significance of perishable, 11, 148–50; springhouses, 129, *130*; terrace placement of, 120–21, 128; waterway orientation of, 121. *See also* Farmsteads

Housework, as subversive politics, 50–51

Humanistic-scientific divide, 70, 84, 87

Hutson, Scott, 59–60

Hydraulic societies, 178–79

Ideology: dominant ideology thesis, 180–82; everyday life formation of, 181–82

Incense burners, 80–81, 158, 160

Inequality, 181–85, 195–96, 202; colonial archaeology and, 60; feminist archaeology focus on, 58

Ingold, Tim, 41–42

Inquiry into the Nature and Causes of the Wealth of Nations, An (A. Smith), 183

Intensive agriculture, 195; Netting on, 187–88, 207n1; population and, 177–78, 179; state control causing, 178–79

Intensive archaeology, 81–84

Irrigation, 129, *130*; hydraulic societies and, 178–79

Jade objects: adorno, 160; with burials, 192; luxury item ownership and, 150; ritual use of partial, 159–60; Xunantunich and, 191–94

Jamaican slaves, eighteenth-century, markets and everyday lives of, 6

Joyce, Arthur A., 62

Juarez, Santiago, *198*

Kalosky, Ethan, 74, *75*

Kant, Immanuel, 32

Keller, Angela, 146

Kestle, Caleb, 80–81, 82, 140, 143

Kingship, 113, 172, 173

Kosakowsky, Laura, 105, 107, 171

Labor value. *See* Decreasing labor value model

Landscape: archaeology, 57; Chan's cultural, 102–5; definitions of, 56; Smith, A. T., dimensions of, 57; space, place and, 55–58

Late Classic period, 126–27; ceramics of, 169–71, *170*

Late Late Classic settlement, 110, *111*

Late Preclassic settlement, 109

Leading families: high-status farmers, 133–35; residences of, 143–48, *144*, *145*, 205n1; shell ornaments and, *151*

Lefebvre, Henri, 21–26, 67; *Critique of Everyday Life* reprint, 22; De Certeau compared with, 31; French countryside analogy of, 23; Heller influenced by, 39; Lévi-Strauss and, 26, 186; Miller and, 43

"Legacies of Collaboration: Transformative Criticism in Archaeology" (Wylie), 73

Lentz, David, 131

Leventhal, Richard, 97

Lévi-Strauss, Claude, 26, 186

Limestone: craft workers, 82–83, 140–43, *141*; fragments, *79*, 79–81; quarries, 82–83; types, 140–41, *141*

Little community, Redfield's, 185–86, 188

Lived space, 58, 65

Longue durée, 6, 21

Lukács, György, 39–40

Luxury items, 158–59; paucity of Xunantunich, 191–94; social stratification and, 150

Macro phenomena, archaeological focus on, xvii, 7–8

Mahogany, 133, 199

Major centers: Belize River valley, 112, 174–75; Chan community center functional similarity to, 94

Malthus, Thomas, 177–78

Manilkara zapota (*chico zapote*), 133, 174, 200

"Man Who Collected the First of September, 1973, The" (Bringsvaerd), 69

Manzanero, Rafael, 71

Marine shell: ornaments, *151*, 167; Strombus beads, 135, 146

Mars Orange Ware, 108

Marx, Karl, 178, 180–81; peasant model, 187; Smith, A., and, 183

Masonry bench, 144

Material remains: community-level production, 143; major classes of Chan, 117, 119; wood, *123*, *132*. *See also* Exotic materials

Material spaces, 41–43; material turn, xx, 41, 43

Maya area. *See* Belize River valley

Measures, site size comparative, 112–13

Medick, Hans, 40

Meierhoff, James, 146

Mesoamerican archaeologists, 52, 81–82

Methodology: discussion overview, 67–69; issues of, 13–14; survey techniques, 98

Microanalysis, 84–85, 117

Middle Preclassic period: ancestor veneration during, 156, 158, 166; ceramics of, 108; community center existence in, 153; settlement, 107–9, *108*

Miller, Daniel, 42–43

Minor centers: Chan as, 11; housing comparison of Chan with other, 149–52, 207n2; temple pyramids of, 112–13

Morality, 40–41; moral economies, 183–85

Morgan, Lewis H., 52

Mound group typology, 102–4, *103*, 205n1; Chaa Creek, 149, 207n3; San Lorenzo, 149, 207n2

Mounds: Central Group residential, 105, 205n1; number of Chan, 102, 205n1; number of residential, 205n1; total number of terraces and, 102

Mt. Maloney Black vessels, 169–70, *170*

Neff, L. Theodore, 190, 207n1

Netting, Robert M., 187–88, 207n1

New Archaeology, of 1960s, 47
Northeast Group, 105, 134, *134*; hearth
   deposit, *136*

Obsidian, 85, 144, 148, 150; blade produc-
   tion, 146; Pachuca, 85, 147, 191–92
Occupation. *See* Settlement
Oppositions: Cartesian and Platonic duali-
   ties, 19–20, 25; De Certeau's sets of, 32–33
Oriental Despotism (Wittfogel), 177, 178–79
Orientation, Central Group, 155–56, 162
Outline of a Theory of Practice (Bourdieu),
   26, 31

Pachuca obsidian, 85, 147; Xunantunich
   lack of, 191–92
Palimpsest, 99–100
Peasants: archaeological perspectives on,
   188–92; persistence of traditional peasant
   model, 188–89; politics and, 35; stereotypes of, 3, 34–35, 186–87; subtle acts of
   resistance by, 34–35. *See also* Farmers
Perception of the Environment, The (Ingold),
   41–42
Phosphorus, *123*
Place: De Certeau's place and space concepts, 33–34; space, landscape and, 55–58
Pole-and-thatch houses, 124, 137
Politics: community center ritual and,
   152–73; everyday life and, 7, 23, 32,
   167–68; exotic items and, 146–47, 148;
   of feminist archaeology, 58–59; group-
   and individual-centered, 166–67, 184;
   group-oriented, 166–67, 174, 184; historical archaeology, 60–61; housework as
   subversive, 50–51; peasant, 35; political economies, 182–85; politico-moral
   economy, 184; religion and, 162; research
   and, 40–41; of spatial archaeology, 59–60
Population: Chan chronology and, 105–12,
   106, 205n1; Chan's period of maximum,
   179–80; decreasing labor values and,
   190–92, 207n1; intensive agriculture and,
   177–78, 179; methodologies for estimating, 207n1; Xunantunich at Chan's peak,
   180
Postclassic period, 172; early, *111*, 111–12
Postholes, 83; testing, 205n1
Postprocessual archaeology, 67, 186
Power: constraints on Xunantunich,

147–48, 180, 195; dominant ideology
   thesis, 180–82; everyday life and, 28–29,
   32; state, 178–79, 181–82
Practical Reason (Bourdieu), 26–27
Practice of Everyday Life, The (De Certeau),
   xviii, 30, 31
Practice of Everyday Life II, The (De Cer-
   teau), 30
Preclassic period: ancestor veneration and,
   156, 158, 166–67; late, 109; middle, 108,
   153, 156, 158, 166–67; terminal, 109
Prehistoric archaeology, 46–47
Prestige objects. *See* Luxury items
Primer for Daily Life, A (Willis), 36
Processual archaeology, 47, 186; data-the-
   ory problem critiqued by, 69
Production: community-level, 143; De Cer-
   teau on consumption and, 32–33; flake
   core, 137; Obsidian blade, 146. *See also*
   Craft producers
Prosaic imagination, 39
Public and private spheres: feminist archae-
   ology and, 53–54; and household archae-
   ology's hidden and public transcripts, 49;
   separation of, 28, 30
Pyburn, Anne, 188

Quality of life, 152, 194
Quincunx patterns, 77, 160–61, *163*; in
   bench, 165

Rabelais and His World (Bakhtin), 39
Rathje, William, 51
Reconstruction drawings: of farmer's
   house, *121*; of farmsteads, *120*, *124*; oflead-
   ing family residence, *145*
Redfield, Robert, 185–86, 188
Red vessels, 165, 169–70, *170*, 171
*Relaciones Histórico-geográficas de la
   Gobernación de Yucatán* (de la Garza et
   al.), 194, 209n2
Religion: everyday life and, 158–62; politics
   and, 162; popular and state, 181–82
Research: on city-rural relations, 185–88,
   202; combined empirical and theoretical,
   25, 192–93; data-theory mutual implication, 67–68; dissertation, 82, 96–97,
   133–35, *134*; ethical and political dimensions of, 40–41; surrealism and, 21. *See
   also* Chan project

Residences: Central Group mounds, 105, 205n1; of leading families, 143–44, *144*, *145*, 205n1; posthole testing and, 205n1. *See also* Households; Mound group typology

Residents, of Chan: composition of, 9; contemporary Succotz, 125; health of, 11, 151; overview of, 92; social classification of, 152. *See also* Craft producers; Farmers; Farming community, of Chan; Settlement

Resistance, 34–35

Revolution: everyday life role in, 24; peasant stereotypes and, 34–35

Ritual practices: and breaking of objects, 77, 79; cardinal directions in, 161–62; community center politics and, 142–73; E-Group site of, 173; farmers as conceiving of, 161–62; focus on individual ancestor in, 156, 158, 166; green objects in, 156; modern reenactment of, 80–81; partial objects used in, 158–59; quincunx patterns in, 160–61, *163*; stelae association with, 172. *See also* Grave revisitation

River cobbles, 76, *78*; in cosmogram, 77, 160–61

Rural producers, cities and, 185–88, 202

Sabloff, Jeremy A., 60

San Jose Succotz, Belize, 72–73, 100, 125

San Lorenzo, 149, 150, 207n2

Sartre, Jean-Paul, 26

Sascab, 165

Scientific-humanistic divide, 70, 84, 87

Scott, James, 34–36, 49, 181; Gramsci and, 35; moral economy term used by, 184

Separation of public and private spheres, 28, 30

Settlement, 92; Chan changing patterns of, *111*; Chan community identification, 100–102; chronology and population, 105–12, *106*, 205n1; diverse population revealed by, 105; implications of, 115; initial investigations, 96–100; mound group typology for Chan, 102–4, *103*, 205n1; techniques, 98; Xunantunich, 100–101, 103, 106–7, 190, 207n1. *See also* Mound group typology; *specific periods*

Sheets, Payson, 85–86

Site size: comparative measure for judging, 112–13; social ideals and cosmology, 156

Smallholders, Householders (Netting), 187–88, 207n1

Smith, Adam, 183

Smith, Dorothy, 27–30; "A Berkeley Education," 38; doxa concept used by, 29; Foucault's influence on, 38

Smith, Monica, 62

Social change: everyday life and, 6, 40; theorists, 6

Social diversity, sustainability and, 148–52

Socialization, 27, 38

Social sciences, 176

Social stratification: dominant ideology thesis, 180–82; lesser degree of Chan's, 150, 193; luxury items and, 150; open-closed communities model and, 193; Scott's focus on class relations, 35–36; social classification of Chan residents, 152

Social sustainability, 174–75

Social theory: archaeology's contribution to, 48; archaeology's exclusion from, xix; everyday life and, 19–44; Maya society interpretations without everyday life in, 188–95

Soft limestone, 140–41, *141*

Soil chemistry, *123*

Space: concept of lived, 58, 65; definitions of, 56; empty, 83; landscape, place and, 55–58; material and spatial practices, 41–43; spatial practices, 34, 41–43; spatial turn, xx, 41, 43. *See also* Ceremonies/ceremonial space

Spatial archaeology, 55–58, 65; politics of, 59–60

Springhouses, 129, *130*

Stasis, everyday life and, 5, 38

State power, 178–79; religion and, 181–82

Stelae: dating of, 80; entry into Chan rituals, 172; limestone fragments identified as, *79*, 79–81

Strombus marine shell beads, 135, 146

Structuralism, 26, 186; De Certeau break with, 37

Stuff (Miller), 43

Surplus extraction, 183

Surrealism, 21

Surveyors, 74, *75*
Survey techniques, 98
Sustainability: agriculture and, 10–11, 131; daily practices of social and, 174–75; forest management and, 131–33, 174, 180, 200; social diversity and, 148–52

Terminal Classic period, 95, 114; Chan decline during, 168–69; settlement, 110–11, *111*; stelae dating to, 80
Terminal Preclassic settlement, 109
Terraces. *See* Agricultural terraces
Thatch roofs, 92. *See also* Pole-and-thatch houses
Theory of Shopping, A (Miller), 42–43
Thompson, Edward H., 52
Thompson, Edward P., 184
Thompson, J. Eric, 72
Tikal, 174–75, 192, 193
Tools: caching of, 142; chert, 137–43, *139*, 158, 207n2
Topography, Chan, *93*
Trade, exotic materials indicating, 136–37, 143
Tradition: colonial period and, 46; everyday life and, 5; persistence of traditional peasant model, 188–89; traditional archaeology, xvii, 61–62, 175
Tribute, 190, 193–94, 209n2
Tyranny of ethnographic record, 75

Vignettes, everyday life, 1–2
Voting with feet analogy, 126–27, 169, 173
Voyeurs, walkers and, 33

Walking: processional, 99; voyeurs and walkers, 33
Water: house orientation to, 121; springhouses for collecting, 129, *130*
Wealth, 183, 185

Weapons of the Weak (Scott), 34
West Plaza, 153, 172
Wild species, 131, *132*, 133
Wilk, Richard, 51
Willey, Gordon, 96, 112
Williams, Raymond, 19–20, 186
Willis, Susan, 36
Wilson, Gregory, 62
Wittfogel, Karl, 177, 178–79, 189
Wittgenstein, Ludwig, 32
Wolf, Eric, 193, 196, 202
Women weavers, Aztec, 5–6
Wood: ash, *123*; forest management, 131–33, 174, 180, 200; remains by time period and weight, *132*
Wyatt, Andrew, 73, 82, 179
Wylie, Alison, 59, 67, 192–93; on collaboration, 71, 73–74; on direct historical analogies, 74–75

X-ray fluorescence (XRF), 85
Xunantunich: allegiance to, 171, 193–94; burials, 191; capital, 10, 104; ceramics of Chan and, 169–71, *170*; Chan distance from, 114; constraints on power of, 147–48, 180, 195; decreasing labor value model tested by, 191–92, 207n1; El Castillo of, 197, *198*; historical overview of, 113–14; luxury items not found at, 191–94; population peak of, 180; rejection of, 172–73; rise and decline of, 94, 113–14; San Lorenzo involvement of, 149; settlement at, 100–101, 103, 106–7; settlement survey data from, 190, 207n1; stelae find and, 79–80; and tribute payments, 190, 193–94
Xunantunich Archaeological Project, 97, 147

Yaeger, Jason, 147, 207n2

Cynthia Robin is professor of anthropology at Northwestern University. Her research focuses on the meaning and significance of everyday life. She studies the everyday lives of ordinary people to illustrate how they make a difference in their societies and are not the mere pawns of history or prehistory. She is particularly interested in understanding how people in the ancient Maya world, through their daily practices, created socially and environmentally sustainable communities. Between 2002 and 2009 she directed the Chan project in Belize, which explored the two-thousand-year history of an ancient Maya farming community. She is the editor of *Chan: An Ancient Maya Farming Community* and coeditor of *Gender, Households, and Society: Unraveling the Threads of the Past and the Present* and *Spatial Theory and Archaeological Ethnographies*. In addition, some of her major articles have appeared in *Current Anthropology*, *Journal of Archaeological Research*, *Journal of Social Archaeology*, and *Proceedings of the National Academy of Sciences*.

CPSIA information can be obtained
at www.ICGtesting.com
Printed in the USA
FFOW03n1724260717
38186FF

9 780813 062105